TREES AT RISK

RECLAIMING AN URBAN FOREST

A Case History of Worcester, Massachusetts

EVELYN HERWITZ

Chandler House Press • Worcester, Massachusetts

TREES AT RISK
RECLAIMING AN URBAN FOREST

Copyright© 2001 by Evelyn Herwitz

All rights reserved. Printed in Canada on recycled paper. No part of this book may be used or reproduced, stored or transmitted in any manner whatsoever without written permission from Chandler House Press, except in the case of brief quotations embodied in critical articles and reviews.

ISBN 1-886284-60-1   paperback
ISBN 1-886284-61-X   hardcover
Library of Congress Control Number: 2001088224
First Edition
ABCDEFGHIJK

Published by
Chandler House Press, Inc.
A Division of Tatnuck Bookseller & Sons, Inc.
335 Chandler Street
Worcester, MA 01602
USA

President
Lawrence J. Abramoff

Director of Publishing
Claire Cousineau

Design by
Atomic Design

Chapter 1-7 Opening Photos by
Robert Nash

Paperback Cover Author Photo by
Louis A. Despres

A portion of the proceeds from the sale of this book will be used to plant trees in the City of Worcester.

Chandler House Press specializes in custom publishing for businesses, organizations and individuals. For more information on how to publish through our corporation, please contact Chandler House Press, 335 Chandler Street, Worcester, MA 01602. Call (800) 642-6657, fax (508) 756-9425, or find us on the World Wide Web at www.chandlerhousepress.com.

FOREWORD

A more modest book, *Trees of Worcester* by Arabella Tucker, published in 1894, inspired this wonderfully researched story of an urban forest by Evelyn Herwitz. Upon arriving at the Worcester County Horticultural Society in 1984, I soon discovered on the shelves of the library the small, thin volume by Miss Tucker. Being a lover of trees, especially trees that have the tenacity to withstand urban conditions, I began a search for the specimens that Miss Tucker described. I quickly learned that a majority of them no longer existed. Due to age, neglect, changing urban conditions and natural disasters, the trees she described mostly had disappeared. I thought of updating the book and highlighting superior specimens of the late 20th century. I quickly realized that I had no time or talent for writing a book. It was a happy day when I was introduced to Evelyn, and she agreed to take on the challenge. As you will soon discover, Evelyn is a meticulous researcher. What was to be a simple update is now a concise and compelling story of an urban forest. The plight of the urban trees of Worcester, Massachusetts has been and is being echoed from Miami to San Francisco and beyond—in effect, throughout the world.

It is important to acknowledge Miss Tucker's inspiration. She was a teacher at what is now Worcester State College. She taught dendrology, but, more importantly, she inspired her students and friends about the wonders of trees. It appears she held no prejudices within the plant kingdom. Trees could be misplaced, but they always had a place within the boundaries of Worcester. It is marvelous when a human being so many generations removed can still inspire and evoke change.

All of Evelyn's fine words would not count for much if they didn't inspire action to change the fate of urban forests. The first byproduct of Evelyn's writing was the organizing of the Urban Tree Task Force, a collection of individuals connected with environmental organizations, neighborhood groups and both state and municipal agencies. Everyone involved recognizes the multifaceted importance of trees and wants desperately to be proactive in a renaissance of green.

I have enjoyed my association with Evelyn during the writing of *Trees at Risk*. I look forward to the positive changes it will inspire.

John W. Trexler
Executive Director
Worcester County Horticultural Society

ACKNOWLEDGMENTS

Young children and pets have a way of forcing you to slow down and look. So it was eleven years ago, when I would take my daughter, Mindi, then a baby, and our dog, Sukki, for afternoon walks around the neighborhood. As we meandered up May Street, pausing to admire dandelions and shagbark hickory nuts, I discovered something I had completely missed in my daily rush—the trees on our street were dying.

That discovery led to a magazine article and, in the process of my research, an interview with John Trexler, Executive Director of the Worcester County Horticultural Society. Within a year, we had teamed up to produce an updated version of Arabella Tucker's 1894 book, *Trees of Worcester*, in honor of the book's centennial and the Horticultural Society's 150th anniversary in 1994. We never made the deadline. What began as a fairly straightforward project soon mushroomed into the much more expansive concept herein realized. To John's great credit, the fact that my research and writing took six years, rather than one as I had naively estimated, never diminished his support for the book. His encouragement and enthusiasm combined with his deep commitment to improving the state of Worcester's urban forest have been an inspiration, and his friendship, a gift. Without John's persistence, this book would never have been published.

Others have contributed in significant ways to the writing of this volume. Ken Moynihan, Professor of History at Assumption College and a colleague from my years producing stories for Massachusetts Public Radio, was an invaluable guide to researching Worcester history. His thoughtful critique of manuscript drafts helped improve both the flow and accuracy of the narrative.

Various individuals gave me access to their research and helped me piece together the story of Worcester's trees—David Foster, Director of the Harvard Forest in Petersham, shared his extensive knowledge of the land-use history of Central Massachusetts; Holly Izard, the Worcester Historical Museum's curator for the Salisbury Mansion, explained the early land transactions of Stephen Salisbury I that had such an impact on land ownership and development in Worcester; William Meyer, then a graduate student in geography at Clark University, gave me his detailed bibliography of late 19th-century newspaper articles on trees in Worcester; and John Anderson, former Worcester mayor and city councilor, lent me his extensive records of environmental issues during his years in office. To all of them, my thanks, and my gratitude to the extraordinary research librarians at the Worcester Public Library's Worcester Room, the Worcester Historical Museum, and that gem of a resource, the American Antiquarian Society.

Bob Nash, nature photographer *par excellence*, contributed his time and talent to illustrating this volume with his beautiful photos of Worcester's trees—making clear in a way words cannot what we are at risk of losing.

David Schuyler, Associate Professor in the American Studies Program at Franklin and Marshall College, gave a thorough critique of the manuscript. His comments helped me to sharpen many sections of the book and avoid some potentially embarrassing mistakes—those that remain are my own doing.

Without Claire Cousineau, Director of Publishing at Chandler House Press, this book would never have been transformed from a manuscript to a published volume. My thanks to her and to Bob Zeleniak and Ingrid Mach for the beautiful design. Thanks, too, to Deborah Sosin, for her careful copyediting of the final manuscript. Ensuring that the book brings its message home, Chandler House President Larry Abramoff had the vision to turn the publication of *Trees at Risk* into a community project to raise money for more street trees in Worcester.

I am grateful to the Nathaniel Wheeler Trust for a generous grant that helped support my research and writing of *Trees at Risk*.

Each word of encouragement from friends and relatives helped me stick to what seemed at times an endless project. Above all, my family kept me going. As this volume grew, so did my daughters. My thanks for their patience during all those long Sundays and evenings when I had to keep writing. Mindi, now adept at computers and searching the Internet, helped me complete the bibliographic references to the book inspired by our strolls up May Street. Emily, who spent many hours on my lap as I composed at the computer, helped select some of the historic photographs that illustrate these pages. My husband, Alan Harris, gave me the gift of faith in the importance of my writing and in my ability to produce a work of lasting value. My love to you all.

To my parents, Paul and Gisela Herwitz, I am grateful for their enthusiastic support of every ambitious project I've ever undertaken. Though my mother did not live to see this book published, there is much of her in it. Were she alive today, I would tell her thank you for all those books she pulled off the shelves and piled on my desk when I had reports to write in high school. Though I groaned then, I now know the value of what she was teaching me—be thorough, be thoughtful and learn from lessons of the past.

DEDICATION

In loving memory of my mother, Gisela Kronenberg Herwitz, who taught me to dig beneath the surface and to value the lessons of history

For my family, Al, Mindi and Emily, who made it possible

And for all the children of Worcester, who will inherit the trees

©Robert Nash

CONTENTS

INTRODUCTION — page 1

CHAPTER 1 — Into Wilderness — page 9

CHAPTER 2 — Clearing the Land — page 23

CHAPTER 3 — Industrial Transformation — page 43

CHAPTER 4 — Greening Worcester — page 69

CHAPTER 5 — End of an Era — page 117

CHAPTER 6 — Under Siege — page 147

CHAPTER 7 — A Legacy Squandered — page 171

EPILOGUE — page 192

BIBLIOGRAPHY — page 194

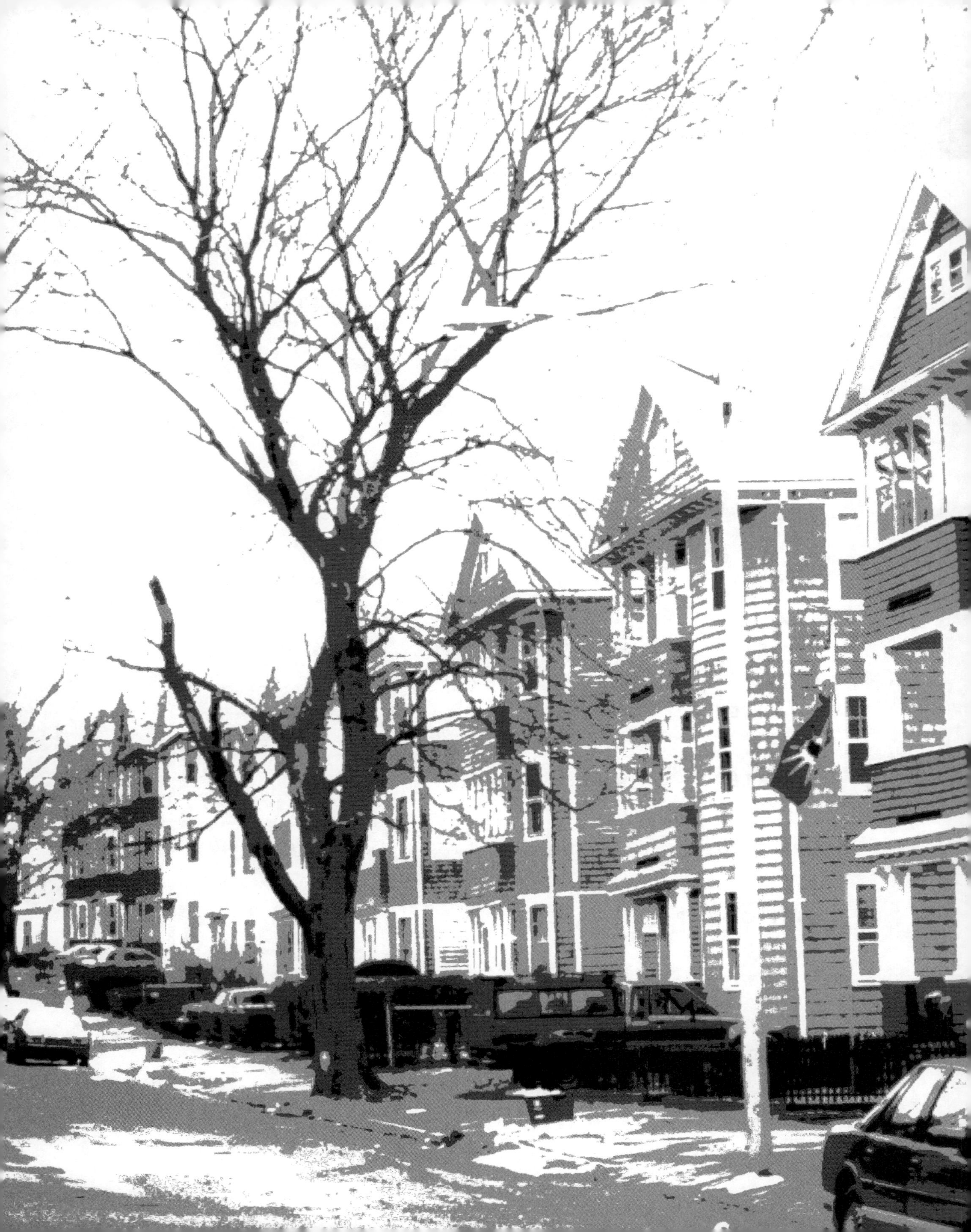

INTRODUCTION

One day Honi, a righteous man, was journeying on the road when he saw a man planting a carob tree.
"How long does it take for this tree to bear fruit?" Honi asked.
"Seventy years," the man replied.
"Are you certain that you will live another seventy years?"
"I found mature carob trees in the world," said the man. "As my forbears planted these for me, so, too, I plant these for my children."
—The Babylonian Talmud, Ta'anith: 23a

On a chill December afternoon when the hardwoods stand barren, their fallen leaves but sodden dregs of autumn's gold, Worcester's hues are clay and stone. Viewed from Mount St. James, once home to native Nipmucs, now to the College of the Holy Cross, the muted city melds with the dun-colored woodlands of surrounding hills—its red-brick factory buildings and cement offices crowding the valley floor, a glass-and-steel bank tower mirroring winter's slate sky, white and brown and beige three-deckers climbing rocky hillsides, the charcoal-gray swath of I-290 snaking over streets.

Come spring, though, there is green. First, a fine misting of chartreuse as the weeping willows unfurl their buds, then a wash of emerald as the sugar and Norway maples, the ashes, oaks and ginkgoes spread their leaves, until Worcester's swarthy face is softened by a sylvan veil. A city of aging factories and dreams of renewal, of ethnic pride and paternalism, of grit, ingenuity and determination, Worcester is also a city of trees.

Like many American cities, Worcester planted the majority of those trees in the mid-19th century, in response to industrialization's ills. Modest planting efforts by private citizens throughout the colonies had predated the revolution by nearly a century. But as the young nation evolved from an agrarian society dependent on foreign trade to a competitive manufacturing economy linked by rail, remote country towns metamorphosed into sooty, congested cities. Dismayed by the transformation, residents yearned for urban greenery to restore a romanticized vision of rural paradise lost.

It was a transformation that could have been anticipated by any traveler to London, where smog and slums were urban fixtures by the early 1800s. In the name of progress, however, Americans ignored warning signs from abroad. Capitalizing on steam-driven turbines, which ended dependence on hydropower, and railroads, which sliced transportation time and cost, industry proliferated during the first half of the 19th century. Obscuring the pastoral countryside near rail hubs and commercial centers, massive brick manufactories lured legions of farmworkers and immigrants in search of a better life. The influx of laborers swelled city censuses exponentially, straining housing and fledgling municipal services. Soon, tenements shadowed factories and sewage choked rivers. Surveying their boomtowns as the nation argued over slavery, civic leaders began to realize the bitter truth their English brethren had learned 50 years earlier—that the price of urban prosperity was pollution, overcrowding and cholera.

Hoping to mitigate health-threatening "miasmas" while re-creating a pastoral ideal, private citizens and local governments set out hundreds of thousands of trees. The results, by the turn of the 20th century, were lush, canopied streets and densely shaded parks. But today, nearly a century later, those urban forests—all the trees within city limits—in Worcester and throughout the United States are dying from neglect.[1]

Despite renewed interest in urban tree planting, inspired by the 20th anniversary of Earth Day in 1990, budgets for tree planting and maintenance have been slashed nationwide as communities struggle to allocate shrinking local resources for basic municipal services. In a 1991 survey of 20 American cities, American Forests (then the American Forestry Association) reported that it would require four times current planting levels to simply maintain the cities' existing tree counts; nonetheless, new plantings would decline by 14 percent in 1992. Substantiating earlier reports that urban forestry programs had been in decline since the mid 1980s, the study also found that 70 percent of the cities surveyed were reducing tree maintenance programs. In turn, crisis management had become the norm.[2]

More recent studies of urban forests in different regions of the United States reveal the impact of such decisions on metropolitan areas surrounded by urban sprawl. Comparing satellite images of Washington, D.C., for 1973, 1985 and 1997, American Forests researchers found a 64 percent decline in areas with high vegetation and tree canopy cover during that 24-year period. During the same span, sections with low tree cover, which accounted for 51 percent of the study area in 1973, comprised nearly 72 percent in 1997. Similar findings were discovered over the same study period in Ohio's Canton-Akron metropolis, where areas of high vegetation and dense tree canopies declined by 40 percent, and areas of low tree density made up 77 percent of the region in 1997, up from 55 percent in 1973. Likewise, in the Puget Sound watershed—encompassing Seattle, Tacoma, Seatac, Redmond, Bellevue and Everett, Washington—researchers found a 37 percent drop in areas with dense tree cover from 1972 to 1996; areas with low tree density more than doubled, from 25 to 57 percent of the study area.[3]

The findings are sobering, since the average life of a city tree is only 32 years—13 years if planted downtown—far short of the 150-year average life span of trees in rural settings. Growing in a highly unnatural environment, bereft of good drainage and rich forest humus, city trees must struggle to survive with even the best of care. Confined to sidewalk pits, their roots cannot spread radially; instead, the roots twist into a Gordian knot by filling every available space in the pit, or tunnel beneath asphalt to a nearby sewer line or catch basin in search of food. Within the pit itself, the soil is often highly compacted and nutrient-poor, more alkaline than natural forest soil, and loaded with chemical by-products from the inorganic fill that underlies most cities. Compounding the problem is a host of urban ills, including noxious auto emissions, root-gouging roadwork, radiant heat from buildings and sidewalks, dog urine, road salt, careless drivers and vandals. Defenses crippled by the hostile environment, those city trees not downed by cars or construction succumb prematurely to their natural enemies: disease, insects, ice, wind and drought.[4]

When such formidable odds for survival are combined with decreased planting and maintenance, the result is a significant decline in the estimated 60 million street trees shading our nation's cities. In New York, perhaps the most extreme example, the metropolis has lost nearly 30 percent of an estimated 700,000 street trees in the past decade alone. A steady drop in funding for tree planting and care since the mid-1980s has rendered the city's Parks Department virtually unable to keep up with regular pruning and disease control, limiting maintenance to dead tree removal—according to a list backlogged more than five years. Roughly 15,000 to 20,000 trees die in New York each year, victims of pollution, malnutrition, vandalism, dogs and cars; to take their place, only about 9,000 new trees are planted annually, with an average life expectancy of seven years.[5]

Urban parks, too, are at risk. Constructed primarily during the mid- to late-19th century, in response to the outstanding success of New York's Central Park, many of the nation's municipal pleasure-grounds today are shaded by mature trees near the end of their life cycles—at a time when maintenance funding is dear. In West Chicago, a survey of the 40-acre Reed-Keppler Park by the Morton Arboretum indicated that the 150-year-old oak forest would be gone by the early 21st century, its natural demise accelerated by intensive recreational use and other stresses on root systems. Similar problems threaten aging giants across the country, from the eucalyptuses in San Francisco's Golden Gate Park to the London plane trees in New York's Central Park.[6]

Though the loss of urban trees does not wreak the same measure of ecological devastation as the destruction of rain forests in the Amazon or ancient forests in the Pacific Northwest, the cost of such losses to the urban environment is both significant and profound. Cleansing the air of pollutants, alleviating extreme temperatures, the billions of leaves that canopy city streets provide a cool, green shelter for humans and animals alike. Root systems stabilize soil and lessen flooding, while trunks and branches block sharp winter winds. In an effort to quantify those benefits, a 1994 study of metropolitan Chicago by the U.S. Forest Service estimated that in 1991 alone, trees performed a service worth $9.2 million by removing air-born compounds such as carbon monoxide and sulfur dioxide from the study area. Were Cook and DuPage Counties to plant an additional 95,000 trees, the researchers estimated that savings in pollution control and reduced expenses for heating and cooling shaded buildings would amount to a $38 million net benefit to the region over the next 30 years.[7]

In contrast to those projected savings, the American Forests researchers who analyzed the deforestation of Washington, D.C., estimated that the loss in tree cover and increase in impervious surfaces, such as asphalt and concrete, from 1973 to 1997 were exacerbating the cost of controlling storm water runoff. During a major storm, the flow of storm water had increased by about 29 million cubic feet, 34 percent more volume than in the early 1970s. To replicate the storm water retention capacity of the lost trees with reservoirs, sand filters and other systems would cost about a quarter of a billion dollars.[8]

In addition to their ecological benefits, urban trees also enhance property values. Nineteenth-century real estate barons were quick to realize the benefits of trees and parks that increased the value of their abutting properties; the battle over the ultimate location of New York's Central Park hinged in part on defining an equitable means to assess park abutters' increased property values in order to finance the project. Today, according to the U.S. Forest Service, trees boost the market value of private homes from 7 to 20 percent.[9]

But the value of urban trees is much more than just dollars and cents. The oldest and largest living things on earth, sources of shelter, food, raw materials, and inspiring beauty, trees are rooted deeply in the human psyche. From the Tree of Life that is the Jewish Torah to the Wisdom Tree, site of Buddha's revelations, they symbolize creation and the source of all insight for the world's religions. Trees are planted as living memorials to loved ones, tied with yellow ribbons to highlight the plight of hostages, named for significant historical figures or events, and grieved when lost to disease or progress. Planted in cities, they provide a spiritual link to the natural world—an oasis from urban stress, a source of moral uplift.[10]

Such connections are difficult to quantify but no less crucial. Writing of the deep relationship between humans and trees in an urban setting, researchers John F. Dwyer, Herbert W. Shroeder and Paul H. Gobster cite the experience of two friends who visited the 1,500-acre Morton Arboretum, west of Chicago, when one was grieving the loss of someone dear:

> We were able to drive slowly and soon came to the densest part of the forest where the sugar maples had turned brilliant colors of yellow and orange. Mingled in with the maples were tall green spruces; the Virginia creeper with its fall red coloring dappled the other colors. It was as if, suddenly, we were inside a large cathedral with stained-glass windows. The feeling was magnificent and awe-inspiring. Almost automatically my car came to a stop. All conversation came to a stop. The "peak" aesthetic experience occurred as the presence of a Supreme Being seemed to engulf us. The beauty of the environment and the solitude of the forest made us become "one." We were quiet and motionless for several minutes. A few tears rolled down the cheek of my friend. Quietly, she said, "Thank you, I feel better—I can face anything now." It was a profound experience for both of us.[11]

So deep is the link between humans and their natural environment that some researchers, including Harvard's Edward O. Wilson and Yale's Stephen R. Kellert, have theorized that *Homo sapiens* may have a genetically based emotional need to be close to trees and other greenery. According to their Biophilia Hypothesis, millions of years of human survival and evolution depended on our ability to cope with the natural world; learning what was safe and dangerous involved the imprinting of strong positive and negative emotional reactions to various natural stimuli. Though late-20th-century American society is no longer so dependent on nature for survival, Kellert theorizes that closeness to the natural world is still crucial for psychological well-being. [12]

The hypothesis is a long way from proven, but anecdotal evidence seems to bolster the theory. To cite just one example, in North Philadelphia, one of the city's worst slums, planting street trees and replacing trash-filled lots with tree-filled gardens have helped to reclaim the drug-infested neighborhood. Philadelphia Green, a nationally acclaimed community-based outreach project of the Pennsylvania Horticultural Society, in 1991 planted hundreds of trees in the ethnically diverse area, teaching residents how to care for the plantings that shaded their apartments. Where neighbors once eyed each other with suspicion, the trees provided a common cause for cooperation, and each newly greened block soon inspired a half-dozen others to follow suit. Orders for new trees quickly outpaced the ability of staff to fill them and, despite some setbacks, vandalism was minimal. In fact, of 543 trees set out in 1991, only 18 had been lost two years later. Since that time, Philadelphia Green has trained about 900 Tree Tenders—private citizens who act as neighborhood tree stewards—representing over 85 community groups, who now care for over 8,000 public trees.[13]

This is the promise of healthy urban forests—and, conversely, the cost of their demise. Lush, well-tended trees shading streets and parks identify a community that is prospering; rows of disease-ravaged trees and snags warn of neglect, decay and the alienation that undermines many urban communities.[14]

Too often, however, the losses go unnoticed until it is too late. Absent a natural disaster such as the devastating hurricane of 1938, or an epidemic like the Dutch Elm blight that claimed millions of American Elms—once the ubiquitous urban street tree—during the first half of this century, untended urban forests take decades to decline. Indeed, with even a quarter of its street tree canopy lost, a city can still look green. Unless its leaders make a commitment to preserve what is left, however, that same city may well discover its streets more barren than shaded within a generation.

Such is the risk for Worcester, which has lost about a fifth of its 20,000 street trees in the past decade. A statewide cap on property taxes passed in the early 1980s effectively eviscerated the city's forestry program; due to budget cuts, new plantings have been limited to private donations and grants, while tree maintenance has been reduced to emergency pruning and removals. Despite impressive efforts in recent years to plant saplings in select business districts, part of a federally funded urban beautification project, the city lacks resources for ongoing care; within months of the young trees' debut, refuse littered their beds of weed-choked mulch. Elsewhere, the Department of Parks, Recreation and Cemeteries has been unable to keep up with the proliferation of diseased and damaged trees along streets and in parks. Compounding the challenge, more than half the city's street trees, the oldest survivors planted over a century ago, are nearing the end of their natural life cycle.[15]

Like so many other cities around the country, Worcester stands to lose not merely a valuable resource but a living legacy from its founding families. Though the names and details are unique to the city, the story of Worcester's urban forest, its creation, nourishment and threatened demise, is also a story of the insight and sensibilities of past generations, of cultural values and political priorities that shaped the nation's urban landscape. Worcester's challenge is a clarion call to all cities to preserve and protect their sylvan treasures before it is too late—before the chartreuse and emerald, the fir green, jade and viridian fade not just seasonally, but permanently, into hues of clay and stone.

[1] Robert W. Miller, "The History of Trees in the City," in Gary Moll and Sara Ebenreck, eds, *Shading Our Cities: A Resource Guide for Urban and Community Forests* (Washington, D.C.: Island Press, 1989), pp. 32–4. Though most cities, like Worcester, were characterized by haphazard plantings until municipal officials instituted systematic beautification efforts in midcentury, some, like Philadelphia and Detroit, were planned with trees in mind long before the industrial transformation. Designed by William Penn in 1682, Philadelphia included five tree-filled open spaces, each between five and ten acres. Also, according to Miller, "A Territory of Michigan law in 1807 specified that trees be planted on boulevards in the city of Detroit and that squares be established and planted with trees."
[2] Bob Skiera and Gary Moll, "The Sad State of City Trees," *American Forests,* Mar./Apr. 1992, pp. 61–64; J. James Kielbaso, "City Tree Care Programs: A Status Report," in *Shading Our Cities*, p. 39.
[3] "The District of Columbia Urban Ecosystem Analysis," *American Forests,* 1999; "Canton-Akron Metropolitan Area Regional Ecosystem Analysis," *American Forests,* 1999; "Puget Sound Metropolitan Area Regional Ecosystem Analysis," *American Forests,* 1999.
[4] Evelyn Herwitz, "For Trees' Sake," *Inside Worcester,* Apr. 1991, pp. 41–44.
[5] Kielbaso, *Shading Our Cities,* p. 45; Douglas Martin, "Mother Nature Never Intended This: Pollution and Not Enough Care Afflict City's Street Trees," *New York Times,* May 30, 1994.
[6] Joseph M. Keyser, "Crisis in Our Urban and Historic Parks," *American Forests,* Mar./Apr. 1988, pp. 61–64.
[7] William K. Stevens, "Money Growing on Trees? No, But Study Finds Next Best Thing," *New York Times,* Apr. 12, 1994.
[8] "Dramatic Tree Loss Costs DC Millions," *American Forests* press release, Nov. 16, 1999.
[9] Ebenreck, "The Values of Trees," *Shading Our Cities,* p. 49.
[10] John F. Dwyer, et al., "The Deep Significance of Urban Trees and Forests," in Rutherford H. Platt, et al., eds, *The Ecological City: Preserving and Restoring Urban Biodiversity* (Amherst: University of Massachusetts Press, 1994).
[11] Ibid., pp. 139–40.
[12] William K. Stevens, "Want a Room with a View? Idea May Be in the Genes," *New York Times,* Nov. 30, 1993.
[13] Tricia Taylor, "The Greening of North Philadelphia," *American Forests,* Jan./Feb. 1993, pp. 23–26; Pennsylvania Horticultural Society web site, www.libertynet.org/phs/.
[14] Ebenreck, p. xv.
[15] Herwitz, "For Trees' Sake"; *Worcester, MA, Street Tree Management Plan Executive Summary,* 1988.

INTRODUCTION

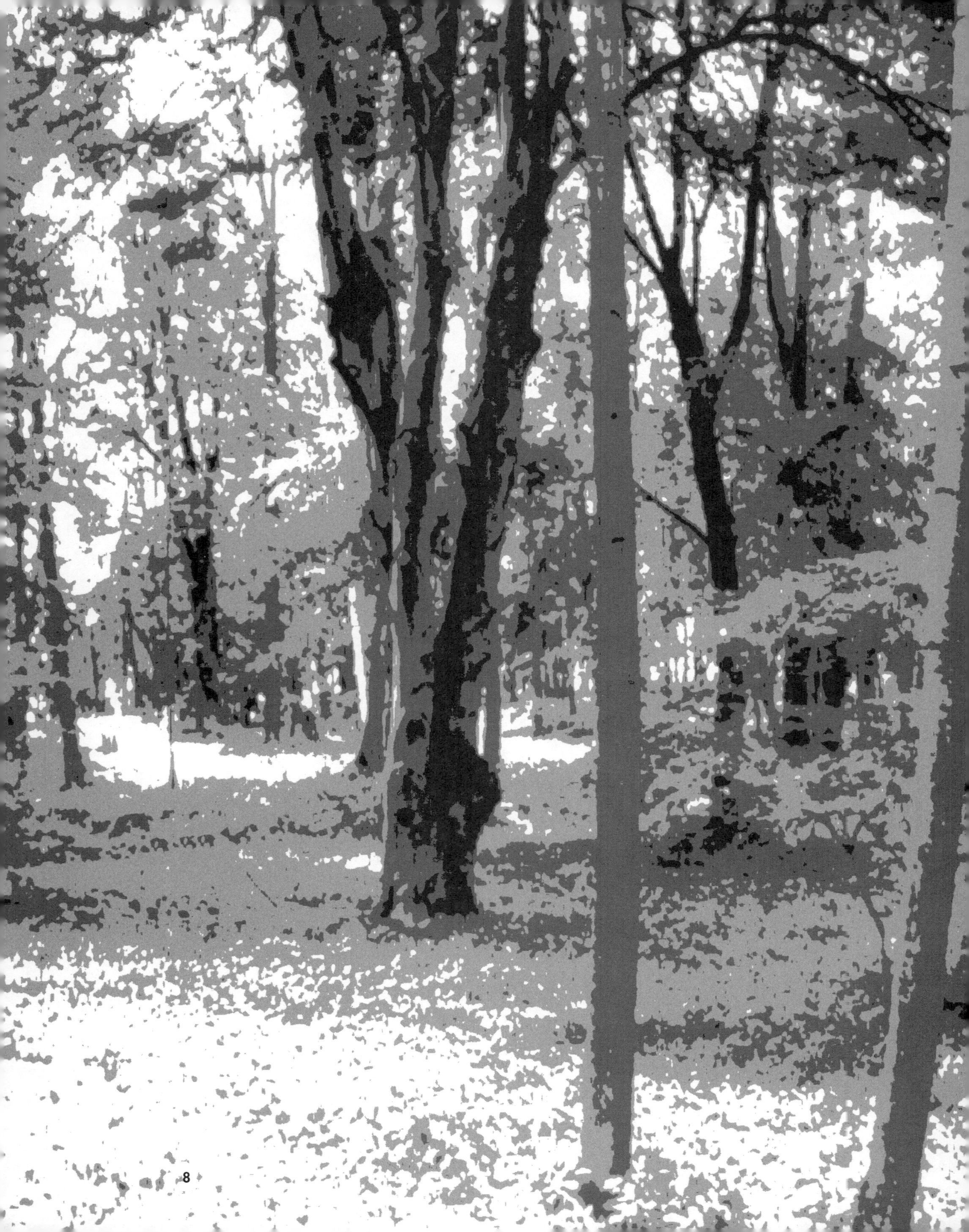

INTO WILDNERNESS
Chapter One

It had been a long day's ride from Boston, a dusty, wearing journey along the road to Springfield. But as Daniel Gookin, Edward Johnson and Andrew Belcher climbed over a ridge about 12 miles west of the frontier town of Marlborough, they finally found their landmark. Glistening before them in the late afternoon sun stretched a long, narrow lake called Quinsigamond by the native Indians.[1]

Farther they rode, past the lake, following the trail through woods flecked copper and gold. Here, just over the next ridge, was the broad valley they had been sent to explore, a promising patchwork of meadows and forest, streams and ponds. A closer look convinced the small party that this land would, indeed, make a suitable settlement. In their report to the Massachusetts Bay Colony's General Court that October, they noted that the site "contains a trract of very good Chestnut tree land, a large quantitye." Meadow and desirable upland were limited not by topography but by previous land claims. Nonetheless, the site was "conueniently scituated & wel waterred with ponds [and brooks] and lieing nearre midway beetwene Boston & Springfeild, about one [day's] ioyrny from either . . ." They recommended creating a plantation, "eight miles squrare," to be named Quinsigamond.[2]

The year was 1668, nearly a half-century after the Pilgrims had landed at Plymouth Rock and begun the European restructuring of New England's landscape. Before their arrival, the rocky soil, abundant forests and rich waters of what was to become Worcester, Massachusetts, were known only by those who called themselves Nipmucs, or "fresh water people," descendants of Asians who first came to central and southern New England 10,000 years ago.[3]

For millennia, the Nipmucs and their ancestors had treaded lightly on that land, clearing patches of forest for planting, hunting abundant wildlife amid the dense woodlands. But within a half-century of the English scouting party's visit, the Nipmucs' ways would be obliterated and the land under siege. No longer shared by members of a tribal community, land would become a commodity for sale or inheritance, its ownership sealed by cultivation. For farmers bent on planting European grains and raising imported livestock, claiming that land would mean years of grueling labor, freeing the soil of rocks and roots—and an all-out war against an enemy even more tenacious than the natives who fought to retain their territory: trees.

Felled, burned and uprooted to make way for cropland and pasture, carelessly consumed for fuel and lumber, the ancient trees that filled the forests would dwindle in number until, by the mid-19th century, two-thirds of the dense woodlands that shaded Massachusetts when Gookin and his companions first surveyed Quinsigamond would be gone. But the bitter lessons of deforestation learned by Europeans centuries earlier—lessons of vanishing wildlife, soil erosion, harsh winters and hot summers, flooding and drought—were easily forgotten in the midst of abundance. For Gookin's scouting party, the chestnut trees were prime timber, the well-watered meadows an opportunity.

As they mounted their war with forests, however, the European settlers of New England also planted trees. Cultivating them in gardens and orchards, planting them along streets and in town commons, the colonists prized trees to beautify their hard-wrought communities. It was a practice both fitting and ironic, one that capped efforts to restore a sense of Europe in the New World by replicating the landscape: once the land was cultivated and tamed, trees reflected refinement, not wilderness.

For Worcester, it would take three tries before the English settlers would establish a lasting settlement and begin to re-create the European countryside. Besieged by Indians, beset by famine, they struggled to redraw the landscape with each attempt, adding roads and lots meeting halls and homesteads that would define the city's skeleton. Their theory of the ideal community, centered on the church and surrounded by shared pasture, would establish Worcester's first open space, the Town Common; and their need for protection via two strategically placed garrisons would determine the north and south poles of Main Street. Only when they felt secure, when the fear of Indian raids was a dim memory, did the settlers begin to beautify their new community and line its common and dusty streets with trees.

So began a new, cultivated forest—a forest that would grow with the community, on human terms. Over the centuries, its guardians would include a physician, a governor, a banker, a newspaper editor, a real estate baron and a farmer. Flourishing by the late 1800s, it would provide a soothing antidote to urban stress, and crucial protection from pollution, heat and harsh winter winds. One hundred years later, it would shade over 1,000 acres of public parks and include nearly 20,000 street trees, as well as tens of thousand of trees on the grounds of private institutions, businesses and homes. Ironically, however, this forest, too, would fall under siege—not from willful destruction but from neglect. And its decline, if allowed to continue, will spell the loss, yet again, of a precious natural inheritance.

Forest Riches—The Landscape of the Nipmucs

In 1668, the wilderness of Quinsigamond, so valued by the native Nipmucs and reviled by the English colonists, reflected the primeval past. Over terrain carved by powerful ancient rivers, then smoothed and tamed by receding glaciers, a succession of plants had sprouted, their evolving mix defined by fluctuations in temperature, wind and precipitation. As climatic conditions settled into temperate patterns about 8,000 years ago, New England's major forest zones emerged: to the north, the mountains were blanketed with conifers, including spruce and white pine; farther south, oak and other hardwoods predominated. [4]

RED SPRUCE
Picea rubens

Among the first trees to shade the landscape of prehistoric Worcester, spruce are members of the Pine family. Like other conifers—cone-bearing trees—spruce evolved when dinosaurs roamed the continent. The first conifers probably appeared about 225 million years ago during the Paleozoic Era; trees shaped as we know them today are more recent arrivals, appearing during the Tertiary period, which lasted from about 38 million to 12 million years ago.

Characterized by scaly bark and drooping cones, spruce are also distinguished by their four-sided, sharp needles that spiral around the branch like bristles on a bottle brush. These needles contain volatile oils; when crushed, they release distinctive aromas particular to each species. The scent of red spruce, among the most common native spruces in the Northeast, resembles ripe apples or orange rind.

A beautifully symmetrical tree that makes a handsome ornamental, red spruce grows to a height of 50 to 80 feet, with a trunk up to two feet in diameter. Its stiff, shiny green needles are about 1/2 inch long; small, red-brown cylindrical cones (1 1/4 to 1 1/2 inches long) grow downward from short, straight stalks and drop when mature. The bark of a red spruce is thin and scaly, with a reddish-brown hue.

Like its Canadian cousin white spruce (*P. glauca*), red spruce is a major pulpwood tree for making newsprint. Its highly resonant wood is also favored for musical instruments, including violins and piano sounding boards. In addition, red spruce was once a major source of chewing gum. Resin from both red and black spruce (*P. mariana*) was collected from bark, boiled, skimmed, rolled and cut into bite-sized pieces by companies like the Curtis Chewing Gum Factory of Portland, Maine, in the mid 19th century. Though the gum's taste left something to be desired by today's standards—it has been compared to the likes of "frozen gasoline"—spruce gum was the forerunner of modern chewing gum. Another treat came from red spruce twigs; boiled with sugar and water, they were used to make spruce beer.

Though red spruce is a New England native, the spruces commonly found in Worcester today are introduced species. Among them, the most popular are Norway spruce (*P. abies*)—a towering European native that reaches heights of 200 feet—and Colorado blue spruce (*P. pungens*), noted for its stiff, ice-blue needles.

In recent years, spruces have become vulnerable as possible secondary hosts to the hemlock woolly adelgid, an insidious insect that is destroying various hemlock species throughout the United States. First detected in the Pacific Northwest 80 years ago, the parasite is now prevalent throughout the Northeast, feasting on sap of host trees to the point of defoliation and ultimate death. Though infestations can be controlled with careful use of insecticides, close monitoring and care of endangered trees are crucial for their survival.

New species, such as red maple, hemlock and beech, migrated to the region during the next three millennia, encouraged by a prolonged period of warmer, drier weather. Pathogens, too, defined the landscape: about 4,800 years ago, most of the region's hemlocks succumbed to some form of organism or insect so devastating it took another 500 years for the species to recover. There were fires, as well; in the region around Quinsigamond, major forest fires swept the hills and valleys every 1,000 years, fostering growth of sunlight-greedy species like white pine in the barren patches they left behind. Severe windstorms also rearranged forests, felling and uprooting trees every 50 to 100 years.[5]

Near Quinsigamond, the resulting mosaic of trees and clearings designed and redesigned by heat, moisture and wind, fire, ice and pestilence was a mix of conifers, oak and other hardwoods—a cross between the conifer and hardwood forests to the north and the oak-hardwood forests farther south. For the Nipmucs who made the woods their home, it was a sensory feast of trees: sugar and red maples whose leaves fired autumn; yellow, gray and paper birch, punctuating the forests with their silver and chalky trunks; smooth-skinned beech; craggy, majestic oak; pungent balsam fir; fruity red spruce; tough hickory; sweet chestnut; lacy hemlock; towering white pine.[6]

Each tree, the natives knew, had a valued use. Nuts from beeches, hickories, oaks and chestnuts, ground into meal or boiled for drink, were important food staples. Sap from the brilliant maple, refined over fire, made sugar. Tannin from hemlock bark cured burns and sores. Paper birch peels waterproofed canoes and wigwams. Resin from spruce trees made a thirst-quenching chewing gum. Balsam resin healed sore nipples of nursing mothers.[7]

Medicine, food, tools and warmth—trees yielded their bounty, and more. They shielded the natives from icy winds and harsh sun, and sheltered choice game. They served as blinds for hunters—and camouflage for warriors.

Even so, trees were not sacrosanct for the region's natives. Throughout southern New England, Indians burned trees to clear land for planting. Toward the coast, they also favored fire to make paths for travel and manage forests for game.[8]

These latter practices created a coastal landscape that was more park-like than densely wooded. Once or twice annually, southeastern tribes would clear a chosen forest area of fallen trees and branches, then set fast-moving ground fires that consumed mostly non-woody plants and smaller trees before extinguishing themselves for lack of fuel. The controlled fires opened up the forests for planting and enabled the native hunters to drive game to a chosen location.[9]

This early form of forest management had several advantages: it accelerated the natural process of nutrient recycling, promoting lush growth of grasses and shrubs in the fire's wake; it nourished an abundance of strawberries, raspberries and other hand-picked edibles; it helped destroy plant diseases and pests, such as fleas; and it created excellent wildlife habitats for a diversity of species, including deer, elk, beaver, turkey and quail—animals valued by the natives, and soon by the colonists, for food, fur and leather.[10]

The resulting mosaic of forest and grassland became denser and darker farther inland, away from major rivers and other water-bodies, where tribes like the Nipmucs restricted their use of fire to clearing patches for planting. The basic technique involved killing trees by igniting their bark. Once the trees were dead and leafless, women would plant in the sunlit spaces around the snags. After several years, the dead trees would fall; their remains were burned, enriching soil and opening more land for planting. This process was repeated every eight to ten years, as the soil became exhausted and a new field was needed.[11]

English Land Claims—A Biblical Imperative

These "Indian broken up lands" were highly prized by the European colonists who came to claim the forested frontier. English farming methods required large open spaces for pastures and planting fields—methods which, combined with an insatiable demand for firewood and building materials, had caused massive deforestation and severe wood shortages in England since the 15th century. Coming to the New World, with its vast forests and abundant wildlife, the colonists discovered a bountiful solution to their problems back home, and a challenge: how to harvest the lush forests for fuel, timber and economic gain, and clear the land to reproduce familiar farming patterns. The most efficient way to get started was to locate new communities where well-watered meadows created a natural break in the forest. And if the arduous process of clearing fields had already been started by soon-to-be-displaced native farmers, so much the better.[12]

The English justified these land-takings—despite their own, recent flight from religious oppression—on what they interpreted as a biblical imperative. Citing Genesis 1:28— "Be fruitful, and multiply, and replenish the earth, and subdue it . . ."—the Massachusetts Court defined land claims in terms of visible improvements. By working the earth, fencing it, building permanent structures on it, a settler staked his claim. The Indians, however, knew nothing of land ownership. Theirs was a culture that shared the land with all who lived on it, animal and human.[13]

Hunters for millennia, farmers for centuries, the Nipmucs shifted sites by season. Spring was a time for planting near the main settlement. As maize grew tall, the community would move on to summer hunting and fishing camps, and glean the forest's nuts and berries. Fall's harvest drew them back to the fields and village. Then it was time to prepare for the trip to winter hunting camps. With each move from the main settlement, the Nipmucs would roll up reed mats and bark covers for their wigwams, leaving behind the frames of bent wooden poles, bound at the top. As firewood and fields were exhausted, they abandoned old settlements for new.[14]

Nipmuc possessions were limited to those things made or grown by their own hands; once the objects had lost their usefulness, they were discarded or given away. Similarly, land was never owned in the European sense, passed from one generation to the next, or purchased for tender. Rather, farming plots were allocated to individuals or families by tribal leaders; when the plots were exhausted, they were left fallow, then reallocated. This nomadic life struck the English as primitive and impoverished, and the Indian lands, with few traces of human activity, seemed to them in no way "subdued." Thus, the colonists believed, they had every right to claim, deed and develop land that was virtually—in their eyes—unused.[15]

As they sought choice sites for cultivation, the English also craved open spaces for deeper, psychological reasons. Fear of wilderness, embodied by dense, dark forest, was embedded in the newcomers' world-view. Coming from a land where pagan beliefs still resonated beneath the surface of Christian culture and religious practice, the Europeans deemed the forest a dangerous place. If not the home of demons and dryads, hungry for human appeasement, it was at least a lair for wild beasts and worse. Forest was feared because it was a place to get lost, a place to be separated from human company and swallowed by the unpredictable. It was a place haunted by the forces of evil—by Satan himself—personified by the Indians who dwelled in its shadow. From forest blinds, the natives would launch guerrilla-like attacks against the encroaching English; colonists soon learned to carry muskets with their hoes and to keep close watch over the dangerous border between field and forest.[16]

To many English settlers, Indian raids served only to reinforce their view of the natives as godless, blood-thirsty heathens who deserved destruction. For the Indians, the coming of the

Metacomet, known as King Philip, sagamore of the Wampanoags of Narragansett Bay
Courtesy,
American Antiquarian Society,
Worcester, Massachusetts

Europeans meant a struggle for survival. Not only did the colonists enrage the natives by claiming their villages, planting fields and hunting grounds but they also undercut the Indian economy and political system with the European fur trade. Christian missionaries, too, chiseled away at native culture with their message of enlightenment. Even more devastating, by the year Gookin, Johnson and Belcher reached the Quinsigamond valley, much of New England's Indian population had succumbed to Old World diseases such as smallpox and tuberculosis; throughout the region, their numbers plummeted. Of an estimated 80,000 Indians living in southern New England before the Europeans' arrival, only 20,000 were left by the last quarter of the 17th century—of those, about a fifth remained in Nipmuc territory. By contrast, English settlers in Massachusetts, Connecticut, Rhode Island and Plymouth colonies totaled around 45,000—more than double the surviving natives.[17]

Overwhelmed by the superior numbers and firepower of the settlers, some tribes—like the coastal Massachusetts Indians and the Pawtuckets of the Merrimack Valley—turned to the newcomers for protection and employment. Others, like militant members of the Wampanoags of Plymouth and Narragansetts of Rhode Island, agitated for an uprising of Indian nations against the encroaching English. The Nipmucs found themselves caught in the middle, torn between a desire to live at peace with the newcomers by adopting Christianity and English farming culture, and an allegiance to their Indian brethren who urged resistance.[18]

"Eight Miles Square"—The First Quinsigamond Settlement

This was the backdrop for the negotiations that led to the purchase of Quinsigamond plantation from the Nipmucs on July 13, 1674. Eight years had passed since Daniel Gookin and company first surveyed the site. The summer after his initial visit, Gookin—who by that time had served nearly 20 years as superintendent of all Indians under Massachusetts jurisdiction—helped develop a plan for settling Quinsigamond. To lure new settlers, the plan promised first-comers the right to use Nipmuc planting fields, even if the "Indian broken up lands" were outside their assigned lots.[19]

A tract eight miles square, including present-day Worcester, Holden and part of Auburn, was divided into 90 lots of 25 acres each. Prospective planters would receive from one to four adjoining lots, depending on their means and "quality, estate, usefulnes and otherr considerations" deemed relevant by the settlement committee. Meadow, woodlots and pasturage would be allocated in proportion to the number of house lots received. Near the proposed town center, the planners allocated land for a meeting house that served as a church, as well as 50 acres nearby for the minister. In addition, they set aside 20 acres for a training field and schoolhouse and another 25 for the schoolmaster. Land near Mill Brook was designated for a corn and sawmill, and 50 acres set aside for the miller's house; in addition, the miller was granted the right to "cut timber vpon any lands to Saw forr the vse of ye towne." The plan also included guidelines for assessing lot owners to pay for new mills and roads and for fairly dividing unassigned land.[20]

This design reflected popular wisdom about arranging new communities, articulated in 1635 by an anonymous New Englander in "The Ordering of Towns." The ideal plantation, according to the author, was an area six miles square divided into six concentric zones. At its center was the meetinghouse, surrounded by a ring of houses and common, or shared, planting fields, in turn surrounded by common livestock pastures. Beyond these were larger, 400-acre lots, set aside for those of higher means and position. Once a community was firmly secured, the plantation's common lands were divided among the settlers and new lots apportioned amid the larger tracts in the outer rings. Even so, the author cautioned, no farmhouse should be located more than two miles from the central meetinghouse. While surrounding swamps and woodlots were well-used, homes were concentrated around the plantation's heart—the church.[21]

Orderly plans and land bonuses notwithstanding, it wasn't until 1673 that a group of 32 English settlers agreed on paper to make the move west to Quinsigamond. Earlier settlement efforts had been thwarted by conflicting land claims; among them, a 1,000-acre tract owned by the Malden church since 1662. In addition, one Ephraim Curtis of Sudbury had acquired title to 500 acres, including a choice tract at the proposed plantation's center, right where the planners had located the meetinghouse, minister's lot, a mill and ten house lots. With the intercession of the General Court, compromises were reached on competing claims and a survey was completed. House lots were assigned, most fronting either side of the "country road to Connecticut" that

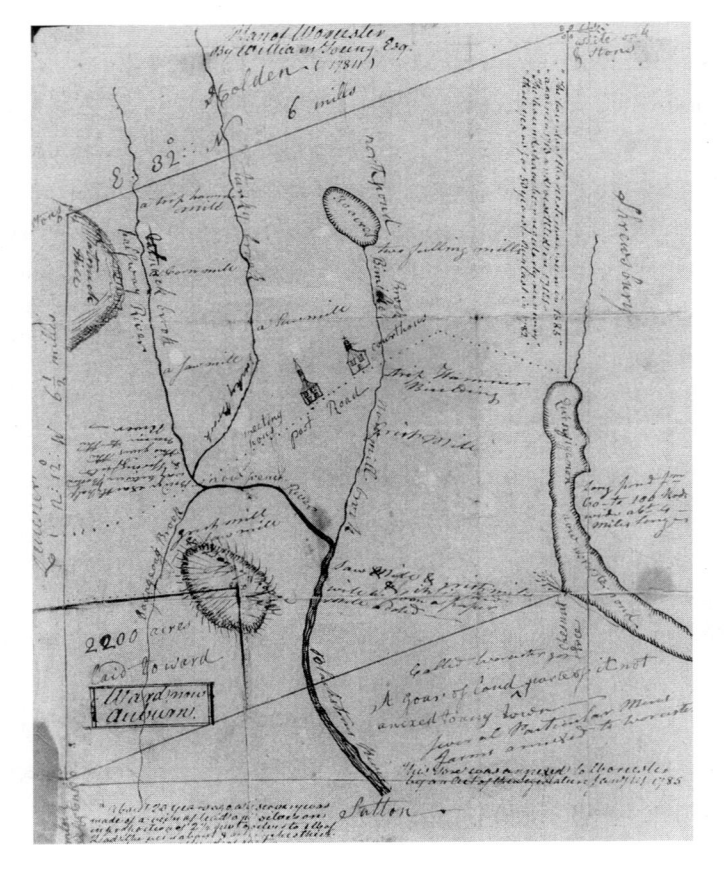

Plan of Worcester, circa 1784,
by William Young
Courtesy,
American Antiquarian Society,
Worcester, Massachusetts

Gookin and company had followed into the valley. Of those 32 lots, however, only 14 were actually paid for by the time the settlement committee was ready to take its next step: the formal, albeit perfunctory, purchase of all land rights from the Nipmucs.[22]

It was Gookin, again, who made the journey in 1674 to Quinsigamond, riding in July's heat up Pakachoag Hill—now Mount St. James, home to Holy Cross College—to meet with two local Nipmuc sagamores, Horowaninit of Pakachoag and Woonaskochu of Tataessit. Pakachoag Hill harbored the largest of three Nipmuc villages on the proposed plantation; Tataessit—later, Tatnuck—was the site of the second village on a hill northwest of Pakachoag, now the location of Worcester's municipal airport. A third, smaller village was situated on a low rise above Quinsigamond's western shore, still known as Wigwam Hill. Together, the three communities numbered between 200 to 300 people.[23]

A loose confederation of tribal villages linked by kinship, the Nipmucs had taken a stance of peaceful coexistence, paying tribute to appease their more powerful Indian neighbors, and not interfering with English territorial claims. Introduced to Christian doctrine two years prior, Horowaninit, called "John" by the English, and Woonaskochu, known as "Solomon," offered no resistance to Gookin's proposal. For a promise of 12 pounds of New England tender, they signed over all rights to the "broken up land and wood land, woods, trees, rivers, brooks, ponds, swamps, meadows, minerals, or things whatsoever, lying and being within the eight miles square" of the Quinsigamond tract. As a down payment, valued at 26 shillings, Gookin presented the sagamores with two coats and four yards of coarse wool cloth, suitable for blankets. The balance was paid in cash two years later, half by Gookin himself, and the rest by a shilling-per-acre assessment on proprietors' house lots.[24]

What Gookin gained for Massachusetts in the transaction was 64 square miles of rich forests, meadows and water. He also gained "extensive" Nipmuc planting fields, including apple orchards set with trees acquired from the English in years prior.[25]

By the following spring, settlement was under way along the Connecticut Road; Gookin and Thomas Prentice, another member of the committee charged with organizing the new plantation, each received 50-acre lots, while 25 acres went to committee member Daniel Henchman. Entrepreneur Ephraim Curtis, who had already set up an Indian trading post and was in the process of building a small house, was assigned 50 acres, in keeping with the earlier court order.[26]

The Connecticut Road was just an east-west path through the forest that skirted the northern tip of Lake Quinsigamond, wide enough for riders on horseback or those who hiked on foot. Within a few months of the settlers' arrival, about six or seven homes stood on either side, including the house of first settler Ephraim Curtis. Though records are scant, it is also believed that Gookin, Henchman, Prentice and proprietor Thomas Brown built houses nearby. Despite this promising start, no more homes were constructed, as most of the planters who signed on for Quinsigamond never made the move.[27]

King Philip's War—The Fall of Quinsigamond

In July 1675, only a few months after building began in earnest, Indians inspired by Metacomet, or "King Philip," sagamore of the Wampanoags of Narragansett Bay, launched an uprising against the English settlers. The ensuing bloody conflict, known as King Philip's War, eventually drew in the Nipmucs. Hostilities surfaced at Quinsigamond plantation during the first summer, when a band of Pakachoag warriors looted Ephraim Curtis's trading post while he was away in Boston. Ironically, the leader of that raid, Matoonus, had been charged by Gookin a year earlier with the responsibility of maintaining English civil order at Pakachoag. But Matoonus had other priorities. Incensed by the execution of his son in 1671 for the alleged murder of an Englishman, Matoonus sought revenge and led the first organized Indian attack against English settlers in Massachusetts Bay Colony, killing five people at Mendon.[28]

A year of tragic losses followed. Hesitant at first to follow Matoonus's lead, the Nipmuc leaders ultimately sided with Indian militants when the English delivered an ultimatum to turn over Matoonus or become enemies. But their resistance was short-lived. The following July, seeking peace for what was left of his people, Sagamore John offered up Matoonus to Massachusetts authorities as proof that his surrender was sincere. Matoonus was shot before a tree in Boston Common by fellow Pakachoags, his head severed and placed on a pole, the gruesome ornament displayed on the gallows, opposite another pole bearing what was left of his son's skull. The Wampanoag leader Metacomet was killed a month later, his body drawn, quartered and hung from a tree, his hand pickled in rum as a war trophy, and his head stuck on a pike for show in Plymouth.[29]

All that remained of Quinsigamond plantation were charred foundations, burned by Indians on December 2, 1675, after English troops had plundered Pakachoag and several other neighboring Indian communities.[30]

Planning for Protection—The Second Quinsigamond Settlement

Another seven years passed before English settlers tried again to settle Quinsigamond. Once more, Daniel Gookin, Daniel Henchman and Thomas Prentice made up the committee charged with organizing the settlement, all three having served as military leaders in King Philip's War. (Gookin, however, temporarily lost his elected post as Assistant to the General Court, a powerful political office, because he sought protection for the Christian Indians during the war.)[31]

The committee had actually commenced plans for resettlement in 1678, but none of the original proprietors was anxious to return to the wilds of Quinsigamond so soon after the Indian uprising. Forcing their hand, the General Court passed an order in October of 1682 that they must move west or forfeit their land grants. The following year, on May 16th, Samuel Andrews of Watertown completed a new survey of the town for the purpose of defining lots. Mapping Quinsigamond plantation as a parallelogram, Andrews marked its four corners by what must have been four remarkable trees—a standard surveying practice of the day. At the plantation's northwest corner stood a birch; at its northeast corner, a white oak; to the southwest, a pine; to the southeast, a chestnut. Within those bounds were 43,020 acres, including 480 acres of meadow. Based on the meadow acreage, the committee decided to divide the entire plantation into 480 lots. Two hundred lots would be set aside for planters, another 80 for public or other specified use, while the balance was allocated to the tract's northern half. Called North Worcester, this half was eventually incorporated as the town of Holden.[32]

Having learned from their first abortive attempt, the settlers planned this time for mutual protection against Indian raids. A citadel would be built on Mill Brook, later called the Fort River, covering a diamond-shaped area a half-mile square, for protection from the Indians. Within its palisades would stand a garrison with a watchtower, as well as six-rod-square hut lots for each settler to use in case of Indian attack. Outside the citadel's wooden walls, the committee laid out a patchwork of ten-acre planting lots and allocated meadow and cedar swamps in proportion to land holdings; those who chose to build homes on their farmland could do so provided they were within musket shot of at least one other home. Lots were also set aside for a meetinghouse, school, and common use, "saw, corn and fulling mills," and the Colony of Massachusetts.[33]

These boundaries were formally confirmed on May 7, 1684. Among the settlers was Captain John Wing, a newly appointed committee member who built the plantation's first corn and sawmills along Mill Brook. Daniel Gookin benefited handily from his years of service to the new plantation, gaining 100 acres on Pakachoag Hill as well as another 80 acres on Raccoon Plain, near the present-day site of Clark University.[34]

That fall, 16 years after he first viewed Quinsigamond, Gookin joined Henchman and Prentice in a petition to the Great and General Court of Massachusetts to rename their plantation Worcester. The new name—used informally since 1668 but made official on September 10, 1684—was, according to tradition, selected to commemorate Oliver Cromwell's 1651 Puritan victory in Worcester, England, over Charles II and the royal House of Stuarts. Derived from the Saxon word *Wegera-ceaster,* or "war castle," the name "Worcester" might also have been an expression of the English settlers' hopes about their new home's security.[35]

Whatever measure of security they enjoyed, however, was short-lived. Two of the community's strongest leaders died within a year of each other, soon after the second settlement's founding: Daniel Henchman in 1686 and Daniel Gookin in 1687. Plagued by Indian attacks, the planters were barely able to cultivate enough crops to feed themselves. Hostilities intensified with the outbreak of Queen Anne's War in 1702, forcing most to flee Worcester. The last holdout, a carpenter-turned-farmer named Digory Serjent who had built his homestead atop Sagatabscot Hill (former site of St. Vincent Hospital), was killed in 1703 or 1704 by Indians, led, according to legend, by Sagamore John of Pakachoag. His wife and five children were taken captive, the wife killed en route to Canada. Two of the children elected to remain with the Indians; the other three were liberated several years later, including Martha Serjent, who married a man named Daniel Shattuck and eventually returned with him to Worcester to build a home on her father's land.[36]

A Town of Two Forts—The Settlement That Stood

In October 1713, several years before Martha's return, Jonas Rice of Marlborough, a planter who had purchased land in Worcester's second settlement, made his way to Sagatabscot Hill with the blessings of the Massachusetts Great and General Court. There he built a new home for himself and began to cultivate the land, including some of the fields once farmed by Digory Serjent. For two years, Rice and his family lived alone on the hill surrounded by forest, celebrating without benefit of friends or other relatives the birth of a new son, Adonijah, on November 7, 1714. The following spring, Jonas's brother Gershom joined him on the hill. And so began the third Worcester settlement.[37]

Five years after Jonas arrived, the new town included several garrisons, the first erected just west of today's city hall. Another of the garrisons stood next to the Connecticut Road, guarding the local mills and providing convenient protection for travelers. These two forts marked either end of the town's main thoroughfare—present-day Main Street—precursors of Worcester's bipolar downtown landscape, bounded by city hall at one end and the courthouse at the other.[38]

Overshadowed by forest, the dirt road was bordered by several homes and businesses. Among them was Deacon Daniel Heywood's garrison house; a pear tree he planted marked the site for more than a century. Nearby was Moses Rice's tavern and the homes of Daniel Ward, Jonathan Hubbard and James Rice. Religious gatherings were initially held at the home of Gershom Rice; by 1717 the town had built its first log-cabin meetinghouse. East of the main thoroughfare flowed Mill Brook, its waters powering saw and corn mills; just south of the stream grew Worcester's first orchard, planted by Gershom Rice. Farther from the town's center, other planters, like Gershom's brother Jonas, staked their claims on choice upland.[39]

All told, in 1718 Worcester was home to 58 log dwellings and about 200 people. A frontier town still struggling to secure its borders from occasional attack by Indians and roving wolves, the "war castle," this time, would stand.[40]

---

[1]William Lincoln, *History of Worcester, Massachusetts, From Its Earliest Settlement to September, 1836: With Various Notices Relating to the History of Worcester County* (Worcester: Charles Hersey, 1862), p. 10; Franklin P. Rice, ed., *Records of the Proprietors of Worcester, Massachusetts* (Worcester: The Worcester Society of Antiquity, 1881), p. 13.

[2]Rice, p. 13; Lincoln, pp. 10–11. Lincoln mentions ten other spellings of Quinsigamond, the one used here being the accepted modern version. Though the October 24, 1668, report of Gookins and company refers to the plantation as "Worcester," the name did not become official until 1684.

[3]Kenneth Moynihan, *Worcester: A New History* (Unpublished manuscript, 1993), pp. 2–4.

[4]Foster, D. R., "Land-use history—four hundred years of vegetation change in New England," in B. L. Turner, A. G. Sal, F. G. Bernaldez and F. DiCastri, eds., *Global Land Use Change: A Perspective from the Columbian Encounter* (SCOPE Publications. Consejo Superior de Investigaciones Cientificas, Madrid: 1995), pp. 253–319.

[5]Foster in B. L. Turner; William Cronon, *Changes in the Land: Indians, Colonists, and the Ecology of New England* (New York: Hill and Wang-div. of Farrar, Straus & Giroux, 1983), p. 32.

[6]Foster in B. L. Turner; Rebecca Rupp, *Red Oaks and Black Birches: The Science and Lore of Trees* (Pownal, Vt.: Garden Way Publishing,1990) pp. 27–28, 226.

[7]Donald Culross Peattie, *A Natural History of Trees of Eastern and Central North America* (Boston: Houghton Mifflin, 1950), pp. 40, 457; Rupp, pp. 18, 27, 41, 76–77, 94, 227, 242.

[8] Cronon, pp. 49–51; According to Foster (in B. L. Turner), no conclusive paleoecological evidence exists of Indians using fire to modify New England forest. Assumptions about Indian land-clearing techniques are based on historical and archeological records alone.

[9] Cronon, pp. 49–50.

[10] Cronon, pp. 50–51.

[11] Cronon, p. 48.

[12] Lincoln, pp. 12, 19–20; Cronon, pp. 20–21.

[13] Cronon, p. 63.

[14] Moynihan, p. 4.

[15] Moynihan, p. 5.

[16] John R. Stilgoe, *Common Landscape of America, 1580 to 1845* (New Haven: Yale University Press, 1982), pp. 7–12; Lincoln, p. 21.

[17] Cronon, pp. 88–89; Moynihan, pp. 3, 5–6.

[18] Moynihan, pp. 6–9, 15.

[19] Lincoln, p. 16; Moynihan, p. 12.

[20] Rice, pp. 14–18; Moynihan, p. 13; Lincoln, pp. 13–14.

[21] Stilgoe, pp. 43–44.

[22] *Celebration of the Two Hundredth Anniversary of the Naming of Worcester, October 14 and 15, 1884* (Worcester: Charles Hamilton Press, 1885), pp. 114–115; Lincoln, pp. 12–16.

[23] Lincoln, p. 31; Moynihan, p. 3.

[24] Lincoln, pp. 16, 17, 22; Moynihan, pp. 13–14.

[25] Lincoln, p. 31; Moynihan, p.14.

[26] Lincoln, pp. 17–19; Moynihan, pp. 12–13.

[27] *Bicentennial*, p. 115; Lincoln, pp. 18–20.

[28] Moynihan, pp. 2, 15–17.

[29] Lincoln, p. 29; Moynihan, p. 34.

[30] *Bicentennial*, p. 46; Moynihan, p. 26.

[31] Rice, p. 33; Moynihan, p. 11, 20–21.

[32] Rice, pp. 33–34; Lincoln, pp. 34–35; Map by Larry A. Bowring, 1975, "The Town of Worcester, Massachusetts, circa 1776—inset of Quinsigamond Plantation, May 16, 1683."

[33] Rice, pp. 34–36; *Bicentennial*, p. 116; Lincoln, pp. 34–35.

[34] Lincoln, p. 35.

[35] Ibid; *Bicentennial*, p. 47.

[36] *Bicentennial*, p. 120; Rice, p. 55; Lincoln, pp. 36–40.

[37] Rice, p. 59; Lincoln, pp. 42–43; Charles Nutt, *History of Worcester and Its People*, Vol. I (New York: Lewis Historical Publishing Co., 1919), p. 215.

[38] Lincoln, pp. 42–44; Edwin Theodore Weiss, Jr., *Patterns and Processes of High Value Residential Districts: The Case of Worcester, 1713–1970*, PhD dissertation, Clark University, 1973, pp. 23–24.

[39] Lincoln, pp. 44–47.

[40] Lincoln, p. 47.

22

CLEARING THE LAND
Chapter Two

It was a day long remembered. On the Town Common, near the liberty pole, flags of the 13 colonies rippled in the breeze. Church bells chimed and drummers beat a rat-a-tat military cadence, enticing more Worcester patriots to join the festivities. Two days earlier, a sedate crowd had gathered near the green to hear Isaiah Thomas read the stirring words from the Old South Meeting House porch. But this Monday, July 15, 1776, was a day for celebrating—a day to rally for freedom and cheer for their new doctrine of liberty, so eloquently stated in the Declaration of Independence.[1]

Joined by town selectmen and Worcester's Committee of Correspondence—which for three years had been nurturing the seeds of rebellion—the crowd greeted the words of the declaration with "repeated huzzas, firing of musketry and cannon, bonfires, and other demonstrations of joy," according to an account that appeared the following week in Thomas's newspaper, *The Massachusetts Spy*.[2]

After incinerating the royal crest of arms that had "in former times decorated, but of late disgraced" the town courthouse, the crowd converged on a former Tory haven, the King's Arms Tavern. There they drank two dozen toasts to their newfound freedom—including "[s]ore eyes to all tories, and a chestnut burr for an eye stone . . . [p]erpetual itching without the benefit of scratching," and defeat to all America's enemies, and enduring freedom and independence for their new country "till the sun grows dim with age, and this earth returns to chaos." Those incendiary words and deeds notwithstanding, the *Spy* reported, "The greatest decency and good order was observed, and at a suitable time each man returned to his respective home."[3]

The first community in America to fete the declaration, setting the tone for future Independence Day celebrations, Worcester had grown in 63 years from a frontier town to a thriving commercial center. Designated the shire of Worcester County in 1731, Worcester now hosted annual sessions of the Superior Court of Judicature, as well as frequent sittings of the Courts of Probate, Common Pleas and General Sessions of the Peace. For the planters and their children who had struggled with bitter winters and hostile Indians to establish a secure settlement, the courts were a welcome boon to commerce. Court sessions became major holidays, a time when farmers and their families throughout the county would travel to Worcester to market goods and produce, to witness court proceedings, and to enjoy diversions such as wrestling, fighting and horse racing down Main Street (until it was outlawed in 1745 as a public nuisance). Crowds gathered, too, for public disciplining of community ne'er-do-wells at the stocks, pillory and whipping post atop Court Hill.[4]

Worcester's designation as a shire town had also attracted new talent to the young community. Among those newcomers, Judge John Chandler, son of a Woodstock, Connecticut, judge by the same name, moved to Worcester when the county was created in 1731. Moderator of town meetings, Chandler filled numerous town and county offices, amassed land holdings and fathered ten children—including the third Judge John Chandler, who carried on his father's tradition of leadership and privilege until the Revolution, when his loyalist leanings cost him his home. Others, like importer Stephen Salisbury, saw promise in the centrally located town and expanded his prosperous Boston businesses to Worcester shortly before the war. Also drawn by good prospects, a young counselor named Levi Lincoln built his legal practice in Worcester after loyalist attorneys fled town; Lincoln's courtroom skill, patriotism and political savvy eventually earned him a post as Thomas Jefferson's attorney general.

With Judge Chandler's fall from grace at the Revolution's outbreak, Lincoln and Salisbury emerged as members of the new community elite—leaders who, along with their descendants, would shape the growing city's political, cultural and physical landscape. But even as revolution reordered the community, another war, a war of centuries, was restructuring the land surrounding Worcester. It was a war against wilderness, a struggle to clear the land of trees and roots and rock—whose impact would be as profound for New England's ecology as the Revolution was for the nation's political system.

Between Meetinghouse and Courthouse—The Landscape of Colonial Worcester

As Worcester celebrated the Declaration of Independence, evidence of that other war was readily visible. Once wild and wooded, the rolling hills and well-watered valleys near Quinsigamond were now a verdant patchwork quilt of meadow, pasture, tillage and hay fields, bordered by forest and woodlot, and seamed by walls of unearthed, all-too-abundant stone. Despite the unwelcome glacial legacy of rocky soil, Worcester farmers had managed to clear and cultivate about 5,550 acres—over a fifth of the town—in just three generations. During the same period, the town census had increased nearly tenfold, to 1,925 inhabitants.[5]

No longer a narrow path through ancient forest, Main Street was now lined with homes, taverns, offices and storefronts. In fact, by the century's second half, the former Connecticut Road was the residential nucleus for the village's wealthiest and most influential citizens. The garrisons that once defined the street's poles were just memories, but houses remained clustered at either end of the street—no longer for mutual protection, but for easy access to the public buildings that had replaced the forts: the meetinghouse to the south and courthouse to the north.[6]

By the time of the July 15th festivities, the bipolar housing arrangement also reflected the split in local politics. Near the courthouse lived several prominent patriots, including *The Massachusetts Spy* publisher Isaiah Thomas and blacksmith Timothy Bigelow, a founding member

EASTERN WHITE PINE
Pinus strobus

Emblazoned on the first flag of America's Revolutionary forces, Eastern white pine is a magnificent tree that towered over New England's forests for millennia until the coming of European colonists. Soaring as high as 150 to 200 feet, with trunks over four feet in diameter, these ancient sylvan giants grew wherever they could stretch to the sun, favoring sandy, well-drained soil on dry ridges or barren patches left by forest fires. So abundant were the virgin stands—by one estimate, East Coast pineries equaled about 750 billion board feet of timber—that winds would carry spring time storms of white pine's yellow pollen hundreds of miles out to sea, dusting decks of approaching vessels. Taller and straighter than any Old World species, *Pinus strobus* was soon prized for ship masts and deemed a critical resource for the Royal Navy.

Noted for its "pagoda-like" tiers of whorled branches, white pine grows clusters of 2- to 5-inch-long, bluish-green needles, typically in clumps of five. Like most gymnosperms (Greek for "naked seed"), it shelters its seeds in cones. Narrow and cylindrical, 4 to 8 inches long, these drooping, yellow-brown cones grow on half-inch stalks; their thin, round scales are flat, flexible and free of prickles. When young, white pine's bark is smooth and green; with age it turns gray, rough and thick, with deep furrows and scaly ridges.

The wood within is close-grained and easily cut. It is also relatively lightweight, about 25 pounds per cubic foot. Those characteristics, coupled with white pine's tendency to grow tall and straight, dropping lower branches as it gains height, make it an ideal timber tree. For European colonists, discovering the blue-green veins of virgin white pine in ancient forests was like striking gold. They felled the giant evergreens for everything from shipmasts to covered bridges, furniture, figureheads and coffins. Depleting virgin pineries first in New England and throughout the Northeast, later near the Great Lakes and into the Appalachians, the harvest lasted three centuries. Easily milled and finished, white pine was used to frame, shingle and panel homes, favored for loom heddles, hobby horses, bobsleds and matchsticks.

The Royal Navy first became enamored with white pine when Captain George Weymouth explored Maine's rivers in 1605. Awed by the towering trees, Weymouth brought home to England mastwood samples and seeds that were planted at Longleat, the estate of Thomas, Viscount of Weymouth. But the so-called Weymouth pine never grew as tall in England as in its native habitat, a major disappointment to the monarchy, which was dependent on foreign powers for its mastwood supply. In 1691, during the reign of William and Mary, the British Crown staked its first claim on the Colonies' finest white pines, reserving them for the Royal Navy. The largest specimens were marked with the King's Broad Arrow—a blaze that soon came to symbolize one more instance of British tyranny.

Defying royal edicts, colonial pioneers deliberately felled the marked trees, destroyed the blaze and cut the timber for milling or export. In 1774, the Continental Congress banned all exports to Great Britain, including mastwood. The grandest white pines were now reserved for the fledgling American fleet; three of the best became masts on the *Ranger,* commandeered by Captain John Paul Jones.

Today, after centuries of exploitation, the tallest white pines average only 100 feet. The ancient giants of old growth forests are gone; *Pinus strobus* is typically found thriving in long-neglected pastures, shading the land once cleared with so much effort and waste.

of Worcester's Committee of Correspondence. As leader of the town's Minutemen, Bigelow headed the march to Cambridge on April 19, 1775, the day shots were fired at Lexington and Concord; his military skills soon earned him a commission as major, then colonel in the Continental Army. It was Bigelow who helped smuggle Isaiah Thomas's printing press from Boston to Worcester in 1775, after *The Massachusetts Spy* was censored. Thomas, who was to become one of the nation's leading publishers, set up his press first in Bigelow's basement, later in an office by the courthouse, and eventually built his own home next door.[7]

Also at Main Street's north end lived merchant Stephen Salisbury, who had established a Worcester branch of the Salisbury brothers' successful Boston importing business near the courthouse in 1767 and developed a farm on land nearby. Salisbury would soon become a leader and major landowner in the community; through his niece's marriage after the Revolution, his family would be linked to another major Worcester family—the Lincolns. Together, the Salisburys and Lincolns would raise a dynasty of politicians and civic leaders who would guide Worcester and New England well into the next century.[8]

Behind Bigelow's property sprawled the 500-acre Chandler estate, owned by Judge John Chandler III. A staunch loyalist who was the town's ranking military officer during the French and Indian Wars, Judge Chandler had inherited the family estate when his father died in 1762; but he made his home and office across town at the south end of Main Street, near the meetinghouse. John's brother Gardiner, who served as sheriff from 1762 until the Revolution, lived near him in a mansion that became a Tory meeting place. Nearby, too, lived the Chandler's brother-in-law, counselor James Putnam. A Tory, like his in-laws, Putnam was a distinguished jurist who alienated his fellow townspeople by using his formidable legal talents to protect the royalist government.[9]

Judge Chandler and James Putnam paid heavily for their politics. In 1774, during a dramatic confrontation at the King's Arms Tavern, they were among a group of loyalists forced to publicly recant a petition they had signed condemning Worcester patriots who opposed the Crown. Putnam eventually fled Worcester to escape the town's wrath. Judge Chandler was banished from Worcester in the summer of 1774 and died in London with only a fraction of his estate—the rest was confiscated.[10]

Still, Chandler left his mark on Worcester's landscape. His home, office and the family store, all located near the meetinghouse, were built on land that had originally been designated as part of the Town Common. As the town's wealthiest and most powerful citizen before the war, Judge Chandler undoubtedly had little trouble converting public land to private use. In so doing, he hastened the erosion of Worcester's only shared open land—a process that eventually prompted the creation of the city's urban parks system a century later.

Chipping Away the Green—Evolution of the Town Common

A trapezoidal plot of green set behind the meetinghouse, the Town Common served as a training field for Captain Bigelow's local militia as well as a public gathering place. The site where Minutemen mustered to march on Concord and patriots joined to cheer rebellion, it was also home to an ancient burial ground and an impoundment for lost cows or "disorderly beasts."[11]

This latter use was the last vestige of the Common's original function as the central, shared plot of land in a corporately owned community. Like other New England towns, Worcester was originally laid out to embody the principle of common effort for the common good. Pasture that surrounded the town's nucleus of meetinghouse, green and homes was to be shared, with the Common designed as a way station for livestock *en route* to or from a day's grazing. The design reflected the intention that the townspeople would bring their animals to the Common each morning; the town herdsman would then lead the livestock to the common pasture, and bring them back to the Common for collection at dusk.[12]

The earliest plans for the first Worcester settlement, drafted in 1669 under Daniel Gookin's guidance, reflected these priorities. Initially, the committee set aside 20 acres at the town's center for a Common, and noted that "large high waies" be left between lot divisions "forr the turning & driuing Catle into the comons and conuinient pastures forr sheep." The plan also specified that the Common be used for "a trayning place" and site for a future "Scoole house," located "as nearre as may bee wherre the meeting house Shalbe placed."[13]

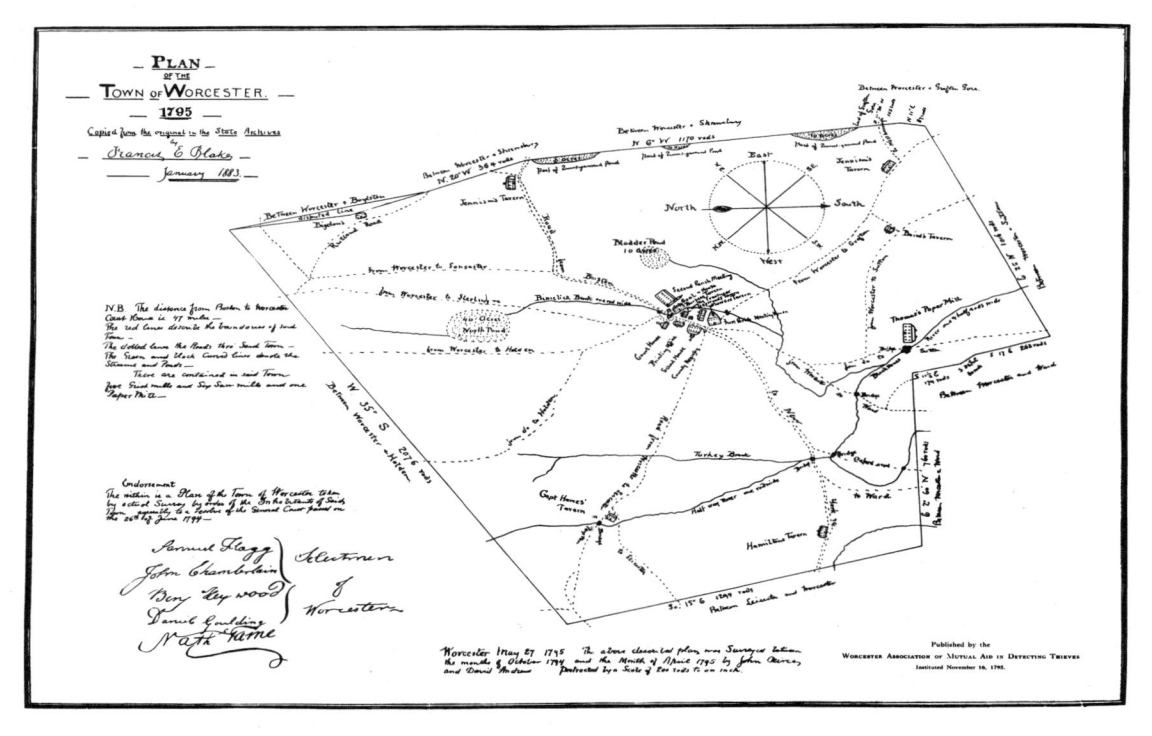

Plan of the Town of Worcester, 1795.

Copy made in 1883.

Courtesy, American Antiquarian Society, Worcester, Massachusetts

27   CLEARING THE LAND

A survey of the Town Common made in 1734 by Benjamin Flagg showed a dog-leg-shaped, 11-acre plot along the Connecticut Road that became Main Street. Bordered to the south by what is now Franklin Street, the Common's lower section, or "foot," included a burial place and meetinghouse. A transverse road radiating from the meetinghouse defined the northern edge of the lower Common; north of the road, the "leg" reached as far as today's Elm Street, wrapping around a square plot of Main Street property owned by Moses Rice. By 1776, additional land uses had devoured the upper Common, including the town's first grammar school and Judge John Chandler's properties. The transverse road had become Front Street, now the Common's northern border.[14]

This erosion of the Common reflected the community's shifting cultural and economic priorities. As markets for agricultural products, both here and abroad, expanded during the 18th century, New England farmers abandoned the principle of common fields and pasture in favor of private land cultivation to meet increased demand. By the century's second half, successful husbandmen like Shrewsbury's Artemas Ward—a leader in town, state and national politics who was commander-in-chief of the Continental Army until replaced by George Washington—no longer limited themselves to producing food and goods for household needs and local exchange. Instead, the prosperous Ward farm, just east of Worcester, diversified its output to include a variety of products for the Brighton market that served Boston, including livestock, meat, butter, cheese and hay.[15]

"The First to Set Out Trees"—Dr. Elijah Dix

As entrepreneurial husbandmen acquired more land for their own crops, cows and sheep, the need for a central gathering place for livestock became an anachronism. Still, the Town Common had its place. Even as commercially minded men chipped away its edges, the Common remained Worcester's core, home to its meetinghouse, a training field for those who would protect its borders, a sanctuary to its departed members.

Worcester Town Common, circa 1903
From the collections of
WORCESTER HISTORICAL MUSEUM,
Worcester, Massachusetts

To enhance this last parcel of shared land, the townspeople planted trees. When the plantings began is unknown, but by 1761 there were enough trees to warrant Worcester's first tree ordinance. At a general town meeting on March 2 led by Judge John Chandler, after debating highway taxes for road repair, how to manage wandering swine and the need for a new meetinghouse, the town passed the following:

> Voted That the Selectmen at the Charge of the Town take proper care for preserving ye growth of ye Trees sett out about the meeting House for shades by Boxing them & that the Inhabitants be desired not to Tye their Horses to them.[16]

Along Main Street, there were other trees, as well. According to one map of Worcester in 1776, a huge, old elm grew at the corner of today's Main and Pleasant Streets—a tree so respected it was left standing as the town developed roads around it; hence, the reason, though the elm is long gone, why Pleasant is slightly offset from Front Street. There was also Deacon Daniel Heywood's pear tree, planted by the town's first minister near his garrison home, shading the corner of what is now Exchange Street well into the 19th century.[17]

Like that legendary elm and pear, some of the trees along Main Street were either remnants of ancient forest or reminders of Worcester's earliest residents. As the town grew, and more land was cleared to make way for buildings and roads, at least one individual took it upon himself to ensure that the streets remained shaded—a physician by the name of Elijah Dix.

A student of Dr. John Green, Sr., the town's leading physician, Dix moved to Worcester in about 1770 to open his medical practice and apothecary shop next to the elm-shaded home he built near the courthouse. Remembered by Massachusetts Governor Levi Lincoln (eldest son of U.S. Attorney General Levi Lincoln) as "a man of robust frame and iron constitution, in a great degree self-educated, and always self-reliant," Dix was a public-spirited individual who found time away from his successful practice for many civic causes. Among them, he helped promote the Worcester & Boston Turnpike to facilitate travel between the two cities, and was a founder of the Worcester Fire Society, a kind of early insurance group whose members banded together to rescue one another's property in case of fire. In addition, Dix was a founder of Worcester's first private academy, the Centre School.[18]

He was also concerned about the physical appearance of his growing community. According to a tribute by his son-in-law, the Reverend Thaddeus M. Harris, Dix's attentiveness to public improvements led him to be "the first to set trees himself, and induce others to plant them, on the borders of Main Street." His interest in trees carried over to horticulture; between ministering to the sick and shepherding civic causes, Dix tended his orchard and developed a pear that bore his name.[19]

Unfortunately, Dix's relentless enthusiasm for tree planting and other civic improvements earned him some enemies. His dogmatic views and strong-willed temperament prompted some

SHAGBARK HICKORY
Carya ovata

Valued for its high energy content, shagbark hickory was a key resource in the colonial economy. Among American trees, it ranks second only to the locust in fuel content; a cord of *Carya ovata*, when burned, produces roughly the same number of BTUs as a ton of coal. Common throughout the eastern United States, shagbark was a premium fuelwood and essential resource for the production of charcoal.

A member of the walnut family, *C. ovata* takes its Latin name from its ovoid nuts. White and sweet, shagbark nuts are encased in a tough, thick husk that ripens to a dark brown before splitting into four sections to reveal its fruit. The tree produces five large, saw-toothed, oval leaflets on each leaf stalk, which turn a deep golden-brown in autumn. Growing to heights of 70 to 100 feet, with a trunk diameter of up to 2 feet, shagbark hickory is most easily recognized by its strips of peeling gray bark, not unlike a shaggy cloak.

Parts of the shagbark have found many uses over the centuries. Indians prized the sweet nuts, pounding and boiling them to make a creamy substance used in cooking and baking; the Indian word for this nut-based staple—*pawcohiccora*—is the root for the English name "hickory." Colonists, in addition to burning shagbark for its fuel content, soon discovered that its tangy green wood smoke enhanced the flavor of meat. They extracted a yellow dye from the inner bark to brighten yarns and used the tough, hard-to-split wood for anything requiring durability, including tool handles, barrel hoops, dowels and door hinges.

The tree's preeminence as a symbol of durability and strength is perhaps best remembered in connection with General Andrew Jackson, nicknamed "Old Hickory" during the War of 1812 for his toughness and stamina. Old Hickory he remained, all the way to the White House, where he served as the nation's seventh president, and beyond to the grave, where his final resting place at The Hermitage is shaded by six giant shagbarks.

In Worcester, shagbarks are still among the most common tree species, flourishing in parks and gardens, shading streets. They can be found throughout the woodlands within and around the city limits, towering over long-abandoned stonewalls that once separated field and pasture.

Looking East from Denny Hill, by Ralph Earl, considered the earliest painting of Worcester.
Courtesy, Worcester Art Museum

of his antagonists to trick him one night with a call for help from a nonexistent patient and to attempt to ambush him *en route*, hoping to drive him out of town. For his tree-planting efforts, Dix was ridiculed. [20]

Eventually, he moved on. The father of eight and grandfather of Dorothea Lynde Dix—who carried on the family tradition of public service by devoting her life to improving care of the mentally ill—Dix built a wholesale drugstore near Boston's Faneuil Hall, then moved to Boston in 1795. He further expanded his pharmaceutical business with a sulfur-refining plant and laboratory in South Boston, investing the proceeds from his successful enterprises in Maine real estate. Tragically, that was to be his undoing; on one of his frequent visits to his holdings in the northern woods, Dix was murdered, according to Lincoln, by "a conspiracy of squatters and fraudulent contractors and debtors." He died in Dixmont, Maine—one of two towns he founded—in 1809.[21]

By Girdling or By Ax—The Farmer's War with Trees

Dix's commitment to planting trees along Worcester's Main Street contrasted sharply with the priorities of neighboring farmers, who were just as committed to ridding their land of trees. Oblivious to the devastating consequences of deforestation learned centuries earlier by their European forebears, husbandmen cleared land with a vengeance.

By girdling or by ax, they felled forests for planting. Girdling was initially favored as the least laborious method: borrowing from the Indian practice of killing a tree by burning away its bark to prevent it from leafing, colonial farmers would strip a swath of bark from around a large tree trunk, then plant maize at its feet. The rotting tree would continue to enrich the soil with nutrients until it toppled—with any luck, missing people, livestock and fences as it fell.[22]

Given those inherent risks, and the fact that many years would pass before a field was completely cleared of unsightly girdled trees, by the late 18th century, farmers preferred the ax. Felling trees in late summer to prevent stumps from sprouting, they would burn the remains the following spring. The resulting ashes would fertilize the newly cleared land, enabling husbandmen to harvest a good crop of maize the first year, winter rye the second and European grains beyond that. Alternatively, by the third growing season, land could be seeded for pasture or mowing.[23]

Any nutritive benefits to soil of these land-clearing practices were short-lived, however. Ultimately, removing trees meant removing the very reason that prime agricultural land was so fertile in the first place. Even as farmers learned to recognize soil quality by the type of forest growing there—favoring hardwood forests of hickory, maple, ash and beech for their rich humus, and avoiding conifer stands of hemlock, spruce, pitch and white pine for their acidic or sandy soil—they failed to acknowledge that the soil was a product of the forest as much as the forest was a product of the soil. By girdling the hickories or felling the maples to make way for crops, they also removed the source of leaves that enriched the forest floor as they decomposed and the network of roots that stabilized soil and trapped moisture in the ground. As a result, the choicest land, once cleared, soon lost its seemingly boundless fertility. As fields wore out, farmers moved on, axes in hand, to the next stand.[24]

Plundering the Wilderness—An Economy Fueled by Timber

Others felled trees, too. Loggers thinned the woods, selecting the largest, choicest trees to meet the voracious demand for lumber both here and abroad. They chopped down soaring white pine for ship masts and house frames; resinous pitch pine for turpentine and tar; sturdy oak for buckets, barrel staves and tannin; dense maple for bread boards, shoe lasts and chairs; tough hickory for roof beams, tool handles and muzzle ramrods; shock-resistant white ash for hay forks and plows; strong walnut for gunstocks and decorative cabinetwork; solid yellow birch for wagon-wheel hubs and ox yokes; humidity-tolerant cherry for clocks and doors; light, rot-resistant cedar for shingles and fence posts.[25]

New England woodsmen cut with abandon, assuming the forest bounty was endless. They used smaller trees to cushion the fall of giant pines, wasting lumber rather than labor. Less-than-perfect felled trees were burned on the spot; only the clearest pine was desired, even for everyday items like shingles and tabletops. Despite edicts from the British Crown, beginning in 1691, to reserve the tallest and straightest white pines for the Royal Navy's ship masts—edicts prompted by the English timber shortage and a series of wars that constrained the Crown's ability to import shipbuilding materials—colonists continued the pine harvest, ignoring the arrow-shaped blaze that marked the Navy's trees. Hardwoods filled in where pines fell; as a result, many of the region's giants—some towering as high as 200 feet, measuring six feet in diameter—were gone by the end of the 18th century. They vanished first from coastal and southern New England, a century later from the deep woods of New Hampshire and Maine.[26]

Cedars, too, were soon depleted. Found primarily in swamps, red and white cedars were valued for their ability to withstand moisture. Milled into clapboards and shingles, they provided the favored means to weatherproof homes. Shaped into posts, they were combined with chestnut rails and pickets to create decay-resistant fencing, prior to the advent of stone walls. For this reason, cedar swamps were valued land holdings; plans for the second Quinsigamond plantation in 1684 carefully allocated cedar swamps along with meadowland. Nearly 50 years later, in 1732, town officials were still concerned with platting and parceling out cedar swamps along Mill Brook. Like white pine, however, felled cedars were unlikely to regenerate; typically, red maples grew in their place. Thus, by midcentury cedars were an endangered species throughout New England. By century's end, they had vanished from Worcester.[27]

Wasting trees was encouraged by the economics of sawmills, which provided an essential service to expanding communities. Though water-powered mills, such as Worcester's first sawmill on Mill Brook built by Captain John Wing during the second settlement, were a cost-effective alternative to the labor-intensive method of hand-sawing boards, mill operation depended on seasonal water supplies. Even under the best of conditions, when snow-melt swelled streams, a colonial sawmill's daily output was limited to perhaps a few hundred board feet, at best. Responding to seemingly insatiable demands of a growing community—by 1784, Worcester had at least four sawmills along Tatnuck Brook, Turkey Brook, Mill Brook and the French (Middle) River—millers had a strong incentive to maximize productivity by minimizing the amount of time and volume of water required to cut each board. That meant, in essence, using only the most knot-free, straight-grained timber, and tossing anything below standard.[28]

Millions of trees were also consumed in the production of potash, a crude form of potassium carbonate derived from wood ashes. A colonial cash crop that gave farmers a profit motive to clear new fields by burning forests and processing the ashes, this chemical salt was used to make a variety of products here and in Europe, including soap, fertilizer, gunpowder, glass and wool. It took about one acre of forest to make two tons of potash, worth $200 to $300 per ton by 1800. Sugar maples were favored for their high ash yield; one cord of maple, when burned, produced about 140 pounds of ash. By treating the ash with water, farmers or manufacturers—like those who flourished near the hardwood forests along Worcester's future Pleasant Street—leached out the potash. The solution was then boiled in large iron kettles until the water evaporated, leaving behind the valuable salt. Nicknamed "black gold," potash put cash in the hands of struggling farmers—and hastened the taking of forests.[29]

Charcoal making to fuel the iron furnaces near ore-rich deposits in western Massachusetts,

Connecticut and Rhode Island furthered forest destruction in southern New England. Hickory, with its high BTU content, and white oak were preferred by the colliers who tended the shallow, covered pits of burning wood. It took about a week or two for the smoldering logs to reduce to charcoal—as much as 40 bushels per cord. Just over six times that amount—250 bushels of charcoal—was needed to produce one ton of finished iron. Since it was not unusual for one furnace to make over 500 tons of iron annually, the growing demand for domestic iron accelerated the pace of deforestation: on average, each colonial furnace claimed over two square miles of forest.[30]

The greatest demand on the region's forest, however, was for firewood. Faced with a seemingly endless supply of trees, New England colonists saw no need to conserve resources, instead favoring large fires in open hearths to warm their homes. During the harsh winters, fires were left burning day and night in every room; the average household consumed from 20 to 40 cords of wood annually—at the high end, using the equivalent of at least an acre of forest to stay warm for a year. To meet that need, many farmers kept an abutting tract of forest as a woodlot; like the colliers, they favored hickory and oak, which burned slowly and produced the most heat per cord. This voracious demand for fuel sometimes caused a local shortage of firewood within less than a generation of a town's founding, though public concern over regionwide fuel wood scarcities didn't peak until the mid-19th century.[31]

For Worcester, the woodlots were still plentiful by century's end. Writing in 1793, Peter Whitney described the town as "well supplied with wood. And as every farmer has his own plat of woodland upon his homestead, so the face of the town appears more woody from the hills, than it is in fact." Worcester's remaining forests, noted Whitney, included "oak, walnut and chestnut, on the higher lands, some pine on the small plains and valleys, and in the swamps and low lands, ash, birch and maple."[32]

Another view of Worcester recorded in 1796 gives a less sylvan impression, however. In what is thought to be the earliest painting of the town, *Looking East from Denny Hill*, by Ralph Earl, shows a rolling rural landscape. In the foreground, farm laborers pitch hay into an ox-drawn cart; beyond, a patchwork of cultivated fields and orchards, broken by an occasional row of trees, blanket hills and valley. The white spires of the Old South Meeting House and Second Parish Church, near Lincoln Square, are barely visible in the distance; overall, the scene is pastoral, a paean to the triumph of farm over forest.[33]

Ecosystem Transformed—The Impact of Deforestation on Southern New England

The cumulative effect of deforestation in southern New England—a process that continued well into the next century—was profound. Bereft of their wooded habitats, once abundant animals like wild turkey, wolf and bear disappeared. Exposed soil, no longer anchored by roots or enriched by decaying leaves, baked in the sun and washed into rivers and streams. That soil erosion, combined with changes in the way soil retained and released moisture, altered drainage patterns and seasonal stream-flows.[34]

In place of ancient trees, European grasses thrived; with them came numerous, prolific foreign weeds, including plantain, Saint John's Wort, couch grass, charlock and cockle. The cows and sheep that grazed amid grass and weeds also wandered into unfenced woodlots, hindering forest growth by nibbling on seedlings. Their browsing habits, along with colonial clear-cutting practices and demand for timber products, altered the mix of trees; around Worcester, hardwoods like beech, sugar maple and oak became scarcer, as did hemlock and pine. In their place flourished stump-sprouting species like chestnut.[35]

In short, as the colonists cleared the land, they radically transformed its ecosystem. Pasture replaced forest, domestic livestock grazed where wild animals once flourished, foreign species of grasses and weeds choked out native vegetation and forest mix changed. In areas where trees no longer stood, temperatures became more extreme and water tables lowered. Soils were less able to retain moisture, causing increased runoff and flooding. Sawmills and gristmills impounded water, altering river levels and fish populations. Sawdust and slag contaminated streams. Poor husbandry exhausted the land and facilitated the spread of crop blights and pests.[36]

Despite those growing problems, landclearing accelerated well into the 19th century. Warnings by observers like the Swedish naturalist Peter Kalm went unheeded. Writing of his New World travels in 1749, Kalm observed, "We can hardly be more hostile toward our woods in Sweden and Finland than they are here: their eyes are fixed upon the present gain, and they are blind to the future."[37]

In Massachusetts, deforestation peaked about 1860, when roughly two-thirds of the state was open land, compared to one-tenth in 1800; many Central Massachusetts hill towns had cleared more than 75 percent of upland areas by midcentury. Some communities quickened that pace: in the farming town of Petersham, about 25 miles northwest of Worcester, half the township was open land by 1800; 50 years later, almost 85 percent of the town's land had been cleared to make way for pasture and crops.[38]

Planting Trees in Tamed Spaces—Orchards and Gardens

Forest thus banished, farmers planted orchards. Pear trees were popular, as well as apple trees, especially for cider making. Typically planted in large, 10- to 15-acre tracts of sandy or gravelly soil unsuited for field crops, the trees were spaced about 20 yards apart so their roots wouldn't interlace. As the orchard matured, livestock were allowed to graze among the shady trees; their tendency to nibble on low branches had the effect of pruning the fruit trees to the "browse line," about six feet up the trunk. That mark became the basis for horticultural pruning standards—today, even when no cows are nearby, fruit trees are often limbed up to the six-foot mark.[39]

The first orchard in Massachusetts was planted around 1625 by the clergyman William Blaxton on Boston's Beacon Hill. Blaxton moved to Rhode Island ten years later and continued planting; the apple he named Blaxton's Yellow Sweeting was probably America's first named variety, today known as the Sweet Rhode Island Greening.[40]

In Worcester, Jonas Rice's brother Gershom planted the first orchard near today's Washington Square, within a few years of the town's founding in 1713. Prior to that time, the Nipmucs had planted apple orchards, possibly in the same vicinity. Their trees were gained in trade with English settlers, who made a practice of growing fruit trees for exchange during the early 17th century.[41]

Gardens, too, were a favored place for trees. While the earliest Puritan gardens in Plymouth Colony were simple and utilitarian—an informal mix of flowers and herbs used for dyes and medicines—gardens of Massachusetts Bay Colony's wealthy landowners were based on the formal style of English manor gardens. A typical manor garden of the 17th or 18th century would include a long central path leading from the main house to an arbor or summer house, flanked by narrow, rectangular beds. Around that central axis were planted L- or T-shaped beds, often bordered by low-clipped hedges; the garden's corners were shaded by trees, its perimeter defined by a decorative fence.[42]

As the colonists prospered, so did their gardens, although few new plant materials were introduced prior to the Revolution. With the war's end, however, as the economy grew and foreign trade flourished once again, a greater variety of species became available. Among the major suppliers of trees in the Northeast was the Prince Nursery, founded in 1737 by Robert Prince in Flushing Landing, Long Island. Run by four generations, the nursery did a brisk business in fruit trees: Prince's first advertisement in 1767 mentioned "apple, plum, peach, nectarine, cherry, apricot, and pear" trees for sale. Prince was also the first American nursery to heavily promote ornamentals. A 1774 ad in the *New York Mercury* listed magnolias, catalpas and mulberries, as well as fruit trees and filberts.[43]

Apple tree, one of the first orchard trees planted by both Nipmucs and settlers.

Hence, domesticated trees were nurtured for food, shade and ornament even as trees in the wild were felled for pasture, fuel and tabletop. To the colonists, there was no contradiction: by taking the forests, they were simply replicating familiar landscape patterns of European farming culture and making proficient use of abundant resources; by planting orchards, they were increasing the land's bounty; by cultivating gardens, they were emulating European aesthetics. As in the Old World, trees, once tamed, were prized. No Indians lurked in the orchard, no shades of dryads or goblins flitted amidst garden walls. Where settlers planted, the land was safe.

So it was that colonists in Worcester and other New England communities embellished their towns with trees even as they felled forests at the perimeter. On April 7, 1783, five months before the Revolution's end, Worcester residents gathered for their monthly 3 p.m. town meeting to discuss, among other priorities, the need to protect the town's trees. Taking a step beyond the 1761 ordinance, they passed the following:

> Whereas a number of persons have manifested a disposition to set out trees for shades near the Meeting house & elsewhere about the Center of this Town, & the Town being desirous of encouraging Such a measure which will be beneficial as well as ornamental. Therefore voted, that any person being an Inhabitant of this town, who shall injure or destroy such trees so set out, shall pay a fine not exceeding twenty shillings for every offense, to be disposed of to the use of the poor of the town.[44]

Those cherished trees would soon symbolize more than just the aesthetic sensibilities of Worcester's revolutionary leaders. With the coming transformation of America from a rural to urban industrial society, city trees would become reminders of a rapidly vanishing, pastoral way of life—that of the "noble husbandman," a romanticized figure whose image still resonates in America's collective unconscious. As factories replaced farms and urban centers grew congested, trees would come to represent an idealized rural past of simplicity, morality and verdant fields. It is perhaps the greatest irony that the very husbandmen whose memory would eventually be hallowed by trees did so much to destroy so many.[45]

Trees Common to 18th-Century New England Gardens

Flowering Almond

Sweet Crab Apple

White and European Ash

American and
 European Beech

Black and River Birch

Box Elder

Butternut

Atlantic White Cedar

Chinaberry

Chinquapin

Cucumber Tree

Bald Cypress

Dogwood

Elm

Balsam Fir

Hawthorn

Shell-Bark and
 Scaly-Bark Hickory

Horse Chestnut

Ironwood

Mountain Laurel

Linden

Honey Locust

Juniper

Kentucky Coffee Tree

Norway, Silver and
 Sugar Maple

Mimosa

Moosewood

Oak

Olive

Osage Orange

Pecan

White, Loblolly and
 Virginia Scrub Pine

Eastern and Lombardy Poplar

Sourwood

Stewartia

Tupelo

Umbrella Tree

Yellow and Weeping Willow

From Favretti, Rudy J., *Early New England Gardens: 1620–1840* (Sturbridge, Mass.: 1966), pp.22–27. Collection of the American Antiquarian Society.

[1] *The Massachusetts Spy*, July 24, 1776, cited in William Lincoln, *History of Worcester, Massachusetts, From Its Earliest Settlement to September, 1836: With Various Notices Relating to the History of Worcester County* (Worcester: Charles Hersey, 1862), p. 103.

[2] Ibid.

[3] Ibid.

[4] W. Lincoln History, pp. 57–58, 103.

[5] According to a 1771 tax census, Worcesterites had claimed and cultivated 22.5% of the town, including 1,184 acres of fresh meadow, 1,884 acres of pasture, 1,184 acres of tillage and 1,298 acres of English and upland mowing land: Bettye Hobbs Pruit, ed., *The Massachusetts Tax Valuation List of 1771* (Boston: G. K. Hall & Co., 1978), pp. 373–79; calculations based on 24,704 acres in Worcester. Holden was incorporated in 1740, comprised of Worcester's northern half; the southwestern corner of Worcester became part of Ward (named for Artemas Ward), later Auburn, in 1778: Lincoln, pp. 139–40. Town census 1775 from Charles Nutt, *History of Worcester and Its People*, Vol. I (New York: Lewis Historical Publishing Co., 1919).

[6] Edwin Theodore Weiss, Jr., *Patterns and Processes of High Value Residential Districts: The Case of Worcester, 1713–1970*, PhD dissertation, Clark University, 1973 (Ann Arbor, Mich.: University Microfilms), p. 27.

[7] Lincoln, pp. 232–35, 240–46, 418–19; S. Triscott, *Map of Worcester, Mass., Showing Oldest Roads and Location of Earliest Settlers*.

[8] Lincoln, 194–95; Charles Nutt, *History of Worcester and Its People*, Vol. II (New York: Lewis Historical Publishing Co., 1919), pp. 172, 221, 253.

[9] Nutt, pp. 75–77; Lincoln, pp. 192–93, Larry A. Bowring, *Map of The Town of Worcester, Mass. circa 1776*, 1975.

[10] Lincoln, pp. 77–87; Nutt, pp. 76–77; Ivan Sandrof, *Your Worcester Street*, (Worcester: Franklin Publishing Co., 1948), p. 47.

[11] Bowring, *Map 1776*.

[12] John R. Stilgoe, *Common Landscape of America, 1580 to 1845* (New Haven: Yale University Press, 1982), p. 48.

[13] Franklin P. Rice, ed., *Worcester Town Records From 1753–1783*, (Worcester: The Worcester Society of Antiquity, 1882), pp. 15, 17. The Common most likely never was as large as the full 20 acres. See Zelotes W. Coombs, *Worcester and Worcester Common* (Worcester: [s.n.], 1945), pp. 30–31.

[14] Rice, pp. 246–47; Bowring, *Map 1776*.

[15] Jack Larkin, "'Labor is the Great Thing in Farming': The Farm Laborers of the Ward Family of Shrewsbury, Massachusetts, 1787–1860," *Proceedings of the American Antiquarian Society*, Vol. 99, Part 1, 1989, pp. 192, 194; Stilgoe, pp. 48, 55.

[16] Rice, pp. 72–73.

[17] Bowring, *Map 1776*; Sandrof, p. 52.

[18] *Reminiscences of the Original Associates and Past Members of the Worcester Fire Society, begun in an Address by Hon. Levi Lincoln, at the Quarterly Meeting, April 1862, and continued in An Address by Hon. Isaac Davis, at the annual meeting, January, 1870* (Worcester: Charles Hamilton, 1870), pp. 22–23; Lincoln, p. 221.

[19] *Fire Society*, p. 23; Lincoln, p. 221.

[20] Percy H. Epler, *Master Minds at the Commonwealth's Heart*, (Worcester: F. S. Blanchard & Co., 1909), p. 123.

[21] *Fire Society*, p. 23; Lincoln, p. 221; Nutt, pp. 98–99.

[22] William Cronon, *Changes in the Land: Indians, Colonists, and the Ecology of New England*, (New York: Hill & Wang, 1983), pp. 116–17.

[23] Cronon, p. 117.

[24] Cronon, pp. 115–16.

[25] Rebecca Rupp, *Red Oaks and Black Birches: The Science and Lore of Trees* (Pownal, Vt.: Garden Way Publishing, 1990), pp. 8–9, 22, 46, 80, 89, 107–8, 144, 168, 209, 220–21; Cronon, p. 112.

[26] Cronon, pp. 109–113

[27] Cronon, pp. 112–13; Rice, pp. 35, 222–23.

[28] Cronon, p. 119; *Map of Worcester by William Young, 1784*, Collection of the American Antiquarian Society.

[29] Cronon, pp. 117–18; Sandrof, p. 124; Rupp, pp. 62–63.

[30] Stilgoe, pp. 155–56, 291–93.

[31] Cronon, pp. 120–21; D. R. Foster, "Land-use history and four hundred years of vegetation change in New England," in B. L. Turner, B. L. Turner, A. G. Sal, F. G. Bernaldez and F. DiCastri, ed., *Global Land Use Change: A Perspective From The Columbian Encounter* (SCOPE Publication.Madrid: Consejo Superior de Investigaciones Cientifica, 1995), pp. 253–319; Stilgoe, p. 198.

[32] Peter Whitney, *Worcester County: America's First Frontier* (Worcester, 1793; Reprinted by Isaiah Thomas Books & Prints, Worcester, 1983), p. 32.

[33] Collection of the Worcester Art Museum.

[34] Cronon, pp. 124, 159–60.

[35] Stilgoe, pp. 199, 202; Cronon, pp. 159–60; D. R. Foster, "Land-use History and Forest Transformations in Central New England," in Mark J. McDonnell & Steward T. A. Pickett, eds, *Humans as Components of Ecosystems* (Springer-Verlag New York, Inc.: 1993), pp. 103–4.

[36] Cronon, pp. 126, 159–60; Stilgoe, pp. 293, 317–18.

[37] Cited in Cronon, p. 122.

[38] Foster, in McDonnell, pp. 95, 97; D. R. Foster, "Land-use history (1730–1990) and vegetation dynamics in central New England, USA," *Journal of Ecology* 1992, 80, p. 756.

[39] U. P. Hedrick, *A History of Horticulture in America to 1860* (New York: Oxford University Press, 1950), pp. 31, 34, 200–1.

[40] Hedrick, p. 30.

[41] Hedrick, pp. 31–32.

[42] Rudy J. Favretti, *Early New England Gardens 1620–1840* (Sturbridge, Mass.: 1966), pp. 5–8.

[43] Favretti, p. 9; Hedrick, pp. 72, 207.

[44] Rice, p. 435.

[45] Leo Marx, *The Machine in the Garden: Technology and the Pastoral Ideal in America* (London: Oxford University Press, 1964), pp. 98–99; David Schuyler, *The New Urban Landscape: The Redefinition of City Form in Nineteenth-Century America* (Baltimore: The Johns Hopkins University Press, 1986), p. 4.

©*Robert Nash*

41   CLEARING THE LAND

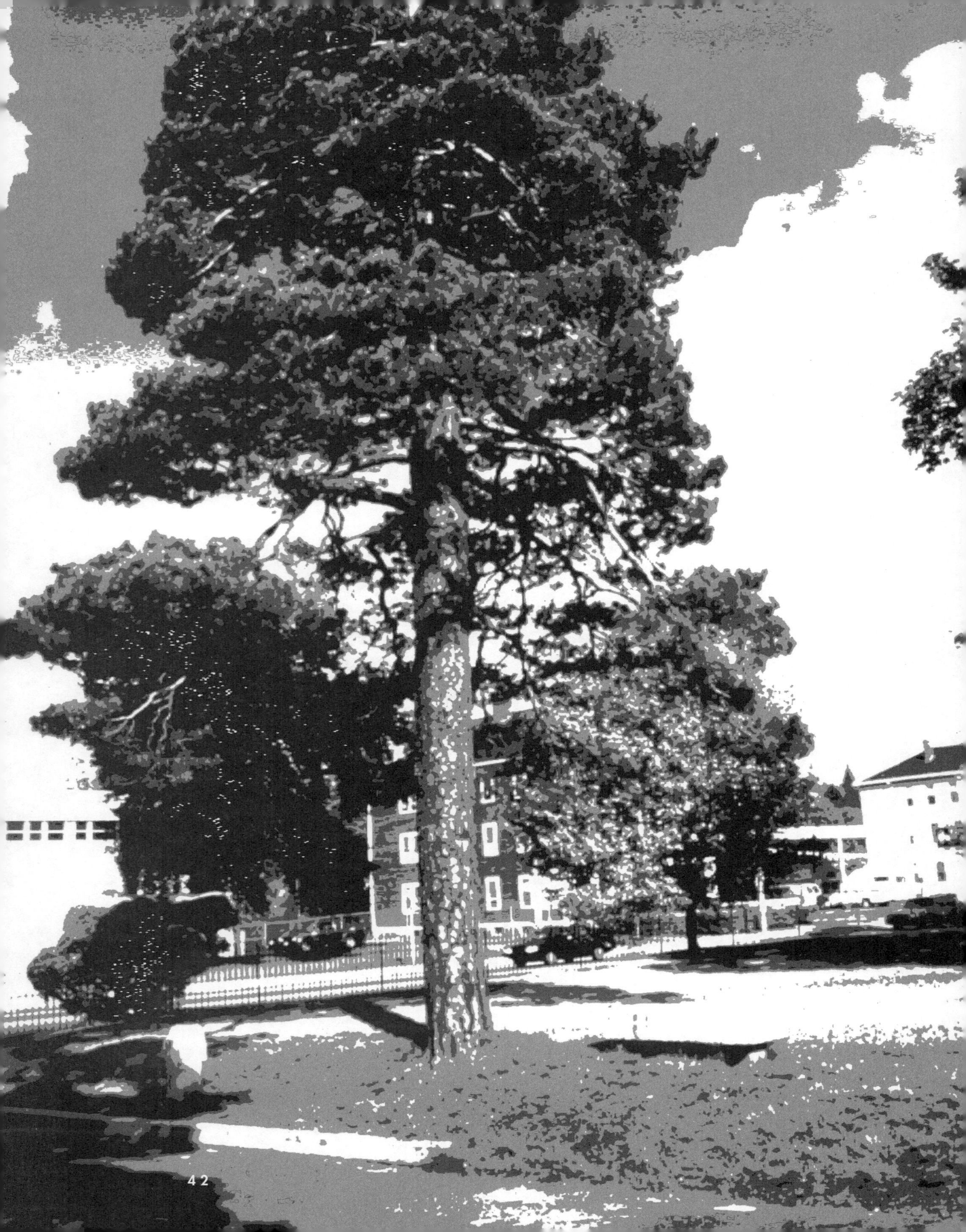

INDUSTRIAL TRANSFORMATION
Chapter Three

Behind the Old South Meeting House, on an unseasonably warm October 7 in 1819, the Common was filled with animals. Lowing and snorting, bleating and bellowing, their voices echoed those of a century past. But unlike their ancestral counterparts, these livestock were not waiting for the town shepherd to lead them out to pasture. Rather, the pride of local husbandmen and gentlemen farmers, the 135 bulls, cows, sheep, swine, boars and oxen penned on the Common that sunny Thursday morning were among the featured attractions of the first Cattle Show and Exhibition of Manufacture of the year-old Worcester Agricultural Society.[1]

By all accounts, the event was an unqualified success. Thousands thronged the grassy avenue between the two ranges of crowded pens to find out who had raised the county's finest livestock. They strolled inside the exhibition hall, specially erected for the day, to admire the mounds of vegetables, broadcloth, satinet, wool hats, cheese and other domestic products proffered for awards. (The weather, unfortunately, was too warm for the butter display, which melted before it could be judged.) Then came the main attraction—a competition among 15 pairs of yoked oxen to see which could best drag a stone-laden cart up a hill and plow rough soil. There were speeches and prayers in the meetinghouse, followed by a public procession, complete with military band, down Main Street to a lavish, packed meal at a nearby hotel. After dinner, awards and premiums were distributed for the finest livestock, produce and wares. Summing up the day, *The Massachusetts Spy* pronounced "that the scholar, the farmer, the manufacturer and the mechanic, have all a common concern in advancing Agriculture to its proper rank in society."[2]

Even as agriculture was being lauded in print and orations, however, the "noble husbandman" who had done so much to transform Worcester's landscape was rapidly becoming an anachronism. Three decades before Worcester's first cattle show, crippled by postwar bankruptcy, Massachusetts farmers who had marched to shut down Worcester's courts and save themselves from debtors' prison during Shays's Rebellion had begun migrating westward. Lured by better, cheaper land and a new life, they traveled to New York, Pennsylvania and beyond, no longer willing to till the rocky soil of Massachusetts. Though the economy stabilized under the newly ratified federal Constitution, and trade resumed with Great Britain and the West Indies toward the century's end, the migration continued. By 1800, in the 25 years following the Revolution's outbreak, Worcester had gained only 500 new citizens, for a total census of 2,411.[3]

Replacing agriculture as the region's economic lifeblood was another European import—textile manufacturing. Beginning with homespun and handwoven cottons and woolens, a cottage industry that flourished during the Revolution when trade with Great Britain was suspended, textile production moved into factories after the war and gained strength during the embargo of 1807 and the War of 1812. By the end of that conflict, Worcester was home to an array of factories along Mill Brook and other Blackstone tributaries, producing cotton yarn, corduroy, carpets, plaids and felt. In addition, the village boasted a paper mill, triphammer, gristmill and clock manufacturer.[4]

There was also the newly founded Worcester Bank. Incorporated in 1804, the bank had quickly replaced private citizens as a major source of credit, financing new manufacturing concerns throughout the county and facilitating the shift toward commercialization of agriculture that had begun prior to the Revolution.[5]

In short, the once rural shire town was emerging as a regional center of commerce and industry. And just as farmers had transformed the land a century earlier, so the new leaders of industrial growth were initiating yet another metamorphosis. Creators of banks, builders of factories, they laid the footings for an economy based on products rather than produce, an economy that would soon entice farm laborers to abandon their fields for the dream of a better wage and easier life in the city. Paradoxically, these very same lawyers, merchants, financiers and manufacturers—the men whose business interests would undermine and undo the region's rural culture—formed the backbone of the Worcester Agricultural Society.

Gentlemen farmers who harkened to their agrarian roots even as they abandoned them, the society's leaders hoped to staunch the flow of westward migration by enlightening their yeoman brethren to the benefits of more efficient and scientific agricultural methods. But in fact, the society's influence was less a matter of farming savvy than of economic and political clout. Many of its founding members were not only the region's leading businessmen but also active in state or local politics; nearly two-thirds of the Worcester County representatives elected to the Massachusetts General Court in 1819 were society members. Many others, both Federalists and Republicans, had previously served in the state legislature. Working together to preserve agriculture as the nation's moral foundation, they became the region's first voluntary society to enable former political rivals to set aside their differences and unite for a common cause. Men used to commanding respect, they comprised a corps of elite civic leaders whose political interests and real estate transactions would mold Worcester's emerging urban landscape.[6]

Westward Migration—The Politics of Agriculture

In its rhetoric, the society shared ideals that had been popularized by sister organizations throughout the young nation since the Revolution's end. With peacetime came a burgeoning of scientific inquiry, much of it focused on ways to improve agricultural yields, because farming was the basis of the nation's economy. Beginning in 1781 with the New Jersey Society for Promotion of Agriculture, Commerce and Art, American scholars sought to glean research and findings from European scientists, and to introduce new crops. As agricultural societies proliferated, however,

FRUIT TREES

Apple *Malus sylvestri*

For 19th-century horticulturists, fruit trees were the rage. By the century's first half, apple orchards were a well-established commercial venture, their fruit valued for cider making. Pear orchards, on the other hand, were prized as a mark of refinement; anyone who valued the title "gentleman" would devote his spare hours to cultivating pears, developing new varieties that would immortalize his name.

Like apples and other popular fruit-bearing trees, including cherry, plum, and peach, pears are members of the Rose family *(Rosaceae)*. With their snowy white petals in spring, shiny green leaves in summer, and sweet, fleshy fruit in autumn, pears have been garden favorites since ancient times. Growing wild in Europe and Asia, pear trees were brought to this country by European immigrants and commercial importers; today's orchard cultivars are all derived from the common pear *(Pyrus communis)*, a native of southern Europe.

Apples, too, were brought to the New World by European settlers. Native to Europe and western Asia, apple trees *(Malus sylvestris)* were a familiar part of the New England landscape by the 1640s, their yields improved by English honeybees imported by the Puritans. Other than using bees to pollinate the trees' pink-tinged blossoms, however, farmers did little to manipulate the quality and characteristics of apples until the early 19th century, despite the fact that orchard techniques such as pruning and grafting had been employed in European orchards for centuries. Instead, most apple trees were grown from seed, with successful variants determined by natural selection; color, texture and flavor were less important than yield, since most of the fruit was used for cider. It was from the colonial cider presses that Jonathan Chapman collected the seeds he freely distributed to create orchards as he walked across the eastern United States during nearly 50 years of travels—a legacy that inspired his nickname, "Johnny Appleseed."

With the rise of horticultural societies, pruning and grafting techniques gained new advocates in the United States. For gentlemen farmers vying to see who could develop the most pear varieties, such skills became essential, because a tree grown from the seed of a particular pear or apple does not necessarily produce fruit with identical characteristics of its parent. Rather, the only way to replicate a given pear is to graft a branch (scion) from its parent tree onto another, similar pear tree (stock). Creating new fruit cultivars involves the complex process of transplanting pollen from the flowers of one tree to another; the resulting fruit combines features of both parents.

Despite their slow start, American horticulturists soon became experts in pomology. In 1845, Andrew Jackson Downing published his third book, *The Fruits and Fruit Trees of America*; edited and revised by his brother Charles, the book immediately became a standard reference that went through 20 editions by the turn of the 20th century. Seven years after *Fruit Trees* appeared, the nation's fruit growers joined to create the American Pomological Society, which quickly became a world-renowned clearinghouse of information on fruit cultivation. The motivation for all this activity was not purely a matter of aesthetics. With the advent of the railroad, fresh fruits could be transported longer distances to market. As city dwellers developed a taste for fresh orchard produce over cooked, demand for new varieties swelled, and pomologists prospered.

Because orchard trees were so valued for their harvest, they were rarely used for wood products. Indeed, in colonial times, apple trees were so important to the local economy that many New England states forbade their felling. By contrast, in Europe fruitwood was prized for its decorative color and texture. French provincial cabinetmakers favored pear trees' light-brown, fine-textured wood for dressers and armoires. For American furniture makers, the fruitwood of choice was a native species, the black cherry *(Prunus serotina)*. Common throughout the eastern United States, cherry trees yield reddish-brown wood whose tolerance for humidity makes it the ideal material for fine cabinets and paneling, as well as clocks and scientific instruments.

FRUIT TREES

Pear — *Pyrus communis*
Black Cherry — *Prunus serotina*

In addition to beautiful wood, tasty fruit and fragrant flowers, cherry trees have another feature in common with apples and pears: all are sources of cyanogens, the chemical basis for cyanide. Found in cherry bark and the seeds of apples, pears, peaches, plums, apricots and almonds, cyanogens become lethal when combined with certain enzymes to produce hydrocyanic acid, a poison that causes respiratory paralysis. Fortunately for all fresh-fruit lovers, the deadly chemical never forms in the fruit itself; Adam and Eve's fate notwithstanding, eating an apple is still one of the few pleasures that's not hazardous to your health.

Pyrus communis

their missions moved beyond the scientific to the patriotic. Echoing the republican sentiments of Thomas Jefferson—"Those who labour in the earth are the chosen people of God, if ever he had a chosen people"—the statesmen-cum-gentlemen-farmers who typically led the societies waxed eloquent on the moral virtues of working the land.[7]

In New England, the fervor of that rhetoric was intensified by the region's stark political realities: as more farmers moved westward, states like Massachusetts were rapidly losing sway in national politics. Slowed population growth, relative to neighboring states like New York, meant comparatively fewer representatives in Congress. (Massachusetts lost so many farmers to its western neighbor that New York's population, less than the commonwealth's in 1790, had swollen to two-and-a-half times that of Massachusetts by 1820.) Such demographics were a major concern at Worcester's 1819 Cattle Show. Keynote speaker Levi Lincoln, Jr., a rising political star, castigated those who would abandon Massachusetts's rocky farmland as lazy and antisocial:[8]

> Ask the returning Emigrant from the *West* or the *South*, which *now* he most highly appreciates—the rough and hard, but vigorous soil of the *East*, with the necessity of labour to subdue and improve it, and the conveniences and pleasures of social intercourse for his recompense—or extent of territory, useless fertility and idleness, in a situation where neighborhood is unknown, the means for the education of children are denied, and opportunities for moral instruction and the publick worship of God unenjoyed?[9]

The yeoman who tilled the land and bore the burdens of crop failures and bankruptcy viewed such high-minded language and associated agricultural reforms with derision. Skeptical of the intensive farming methods being promoted—British practices such as barnyard feeding instead of pasture grazing, methods that facilitated maximum yield from each acre of precious land—yeomen ridiculed their gentry counterparts as book farmers who bred cattle and made manure "in their libraries."[10]

In turn, the gentlemen farmers viewed their stubborn pupils as fools and "clodhoppers" who failed, or simply refused, to see the wisdom of advanced farming practices. Frustrated by resistance to what they believed were true scientific reforms that served the public interest, stymied by the continued westward movement of farmers, the statesmen and merchants nonetheless continued their agricultural crusade via publications and exhibitions. In the process, political archenemies of decades past found a common purpose; for Worcester, the Agricultural Society became an important vehicle for uniting and solidifying the community's elite.[11]

Raising a Dynasty of Gentlemen Farmers—Levi Lincoln, Sr.

Chief among them, and not coincidentally the society's first president, was the renowned attorney and national statesman, Levi Lincoln, Sr. A Harvard College graduate who studied law in Newburyport and Northampton, Massachusetts, before settling in Worcester in 1775, Lincoln was drawn to the rural county seat by the void left at the Revolution's outset, when all but two of the community's lawyers fled town, shunned for their Tory sentiments. Admitted to the bar, he soon became the region's most prominent attorney, dominating the Worcester, Hampshire and Middlesex County courts from the Revolution's end until the turn of the century. A skillful trial lawyer, Lincoln successfully argued a landmark case in 1781 that helped to establish the legal basis for outlawing slavery in Massachusetts—a principle reaffirmed some 80 years later on a national scale by his distant cousin, President Abraham Lincoln.[12]

Holding numerous elected and appointed government posts, Lincoln served as a Massachusetts Supreme Court justice, state representative (in 1797 he was both an elected state representative and senator), and U.S. congressman. Shortly after he took his seat in the Sixth Congress, Lincoln was tapped by President Thomas Jefferson in 1801 to serve as his attorney general, a position he filled, after a brief stint as acting secretary of state, for almost four years. His resignation, reluctantly accepted by Jefferson, afforded him only a short retirement; Lincoln was soon back in the public eye, serving as a member of the governor's council, lieutenant governor under James Sullivan and acting governor of Massachusetts following Sullivan's death in 1808. Only his failing eyesight prevented him from accepting the most prestigious post of his distinguished career—an appointment as associate justice of the Supreme Court by President James Madison.[13]

Retirement this time enabled Lincoln to devote time to his other passions: farming and the classics. A wealthy man now in his sixties, Lincoln had amassed a 152-acre farm on either side of the County Road, later renamed Lincoln Street. In addition, he owned several sheep farms throughout the county; when he died, Lincoln's farm holdings were valued at $54,000. A meticulous record keeper who made a practice of surprise visits to his farms to see if any of his laborers was stealing, Lincoln developed one of the nation's first significant collections of Merino sheep, a breed of Spanish ancestry noted for its fine, long wool. A student of selective breeding, he strove to improve the bloodlines of his flocks, hoping to increase their value and reinvest any profits in more land and livestock.[14]

U. S. Attorney General Levi Lincoln, Senior Courtesy, American Antiquarian Society Worcester, Massachusetts

At the same time, Lincoln was no hands-on farmer. Even as he strongly believed that scientific farming methods would further the national interest, he left the daily business of managing his herds to his farmhands, untrustworthy though they might be. Spending most of his days at his Worcester estate, the Home Farm, Lincoln enjoyed the company of his social peers, confining his agricultural pursuits to reading current reports of farming improvements and recording his experiments with fruit trees. He was no longer active in politics, but he kept abreast of the latest developments and legal cases until his death, one month shy of his 69th birthday in 1820, the year after he had assumed presidency of the Worcester Agricultural Society.[15]

Lincoln's commitment to public service and his republican idealism about agriculture were not lost on his children. With his wife, Martha Waldo—a descendant of two of Worcester's most prominent mercantile families, the Waldos and Salisburys—he sired ten sons and daughters, of whom seven lived to adulthood. Among them, three sons rose to public office: the eldest, Levi, Jr., became governor of Massachusetts; Enoch served as governor of Maine; and John Waldo as state senator. Another son, Daniel Waldo, became county attorney of Cumberland County, Maine, before his death at 29. In addition, Lincoln's daughter Martha married an attorney, Leonard Parker, who became a state senator. Like their father, both Levi, Jr., and John Waldo served as presidents of the Worcester Agricultural Society, and Enoch also maintained an interest in farming. Lincoln's youngest son, William, served four terms as a Massachusetts state

Announcement for the first annual Cattle Show and Exhibition of the Worcester Agricultural Society. Courtesy, American Antiquarian Society, Worcester, Massachusetts

49 INDUSTRIAL TRANSFORMATION

representative. In addition, he became a noted Worcester historian and officer of the newly formed American Antiquarian Society, as well as a family genealogist and agriculturist who helped his aging father supervise his Merino sheep farms.[16]

Inspired by his father's love of the land, William eventually started his own tree nursery. His clients included the Antiquarian Society; Christopher Columbus Baldwin, the Society's first librarian, noted in a March 1834 entry to his diary that he planted "ten locust trees" procured from Lincoln's nursery "in front of the Antiquarian Hall." An avid horticulturist, William developed an elaborate garden at the Home Farm estate, including a lover's lane dubbed Lincoln's Grove and a fishpond large enough for him to navigate in his birch-bark canoe.[17]

Political Acumen and West Side Elegance—Levi Lincoln, Jr.

William's eldest brother, Levi, Jr., was also devoted to the land. Like his father, an accomplished trial lawyer who filled a prodigious array of public offices, both elected and appointed—including eight consecutive terms as Massachusetts governor—Levi carried on the family tradition of farming and livestock breeding. Admired for his elegant estate on Elm Street, he was remembered by his peers for "his love of trees and his care for their culture and preservation . . . his almost poetical fondness for flowers, and the beautiful things which make the garden so attractive to the man of refined taste."[18]

The Lincolns' Elm Street mansion and grounds were on display each fall, when the governor and his wife, Penelope Winslow Sever, opened their home to the statesmen, scholars and entrepreneurs who crowded Worcester for the Agricultural Society's annual exhibition. The Cattle Show Ball was, in fact, the social event of the year for the region's republican gentry—an irony not lost on the farmers who were supposedly the Society's *raison d'être*. Voicing frustration over widening gaps in the community's social fabric, one writer to the Jacksonian Worcester County *Republican* complained in 1831 that while the elite could gain entry to the Ball "without much ceremony . . . a farmer or mechanic . . . would stand a poor chance against the body aristocratic in Worcester."[19]

Lincoln's 28 years as Worcester Agricultural Society president, from 1824 to 1852, coincided with the height of his political career. A Madison Republican who supported the War of 1812, he was elected to the Massachusetts senate during that same year, speaking for the minority in the antiwar, federalist-controlled state legislature. With the weakening of the Federalist Party after the war's end, Lincoln's political future brightened. Elected representative to the General Court from 1814 through 1822 (excluding three years when he chose not to run for office), he ascended to speaker of the house during his last term in the state legislature, even though he was a member of the minority party. In 1823, he was elected lieutenant governor, and was also picked to be a presidential elector for John Quincy Adams. Briefly serving as associate justice of the Massachusetts Supreme Judicial Court the following year, Lincoln was soon nominated for governor by both the Federalist and Republican Parties; his landslide victory in 1825—35,000 of 37,000

CUCUMBERTREE
Magnolia acuminata

Even as Americans benefited greatly from European knowledge of horticulture and imported plant species at the turn of the 19th century, the botanical riches of North America were also a source of fascination in the Old World. In particular, American magnolias were a hot export item for French and English collectors; native to the eastern United States, this genus of deciduous trees was unknown in Europe until a few samples of the cucumbertree *(Magnolia acuminata)* were transplanted in the mid-18th century at Thorndon Hall, England's finest garden of that era.

Widely admired for its symmetrical shape and green, cone-shaped fruit, the cucumbertree was a top priority for French botanist François André Michaux as he explored the North American wilderness in the early 19th century. Seeking to discover and document the continent's plant species and collect their seeds—research that formed the basis of his seminal work, *North American Sylva*—Michaux located a cucumbertree along the Juniata River in Pennsylvania during his travels in 1802. Writing in his journal, he noted:

> *The inhabitants of the remotest parts of Pennsylvania and Virginia and even the western countries, pick the cones when green, to infuse in whiskey, which gives it a pleasant bitter. This bitter is very much esteemed in this country as a preventative against intermittent fevers, but I have my doubts whether it would be so generally used if it had the same qualities when mixed with water.*[1]

Whatever their medicinal value, the cones of the cucumbertree are actually clusters of pointed fruit. Green when they first emerge, dark red when ripe, the fruits burst toward summer's end, each releasing two seeds that dangle by threads until ready to drop. The tree itself grows tall and straight, reaching heights from 60 to 90 feet and a diameter of up to 2 feet. Its yellow-green, ovate leaves are large, measuring 5 to 10 inches long and 3 to 6 inches wide. In spring the cucumbertree bears yellow, bell-shaped flowers—much harder to see than the fragrant white blossoms of its showy cousin, the southern magnolia *(Magnolia grandiflora)*. Instead, what distinguishes the cucumbertree is its scarlet fruit, graceful symmetry and shiny foliage.

Wood from the cucumbertree resembles another member of the Magnolia family, the yellow poplar or tuliptree *(Liriodendron tulipifera)*. Both produce fine, lightweight hardwood with many commercial applications, including furniture, crates, boxes, musical instruments, toys, interior finish for homes and pulpwood. Like cucumbertrees, tuliptrees were a prized American export; both were introduced to Europe from Virginia by early settlers. Among the tallest of Eastern hardwoods, distinguished by its unique, cup-and-saucer-shaped leaves, the tuliptree is also among the hardiest of urban transplants, highly resistant to pollution, disease and drought. Fine examples of both Magnolia species grace the grounds of Worcester's Rural Cemetery.

---

[1] Cited in Donald Culross Peattie, *A Natural History of Trees of Eastern and Central North America.* (Boston: Houghton Mifflin Co., 1950), pp. 276–77.

Massachusetts Governor Levi Lincoln, Jr.
Courtesy,
American Antiquarian Society
Worcester, Massachusetts

votes cast—ushered in a period of political unity and economic prosperity.[20]

A dignified statesman, widely respected for his impartiality and integrity, Governor Lincoln was reelected seven times before he withdrew his name from consideration for the governorship in 1833. But his political retirement, like his father's, did not last long; when Worcester's congressman John Davis was elected to fill Lincoln's seat as governor, Lincoln accepted the honor of filling Davis's place in Washington. There he served in three successive Congresses until 1841, when he was appointed by President William Henry Harrison as collector for the Port of Boston. Refusing to fulfill the patronage requests of President John Tyler two years later, Lincoln resigned with the hope that he would be able to finally enjoy the pleasures of tending his Worcester estate. Again, however, he postponed his retirement, this time to serve two terms in the state senate, the last year as senate president.[21]

Officially, Lincoln ended his public career in 1845, though he continued to accept special positions of public responsibility for nearly two more decades: among them, Lincoln served as Worcester's first mayor in 1848, member of a state commission to investigate the status of the mentally ill in 1854, and twice again as presidential elector—including the year 1864, when he cast a vote for his kinsman, Abraham Lincoln. A member and officer of numerous societies, popular orator and gracious host, Lincoln remained active and involved with his community until his death, following a stroke, at the age of 86 in 1868. On the day of his funeral businesses in Worcester closed, and the streets were lined with mourners who came to pay their last respects to one of the city's most influential and well-loved citizens.[22]

For all his political and social contributions to Worcester, however, Governor Lincoln left his most enduring mark—both directly and indirectly—on the city's landscape. A major landholder, the governor owned extensive acreage west of Main Street, including the old Sever Farm acquired from his wife's family. When he decided in the early 1830s to build his estate, the governor created a street to go with it, carving the new road out of the 80-acre tract that stretched up the hill beyond his three-story brick mansion on Main Street. Clearing away stone and brush alongside his laborers, Governor Lincoln named the street Elm; six other streets built on his land, he also named for trees: Chestnut, Walnut, Maple, Cedar, Linden and Oak.[23]

Setting the standard for his new neighborhood, Governor Lincoln created stately grounds around his Classical Revival mansion, designed by Worcester architect Elias Carter. Because he owned all the surrounding lots, the governor maintained total control of the growth and style of what soon became the city's elite residential nucleus. Elegant homes and gardens, shaded by luxuriant trees, set apart from what was fast becoming a congested, commercial Main Street, were the new status symbols of Worcester's West Side.[24]

Reshaping the Industrial Landscape—The Arrival of Railroads

Governor Lincoln's real estate transactions did much to design the city's most fashionable neighborhood; however, his promotion of commerce via the governor's office had an even more significant impact on Worcester's landscape. In particular, the governor's support for new means of transportation fueled Worcester's economic expansion, accelerating the city's transformation from provincial village to industrial center.

In his first inaugural address in 1825, Governor Lincoln set the tone for his administration, arguing that the corporate debt liability of stockholders should be eased to improve the climate for business investments. He also promoted the creation of a canal system linking Boston to the Connecticut River, an idea first floated in 1796, but soon abandoned after initial surveys were completed. Reviving the notion as a way for Massachusetts businesses to remain competitive in response to the recently completed Erie Canal, the governor chose not to promote another canal already in progress—one linking Worcester to Narragansett Bay via the Blackstone River. Built with the sweat and muscle of Irish immigrants, the Blackstone Canal (sidetracked 30 years by the first proposal for a Massachusetts Canal) was completed in 1828. But for all the high hopes of the canal's investors, the ill-fated waterway—plagued by millowners who impounded water supplies, a complex lock system and impassable ice five months out of the year—was soon supplanted by what became Governor Lincoln's new hope for Massachusetts commerce: railroads.[25]

Ironically, it was the potential success of the Blackstone Canal that prompted Lincoln to explore the newfangled notion of rail transportation: fearing that Boston would lose commerce to points west, once businesses could transport goods via the Blackstone to Narragansett Bay and Long Island Sound, Governor Lincoln began pushing the idea of building railroads in 1827.

The following year, when his hometown's canal opened to much pomp and flourish, the governor assumed leadership of a new Board of Internal Improvements, with the mission of developing a statewide rail network. Ultimately, however, Lincoln's apparent abandonment of Worcester's interests became the city's economic windfall: when the Boston & Worcester Railroad commenced operations on July 4, 1835, it became the first of six railroad lines completed within 15 years that would power the city's industrial boom throughout the 19th century.[26]

The swiftness of that industrial transformation is well illustrated by the city's census: it took the first 30 years of the new century for Worcester's population to nearly double, expanding 73 percent to about 4,200 residents in 1830; but it took only another ten years for the city to replicate that growth rate to just under 7,500—a 78 percent jump in half a generation. Even more dramatically, by 1850, Worcester had ballooned to over 17,000 residents, more than doubling its population in a decade.[27]

Abandoning the rocky farmland cleared with such toil and ardor by their European forebears, the sons and daughters of Massachusetts farmers streamed to Worcester's new, red-brick factories, hoping for an easier life. They were joined by waves of immigrants, escaping poverty and starvation in Europe for the dream of a fresh start in America. In Worcester of 1836—a year after the Boston & Worcester's first train chugged into town, and the same year that Governor Lincoln's brother William published his seminal *History of Worcester*—job seekers could find work in a wide variety of factories: "two mills for the manufacture of broadcloths, six for satinets, one for cotton sheeting and shirting, two for satinet warps, one for pelisse wadding, two paper-mills, seven machinery works, a wire mill, an iron foundry, several manufactories of sashes and blinds, one lead pipe works, paper hangings, cabinet furniture, chairs, brushes, trunks and harnesses, ploughs, hats, shoes, watches, umbrellas, cutlery, piano-fortes, and wagons." In fact, industrial growth had been so rapid that the city had gained 300 new buildings in just the previous two years.[28]

That expansion, further evidenced by a more than twofold increase in Worcester's property valuation in one generation—from $2 million in 1820 to $4.3 million in 1840—was a direct outcome of new, cheaper means to transport goods, first by canal and then by rail, as well as the advent of steam power, a technological innovation that freed manufacturers from dependence on rivers and streams. It was also fostered by Worcester's ability to attract inventors with entrepreneurial talent—men like Ichabod Washburn, whose wire-drawing mill would prosper from the growing demand for barbed wire to fence the nation's prairies, and George Crompton, who built patented power looms, designed by his father, that could weave intricate designs into textiles. Both manufacturers benefited from the era's equivalent of venture capitalists: Washburn from Steven Salisbury II, heir to the Salisbury mercantile estate and Governor Lincoln's cousin, who built a mill for the wire maker in 1834 to launch his enterprise; and Crompton from William Merrifeld, son of another early Worcester family, who purchased land on Union Street in 1839 to erect factory space that he rented to fledgling businesses.[29]

As factories mushroomed, however, so did tenements. Just as the West Side neighborhood of Governor Lincoln was fast becoming the center of Worcester's elite, so the city's East Side was gaining a disproportionate number of lower income residents, many of them immigrants, seeking homes within walking distance of their factory jobs. Much of the poorer section of town was centered east of the Blackstone Canal, around Temple, Water and Summer Streets. Main Street, no longer characterized by elegant homes of founding families, reflected instead the city's burgeoning commercial interests.[30]

With industrialization, too, came dirt. Factories and trains belched soot and smoke. Manufacturers and homes dumped effluent and raw sewage into Mill Brook and the Blackstone Canal. Brick factory walls blocked vistas of Worcester's rolling hills, and Main Street was splattered with horse dung.

Redefining the Rural Past—The Romance of Trees
Moved by the loss of their community's provincial character, residents placed an increasing value on the symbol of their rural past: street trees. For three generations, private citizens had followed in the footsteps of Elijah Dix, planting and caring for trees on public thoroughfares and grounds at their own expense—and whim. Even though tree protection ordinances had been on the town books since the mid-18th century, it wasn't until 1824, the year before Governor Lincoln's first term, that town selectmen first voted to authorize public funds for street tree maintenance within the Centre School District and on the Common. In 1832, four years after the Blackstone Canal opened, the selectmen took the next step of authorizing the use of public funds for tree plantings, for Worcester's new burial ground.[31]

The following year, the town selectmen approved an updated set of tree by-laws for consideration by the county commissioners that would invoke a fine of $1 to $10 for tying "any horse, cattle or team to any of the trees planted in any publick highway or street or on any publick lands in said town, for shade or ornament, or to any iron or fence put up for the protection of said trees." The fine for damaging or removing any trees without the selectmen's consent was steeper—$10 to $20 per offense, up from $3 at the turn of the century. Restating their civic responsibility for public tree plantings at the same meeting, the selectmen passed several ordinances over the course of the next decade authorizing tree maintenance and new plantings on downtown streets and the Common.[32]

The community's growing concern for its greenery echoed a reaction to industrialization throughout the United States, as city after city shed fields for factories, only to mourn the loss of a rural past and the idealized virtues of life on the farm. Inspired by European romanticism, the nation's pastoral yearnings found voice in the popular publications of rural landscape designer Andrew Jackson Downing, and visual expression in the Hudson River paintings of Thomas Cole. Writing in the 1840s and early 1850s from his Hudson River estate in Newburgh, New York, Downing, like Jefferson, canonized the farmer as essential to the preservation of America's economy and republican institutions. Cole, too, glorified agriculture and nature: his five-canvas series of 1836, *The Course of Empire*, is an allegorical depiction of the rise and inevitable fall of urban society bent on bending nature to its will.[33]

Pastoral life was glorified, as well, in the writings of the transcendentalists. In his 1844 lecture "The Young American," Ralph Waldo Emerson extolled the "sanative and Americanizing" influence of working the land:

> Any relation to the land, the habit of tilling it, or mining it, or even hunting on it, generates the feeling of patriotism. He who keeps shop on it, or he who merely uses it as a support to his desk and ledger, or to his manufactory, values it less. The vast majority of the people of this country live by the land, and carry its quality in their manners and opinions. . . . How much better when the whole land is a garden, and the people have grown up in the bowers of paradise.[34]

By midcentury, pastoral nostalgia and anti-urban sentiment had evolved from a critique of countryside lost to the conclusion that cities were bad simply because they were the antithesis of rural landscapes, the romanticized embodiment of good. Writing in the 1850s, urban reformer Sylvester Judd asserted that the only way to salvage cities was to "countrify" them by creating wide open spaces and lining streets with trees: "There should be trees in every street, without exception—trees about the markets, trees in front of the shops, and on the docks, and shading the manufactories."[35]

But even as belief in the "evil city" gained momentum—fueling nativist sentiments in rural areas—there were those who maintained a more balanced view of urban centers, recognizing not only their problems but also their cultural and educational attractions. Emerson himself wrote in his personal journal of his desire for his children to have the best of both worlds: "rural strength and religion" as well as "city facility and polish."[36]

In Search of a Pastoral Ideal—The British Landscape Gardening School

For those who could afford it, one way to resolve the rural-urban dichotomy was to build country homes close enough to the city to enjoy its riches without enduring its vices. No simple farmhouses embodying rural virtues, the country homes that blossomed around Boston and along the banks of the Hudson were really estates, distinguished from those of centuries past by their grounds. Instead of farmland, the elegant houses were surrounded by the artifice of farmland, a nostalgic interpretation of rural vistas made popular by the British landscape gardening school.[37] Developed in England during the 18th century, landscape gardening was in part a reaction to the highly stylized designs of 17th-century Dutch and French gardens, and in part a physical expression of the shift toward a romanticized conception of nature. Its proponents—most notably, Humphry Repton—favored curved lines over straight and "natural" clusters of vegetation over ornate groupings; in this way, they strove to create landscapes that emulated rural countryside. Indeed, by the turn of the century, this pastoral ideal had become equated with nature, as factories blackened the horizon and memories of long-gone wilderness quietly vanished.[38]

Overlooking inherent contradictions, the landscape gardening school prized country scenery that showed no evidence of human involvement; anything manmade was considered inferior to nature's designs, despite the fact that nature, in this case, was actually a very human fabrication. This false dichotomy of the romantic era, setting humans apart from nature rather than viewing humans as part of nature, would continue to resonate well into the 20th century, defining environmental values up to the present day.[39]

Among those who helped import the landscape gardening philosophy to the United States was André Parmentier, a nurseryman who immigrated to New York from either France or Belgium in 1824 and started a nursery on Long Island. Until his death six years later, Parmentier landscaped numerous Hudson River estates, including Hyde Park. Though his efforts were cut short, the results were significant enough to catch the attention of Downing, an accomplished horticulturist who wrote the nation's first statement of landscape design, *A Treatise on the Theory and Practice of Landscape Gardening Adapted to North America*. Published in 1841, when Downing was 26, the immensely popular and influential book made a persuasive case for the value of improving private grounds.[40]

Downing also implored his readers to plant street trees in rural towns and villages. He emphasized their practical attributes as fire barriers and sources of shade, as well as the aesthetic advantages of tree-lined thoroughfares, citing examples of old New England communities as models of graceful, tasteful landscapes. Praising private individuals who had taken the initiative to plant trees, such as James Hillhouse, whose planting efforts in New Haven during the early 1800s had earned that community recognition as the "City of Elms," and those who offered tree bounties to encourage plantings, Downing also lauded organizations that brought citizens together to improve their communities, such as the Ornamental Tree Society in Northampton, Massachusetts. Writing in 1850, he extolled tree planting and the art of landscape refinement as "the outward mark of education, moral sentiment, love of home, and refined cultivation."[41]

Creating Sacred Landscape—The Rural Cemetery Movement

For all its flawed reasoning, this growing appreciation of landscape aesthetics in America was a primary force behind the first major effort to offset urban squalor with green open spaces: the rural cemetery movement. A response to public health concerns over burial practices, the rising real estate value of center city graveyards, and changing religious values about death, the push for landscaped, park-like cemeteries on city outskirts was both a pragmatic answer to urban congestion and the embodiment of romantic sentiment toward nature. No longer would loved ones be interred in a crowded, weed-choked graveyard, their headstones plastered with handbills or toppled by vandals, their memories smudged with soot. Rather, removed from factory grime, they would be placed to rest in a cemetery—a deliberate shift in terminology, derived from Greek for "a sleeping place"—that was airy and green, shaded by stately trees and flowering shrubs.

The rural cemetery movement did not gain force until the 1830s, yet the idea of creating an ornamental graveyard had first surfaced in New Haven in 1796, when the Connecticut port town declared its Old Burying Ground overcrowded. To replace it, federalist senator James Hillhouse designed the New Burying Ground, a ten-acre field of leveled land enclosed by fencing and divided into "handsomely railed," tree-shaded, square lots. These in turn were divided into square family plots, ornamented with marble headstones that were adorned with chiseled urns and willows, symbols of mourning. Alleys were laid between the burial plots, wide enough for two carriages to pass.[42]

Hillhouse's design was a deliberate departure from the graveyards of New England's past. Symbols of the Puritan conception of death as chaos, 17th- and 18th- century communal graveyards were typically ill-tended, haphazard collections of tilting tombstones. Placed at the town's heart—in the town Common, near or alongside the meeting house, or in a churchyard—they served as unavoidable reminders of life's frailty and the unknown wilderness that awaits the departed. Headstones, too, reflected the dark side of death: skulls and hourglasses hovered over epitaphs, warnings of numbered days before the ultimate reckoning.[43]

With the advent of Unitarianism in New England at the end of the 18th century, however, the Puritan hell-and-brimstone dogma lost favor, and graveyards were no longer conceived as public object lessons about the threat of eternal damnation. New Haven's New Burying Ground signaled that shift, its broad paths an invitation to visitors, its shaded, ornamental graves symbolic of peaceful rest. The design was applauded by European visitors, who typically had little positive to say about American landscape, particularly urban landscape, with its dearth of greenery. They were even more impressed 35 years later, when a bolder adaptation of Hillhouse's innovation,

Judge Story's Monument at Mount Auburn Cemetery in Cambridge, Massachusetts, the prototype of the rural cemetery movement. Printed in Boston.
Courtesy,
American Antiquarian Society
Worcester, Massachusetts

the 72-acre Mount Auburn Cemetery, opened its gates along the Charles River near Harvard College in 1831.[44]

The prototype of the rural cemetery movement, Mount Auburn was conceived by Dr. Jacob Bigelow, a physician who, at the request of the Boston city council, had authored a special study about the health risks of overcrowded city burial grounds in the mid-1820s—a hotly debated topic after an 1822 yellow fever epidemic in New York City claimed 16,000 lives, striking hardest those who lived near the Trinity Church burying ground. Echoing concerns voiced by the New York City Board of Health (and ignored by the public), Bigelow recommended that Boston cease burials within the city to avoid public health risks from contaminated corpses; he also suggested creating a cemetery outside of Boston, modeled after New Haven's.[45]

His report fell on deaf ears. Undaunted, in 1825 Bigelow started his own crusade to build the cemetery. After some searching, he and his followers discovered the ideal site, a rolling, forested tract in Cambridge known as Stone's Woods, popular among Harvard students for hikes and picnics. Teaming up with the newly founded Massachusetts Horticultural Society (MHS), Bigelow purchased the land in 1831. Initially, the private, nonprofit partnership enabled the MHS to create an experimental garden on about half the cemetery grounds. By 1835, however, disputes over finances and authority forced a rift, and the MHS abandoned the project, albeit with a lucrative settlement.[46]

Even without the MHS, Mount Auburn soon became renowned for its striking landscape, breathtaking vistas of Boston and the Charles and naturalistic gravesites. Winding carriage paths, named for trees, curved around the carefully tended plots. Only metal and stone could be used for railings, and stone for markers—the wood fences and slate headstones of old graveyards were prohibited. Strict decorum was enforced: carriages moved no faster than a walk and food was forbidden, as were flower picking and boisterous behavior.[47]

Mount Auburn's beautiful grounds and behavior codes manifested the romantic ideal that a cemetery should be an outdoor cathedral. Here mourners could seek solace and inspiration by communing with nature, finding comfort in God's presence as evidenced in the pastoral landscape. Here, too, as it turned out, visitors could enjoy a pleasant Sunday stroll amid the tastefully arranged trees and flowers and forget the stresses of city life. Indeed, Mount Auburn was such a welcome alternative to Boston's congested urban landscape that it soon became a popular tourist attraction—so popular that in 1876 James Russell Lowell quipped that Bostonians "seemed to have only two ideas of hospitality: a boring dinner party followed by a ride in Mount Auburn—'Your memory of the dinner is expected to reconcile you to the prospect of the graveyard.'"[48]

Cynics notwithstanding, Mount Auburn's successful design was soon emulated around the country. Laurel Hill Cemetery in Philadelphia was the first to copy the Boston model in 1836, followed two years later by Greenwood Cemetery in Brooklyn, Greenmount in Baltimore, and Mount Hope—the first municipal rural cemetery—in Rochester, New York. By midcentury, there were also rural cemeteries in Pittsburgh, Cincinnati, Louisville, Richmond and Charleston.[49]

"A Temple in Every Grove"—Worcester's Rural Cemetery

Worcester was no exception to the national trend. The year Mount Auburn opened, the town had three public burial sites: the century-old burial ground on the Common, neglected and overgrown, where many of the community's founding pioneers and revolutionary heroes were interred; the crowded Mechanics Street graveyard, opened in 1796, when dysentery claimed the lives of many Worcester children; and the Pine Meadow burial ground, laid out in 1828 just southeast of the town's congested core. Worcester's original burial place, located in a grove of oak trees a short walk east of Main Street, was used from 1717 to 1730; the unmarked graves of more than two dozen of Worcester's founders were eventually obliterated at the turn of the century, when the town decided to fell the oaks and move the schoolhouse from the Common to the ancient plot—over the objections of several townspeople, "especially those of color, who apprehended, that the site covered the remains of some of their race."[50]

Barely ten years after the new Pine Meadow burial ground opened, what had been a secluded site was now bisected by railroad tracks. The Mechanics Street graveyard, filled to capacity, was enclosed by commercial buildings. An effort in 1835 to solve the space problem with a purchase of 20 acres west of town for a public cemetery had failed when those who died with no surviving family were banned from burial there; outrage was so overwhelming that after just one interment, the town voted to sell the land. Two other burial sites were created within the city, but the underlying problem remained: given the pace of urbanization and industrial development in Worcester, and associated rise in real estate values, no public burial ground was truly sacred.[51]

Those issues deeply concerned one of Worcester's leading citizens, Edward D. Bangs. The son of a respected judge, who became state representative, county attorney and Massachusetts secretary of state, Bangs was a persuasive speaker who worried that the rapidly expanding town was neglecting its moral responsibilities to the dead. In an 1837 lecture to the Worcester Lyceum, a society formed just eight years earlier by the town's Unitarian elite for "mutual instruction and improvement," Bangs decried the sorry state of Worcester's burial grounds. The only way to solve the problem, he urged, was to create a cemetery where anyone could purchase a private plot and the right to perpetual occupancy.[52]

Inspired by Bangs's lecture, banker Daniel Waldo decided to act. A wealthy bachelor who had succeeded his father as president of the Worcester Bank and was also first president of the Worcester County Institution for Savings, Waldo owned a considerable amount of local real estate. Like his nephew, Governor Lincoln, he had a strong sense of public duty and served as an officer of many local organizations, including four years as president of the Worcester Agricultural Society (WAS). With $1,400, Waldo purchased a nine-acre tract about 1.5 miles from the courthouse, just north of the mill his cousin Stephen Salisbury had built for Ichabod Washburn, bordering the Holden Road. Abutting the Salisbury estate to the west and land owned by Worcester's medical dynasty, the Greens, to the east, the heavily wooded tract was split by a brook and spring-fed pond. Its rolling contours and majestic trees seemed to Waldo the perfect attributes for a cemetery like Mount Auburn; in the following year, 1838, he donated the land to a newly chartered cemetery association that was created to receive his gift for a secure burial site in a pastoral setting. Waldo's only request was that a 20-square-foot lot be reserved for himself.[53]

As the weather warmed, work on the new cemetery commenced. The trustees—Governor Lincoln, Edward Bangs, Stephen Salisbury and William Lincoln among them—hired James Barnes, a respected engineer for the Western Railroad, to conduct a topographical survey and develop a plan for the grounds. Working alongside landscape gardeners, the trustees spent the summer clearing and smoothing the tract. By August, streets and paths were laid out and named; that same month, Salisbury donated a half-acre of forested land, enhancing the parcel with needed road frontage. Finally, on a brilliant, clear September 8, 1838, Worcester's Rural Cemetery was ready for its official consecration.[54]

Following a dedication service led by Unitarian minister Alonzo Hill, Governor Levi Lincoln (elected president of the cemetery association when Waldo declined the honor) addressed the sizable crowd:

> We come from the bustling scenes of business, from the crowded streets, the noisy resorts of labor or of pleasure, to this secluded grove, the quiet repose of nature; to that stillness and peace, which reigns uninterrupted by the controversies of the world, and is undisturbed by the restless strivings and the unsatisfied competitions of men . . . Religion shall find here, a temple in every grove, and prayer an altar on every mound. The throng of the idle multitude shall not obtrude within these walks, nor the din of the world's cares disturb the quiet of these shades, nor the footsteps of business cross the pathway to the tomb, nor the swift heel of pleasure press the bosom of the fresh tenant of the grave.[55]

Worcester's Rural Cemetery, founded in 1838, one of the city's finest arboretums.
©Robert Nash

INDUSTRIAL TRANSFORMATION

Those high ideals were soon challenged, however. Twelve-and-a-half years later, Governor Lincoln, still president, bemoaned the urban congestion that had rapidly engulfed the once secluded spot; now wedged between two major roads, Rural Cemetery had become a popular place to play and dally. Writing in the annual trustees' report for 1851, Lincoln noted, "it is hoped, that the place may be held more sacred from profanation by idle, and thoughtless, and rude indulgences in mere amusement or recreation." To solve the problem and separate the cemetery "from scenes so incongruous with its designs," he recommended constructing a "closed gateway" and "dense border . . . of lofty forest trees."[56]

And there were other problems. Within a few years of the cemetery's consecration, minimal restrictions on lot ornamentation and upkeep had fostered an indiscriminate arrangement of headstones and vegetation; because maintenance was left to the lot owners, landscape aesthetics were more a function of individual choice and income, rather than cohesive design. The issue was a major concern for trustee Frederick Paine, a descendant of the family that originally owned the cemetery tract and avid horticulturist, who took it upon himself to unify the cemetery's landscape. In 1844, the trustees named Paine and two others to a new committee that would supervise the grounds, a responsibility that Paine readily shouldered for many years. His efforts laid the groundwork for what is today the city's finest arboretum.[57]

Cultivating Pears—The Growth of Horticultural Societies

Rural Cemetery was not the only place where Paine invested his horticultural talents. At his Lincoln Street family estate, The Oaks, Paine created extensive gardens that were widely admired. His flowers were a regular feature at exhibitions of the Worcester County Horticultural Society (WCHS), which he helped incorporate in 1842, serving as its treasurer for 29 years.[58]

Like many horticultural societies that flourished during this period, the WCHS was formed in reaction to the changing focus of agricultural societies. By the 1830s, no longer fired by the ideals of rural republicanism, societies like the WAS and its Boston cousin were more interested in the fine points of farming and stockbreeding than the practical problems of cow feed and fertilizer. Indeed, by midcentury, most agricultural societies were obsessed with how to breed the finest racehorses.[59]

By contrast, the social elite who flocked to horticulture were obsessed with aesthetics. Seeking to prove that they were more than just materialists, these manufacturers, financiers, merchants and professional men who had built their fortunes on an industrial economy invested their considerable wealth in elaborate gardens and orchards. Cultivating their pears and dahlias, meticulously landscaping their grounds, they vigorously pursued nature's beauty to convince themselves and their neighbors that money was not their supreme value.[60]

Aesthetic ideals notwithstanding, materialism had a way of shading the picture. At its 1845 annual exhibition in Faneuil Hall, the Massachusetts Horticultural Society featured a gala dinner for 600 of Boston's finest; elaborate floral decorations included "a Gothic pyramid, a Chinese temple and a Newfoundland dog executed in hollyhocks and moss." On display were 1,400 dishes of fruit—one exhibitor, alone, contributed 240 pear varieties.[61]

Such excesses were only the beginning. In 1852, prosperous banker and railroad magnate Horatio Hunnewell bought a 500-acre Wellesley estate, which he transformed over several years into one of the era's most extravagant horticultural displays. In addition to a series of ornate Italian gardens, the grounds included 12 greenhouses—half for fruits and half for flowers—dozens of ornamental flower beds and elaborate fruit and vegetable gardens, long allays of native and exotic trees, an abundance of fountains, and a $1,200 steam engine to power them all.[62]

Worcester's elite never rivaled that extreme, but they still took their horticulture quite seriously. It was William Lincoln, whose idyllic gardens on the Home Farm estate had earned him considerable respect, who first pushed to create a local society modeled after the MHS. Annoyed by the Worcester Agricultural Society's growing disinterest in produce and flowers, Lincoln persuaded several like-minded gentry—including Dr. John Green, whose extensive garden and meadow of wildflowers stretched far behind his Main Street home—to join him in exhibiting their best flowers and fruits on October 13, 1840, upstaging the WAS's annual cattle show by a day.[63]

Fortunately for William, his older brother Levi—then president of the WAS—didn't take the gesture personally. In fact, in a show of good will, he contributed several specimens of the Rohan potatoes he had been nurturing on his Elm Street estate. Neither he nor Governor John Davis earned any awards for their potato entries, prompting the *National Aegis*, a newspaper edited by William, to chide that although "[m]en who grow to be Governors might reasonably be expected to grow great potatoes . . . [t]he nutritious qualities of this species of potato have not been sufficiently tested in this part of the country to determine their value. It is pretty well ascertained that they are not fit for the tables of horticulturists."[64]

Despite that snub, Governor Davis two years later signed the legislation that officially created the Worcester County Horticultural Association. Dr. John Green was the organization's first president, Dr. Samuel Woodward and Stephen Salisbury II, vice presidents. William Lincoln, who had done so much to pull the group together, chose the lesser role of corresponding secretary. Although he died in 1843 at 42 years, his kinsmen would continue to dominate the society for the balance of the century. Among them, William's nephew Daniel Waldo Lincoln, president of the Boston & Albany railroad and mayor of Worcester during the Civil War, became one of the city's most prominent horticulturists and the society's head from 1857 to 1860. His running competition with *Worcester Spy* editor John Milton Earle for top honors in pear cultivation dominated the society's midcentury exhibitions: at one show, Lincoln contributed 160 varieties. In addition to pears, his vast West Side orchards and grounds featured a pond filled with Victoria Regia—a giant water lily whose three-feet-wide lily pads could support the weight of any small child willing to pay Lincoln a quarter for the privilege.[65]

In his love of pears, Daniel Waldo Lincoln and his fellow horticulturists were not alone.

Indeed, cultivating pears was the mark of a cultured 19th-century gentleman. Nurseries like Robert Manning's Pomological Garden in Salem, Massachusetts, founded in 1823, supplied more than 2,000 varieties of fruit trees—including about 1,000 pear variants by 1842—to wealthy men throughout the northeast. Much of the pear-growing culture focused on the MHS, which served as an information clearinghouse and exhibition center for the popular fruit.[66]

Mulberries, too, became a national obsession. Spurred by an 1825 Act of Congress that encouraged the notion of harvesting mulberry-loving silkworms to develop a national silk industry, entrepreneurs set down mulberry trees as fast as the Linnæen Gardens in Flushing, New York, could import them from China and the Philippines. Planted from Boston to Charleston, most extensively on Long Island, the mulberries struggled in the inhospitable North American environment until the craze ended with a severe winter in 1844 that wiped out any remaining plantations.[67]

The explosion in horticulture and ornamental gardening was further inspired by the work of botanic explorers. Naturalists like François André Michaux, who wrote the *North American Sylva*, a classic reference on trees of the eastern United States, David Douglas, who discovered the Douglas Fir in 1825, and Charles Christopher Perry, who found the Colorado Blue Spruce on Pike's Peak in 1862, all were part of a broader movement during the century's first half to collect and classify native and exotic flora. Through experimental gardens, such as the one founded by MHS in conjunction with Mount Auburn Cemetery, newly discovered plants were tested and the results disseminated throughout the world.[68]

Even as the gentlemen farmers tended their orchards, however, the economic forces their worldly pursuits had set in motion devoured much that was left of New England's forests. Just as their romanticized agrarian forebears had begun the process of deforestation by clearing the land for crops, so these manufacturers and financiers accelerated the felling of trees—not only for fuel but for railroad ties and raw materials. Writing in 1846, botanist George B. Emerson warned that Massachusetts's wood-based industries—such as ship building and furniture manufacturing—had so depleted native forests that the state was rapidly becoming dependent on timber imported from Maine and New York, a risky situation:

> Even these foreign resources are fast failing us. Within the last quarter of a century, the forests of Maine and New York, from which we draw our largest supplies, have disappeared more rapidly than those of Massachusetts ever did. In a quarter of a century more, at this rate, the supply in many places will be entirely cut off.[69]

In Worcester, he noted, deforestation was causing problems for horticulturists: "[A] most intelligent gentleman in Worcester [Stephen Salisbury II] tells me, that he attributes the greater difficulty now experienced in the cultivation of the more delicate fruits of the town, to the fact that the encircling hills, formerly crowned with [climate moderating] trees, are now, to a considerable degree, laid bare."[70]

Not until 1875, the same year that the second edition of Emerson's massive survey of state trees and shrubs was issued, would the trend begin to reverse. In the meantime, however, the urban elite whose orchards suffered while their bank accounts swelled from the profits of deforestation became interested in a new application of landscape architecture. Inspired by the popularity of rural cemeteries, they began to think about creating green spaces within cities—not for burial but for peaceful contemplation and exercise. Urban parks would bring the rural countryside back into the city, albeit in a controlled fashion. Only in these manmade settings, not nature's wilds, would trees be appreciated as "the most magnificent among the material works of God."[71]

[1] Levi Lincoln, Jr., *Address, Delivered Before the Worcester Agricultural Society, October 7, 1819, Being Their First Anniversary Cattle Show and Exhibition of Manufactures* (Worcester: Manniner & Trumbell, 1819).

[2] Levi Lincoln, Jr., *WAS Address*; Charles A. B. Nutt, *History of Worcester and Its People*, Vol. II (New York: Lewis Historical Publishing Co.: 1919), p. 1049; *The Massachusetts Spy*, Oct. 13, 1819.

[3] *Celebration of the Two Hundredth Anniversary of the Naming of Worcester, October 14 and 15, 1884* (Worcester: Charles Hamilton Press, 1885) p. 143; William Lincoln, *History of Worcester, Massachusetts From Its Earliest Settlement to September, 1836: With Various Notices Relating to the History of Worcester County* (Worcester: Charles Hersey, 1862), pp. 119–131; John L. Brooke, *The Heart of the Commonwealth: Society and Political Culture in Worcester County, Massachusetts, 1713–1861*, (Amherst: The University of Massachusetts Press, 1989), pp. 201, 272–73; Russel Blaine Nye, *The Cultural Life of the New Nation 1776–1830*, (New York: Harper & Row, 1960), p. 116; Tamara Plakins Thornton, *Cultivating Gentlemen: The Meaning of Country Life Among the Boston Elite 1785–1860* (New Haven: Yale University Press, 1989), pp. 122–23.

[4] Brooke, p. 272; *Celebration*, pp. 144–45.

[5] Brooke, p. 269.

[6] Brooke, p. 268; Thornton, p. 68.

[7] Thornton, p. 108; Nye, pp. 72, 82–83; Jefferson cited in Leo Marx, *The Machine in the Garden: Technology and the Pastoral Ideal in America* (London: Oxford University Press, 1964), p. 122.

[8] Thornton, pp. 122–23.

[9] Levi Lincoln, Jr., *WAS Address*, p. 8.

[10] Thornton, pp. 119, 125.

[11] Thornton, p. 122; Brooke, p. 268.

[12] Waldo Lincoln, *History of the Lincoln Family* (collection of the American Antiquarian Society) pp. 157–58, 161–62; Emory Washburn, *Memoir of Hon. Levi Lincoln, Prepared agreeably to a Resolution of the Massachusetts Historical Society* (Cambridge, Mass.: John Wilson & Son, 1869), p. 4 (Collection of the American Antiquarian Society).

[13] Waldo Lincoln, pp. 158–161. On p. 159, Lincoln notes, "In [1797 Lincoln] was elected senator and seems to have served in both capacities, his name being recorded both as senator and representative in the Journals of the General Court, and while holding these offices 'exerted strong influence in the legislative action, particularly in the modification of the judicial and school systems.'"

[14] Richard B. Lyman, Jr., "'What is Done in My Absence?' Levi Lincoln's Oakham, Massachusetts Farm Workers, 1807–20," *Proceedings of the American Antiquarian Society*, Vol. 99, Part 1, 1989, pp. 158–168.

[15] Ibid.

[16] Nutt, *History* Vol. I, pp. 172–74.

[17] "The Diary of Christopher Columbus Baldwin, Librarian of the AAS 1829–1835," *The Transactions and Collections of the American Antiquarian Society*, Vol. VIII, 1901 (London: Johnson Reprint Corp., 1971), p. 282; Mildred McClary Tymeson, *Rural Retrospect: A Parallel History of Worcester and Its Rural Cemetery* (Worcester: Albert W. Rice, 1956), p. 8.

[18] Washburn, p. 29; Tymeson, p. 53.

[19] Washburn, p. 29; *Republican* letter cited in Brooke, p. 311.

[20] Brooke, pp. 303–4; Charles Hudson, "Character of the late Hon. Levi Lincoln of Worcester, Mass.," 1870, (Collection of the American Antiquarian Society).

[21] Hudson; Waldo Lincoln, pp. 278–79; Washburn, p. 11.

[22] Washburn, p. 30; Waldo Lincoln, p. 279.

[23] Edwin T. Weiss, Jr., *Patterns and Processes of High Value Residential Districts: The Case of Worcester, 1713–1970*, PhD dissertation, Clark University, 1973, pp. 82–83;

Ivan Sandrof, *Your Worcester Street* (Worcester: Franklin Publishing Co., 1948), p. 47.

[24] Weiss, ibid.

[25] Washburn, pp. 15–16; William Lincoln, pp. 282–83.

[26] Washburn, ibid; *Worcester City Documents* #4, p. 6: The railroads were Boston & Worcester (1835), Western (1839), Norwich & Worcester (1840); Providence & Worcester (1847), Worcester & Nashua (1848), Worcester & Fitchburg (1850); Tymeson, p. 23.

[27] *City Documents* #4, p. 6.

[28] *Celebration*, p. 146.

[29] *City Documents* #4, p. 6; Tymeson, pp. 22–23, 49; Weiss, pp. 69–70.

[30] Weiss, pp. 70–79.

[31] Franklin P. Rice, ed. *Worcester Town Records 1801–1816*, (Worcester: Worcester Society of Antiquity, 1895), pp. 21, 24; *Town Records 1817–1832*, entries for Aug. 23, 1824 and Mar. 5, 1832.

[32] *Town Records 1833–1848*, p. 30: The tree fine compared with recommendations for a $2 fine for playing ball in the street, $2 for throwing stones or bricks, $2 for rolling a hoop on the street, $1 for smoking a "segar" or pipe in the street or roads within School District One, and $2–$10 for swimming nude between one hour before sunrise and one hour after sunset within view of public streets or private homes; *Town Records 1801–1816*, p. 24.

[33] David Schuyler, *The New Urban Landscape: The Redefinition of City Form in Nineteenth-Century America* (Baltimore: The Johns Hopkins University Press, 1986), pp. 24–36.

[34] Joel Porte, ed, *Ralph Waldo Emerson: Essays & Lectures* (New York: Library Classics of the U.S., Inc., 1983), pp. 216–17.

[35] Judd cited in John R. Stilgoe, *Common Landscape of America, 1580 to 1845* (New Haven: Yale University Press, 1982), pp. 207–8.

[36] Schuyler, p. 32; Stilgoe, p. 263.

[37] Norman T. Newton, *Design on the Land: The Development of Landscape Architecture* (Cambridge, Mass.: Harvard University Press, 1971), p. 260.

[38] Newton, pp. 197, 208–9, 216–17.

[39] Newton, p. 209.

[40] Newton, pp. 260–266.

[41] Follows discussion and citation in David Schuyler, *Apostle of Taste: Andrew Jackson Downing 1815–1852* (Baltimore and London: The Johns Hopkins University Press, 1996), p. 118.

[42] Stilgoe, p. 228; Stanley French, "The Cemetery as Cultural Institution: The Establishment of Mount Auburn and the 'Rural Cemetery' Movement," *American Quarterly*, 18 (Fall 1966), p. 43.

[43] Stilgoe, pp. 227–28.

[44] Neil Harris, *The Artist in American Society: The Formative Years 1790–1860*, (New York: George Brailler, Inc., 1966), p. 199; Stilgoe, p. 228; French, p. 44.

[45] French, p. 42.

[46] Thornton, p. 160; U. P. Hedrick, *A History of Horticulture in America to 1860*, (New York: Oxford University Press, 1950), p. 428; French, p. 44–45.

[47] French pp. 45, 48, 52.

[48] Harris, pp. 199–202; Lowell cited in French, pp. 37–38.

[49] French, p. 53.

[50] William Lincoln, pp. 250–51, 260; Levi Lincoln, Jr., "An Address Delivered on the Consecration of the Worcester Rural Cemetery," (Boston: Dutton and Wentworth, 1838), pp. 8–15.

[51] Levi Lincoln, Jr., "Consecration," pp. 29–30; Tymeson, p. 30.

[52] William Lincoln, pp. 207, 275; Tymeson, p. 30; Levi Lincoln, Jr., "Consecration," p. 31.

[53] Nutt, Vol. II, pp. 254–55; Tymeson, p. 31; Levi Lincoln, Jr., "Consecration," p. 31.

[54] Levi Lincoln, Jr., "Consecration," pp. 31–32; Tymeson, pp. 34–38.

[55] Levi Lincoln, Jr., "Consecration," pp. 5, 21.

[56] "Thirteenth Annual Report of the Trustees of the Rural Cemetery in Worcester," (Worcester: C. Buckingham Webb, 1851), pp. 8–9.

[57] Tymeson, pp. 67–68

[58] Worcester County Horticultural Society Collection; Frances Herron, "The Worcester County Horticultural Society—A Look at the Early Years," in "The Worcester County Horticultural Society: Celebrating 150 Years," p. 14.

[59] Thornton, p. 180.

[60] Thornton, pp. 161–62.

[61] Thornton, pp. 158–59.

[62] Thornton, p. 153.

[63] Eugene and Margaret Parsons, "One Hundred Years of Worcester Horticulture," *Sunday Telegram*, Sept. 15, 1940; Herron, p. 11.

[64] Cited in Herron, p. 14.

[65] Herron, p. 21; Nutt, Vol. II, pp. 174, 1051.

[66] Hedrick, pp. 211–12, 235.

[67] Hedrick, pp. 216–17.

[68] Hedrick, pp. 400, 412–13, 417–18, 421–22, 428.

[69] George B. Emerson, *A Report on the Trees and Shrubs Growing Naturally in the Forests of Massachusetts*, Vol. I, 2nd ed. (Boston: Little, Brown and Co., 1875), pp. 17–18.

[70] Emerson, p. 6.

[71] Emerson, p. 42.

©*Robert Nash*

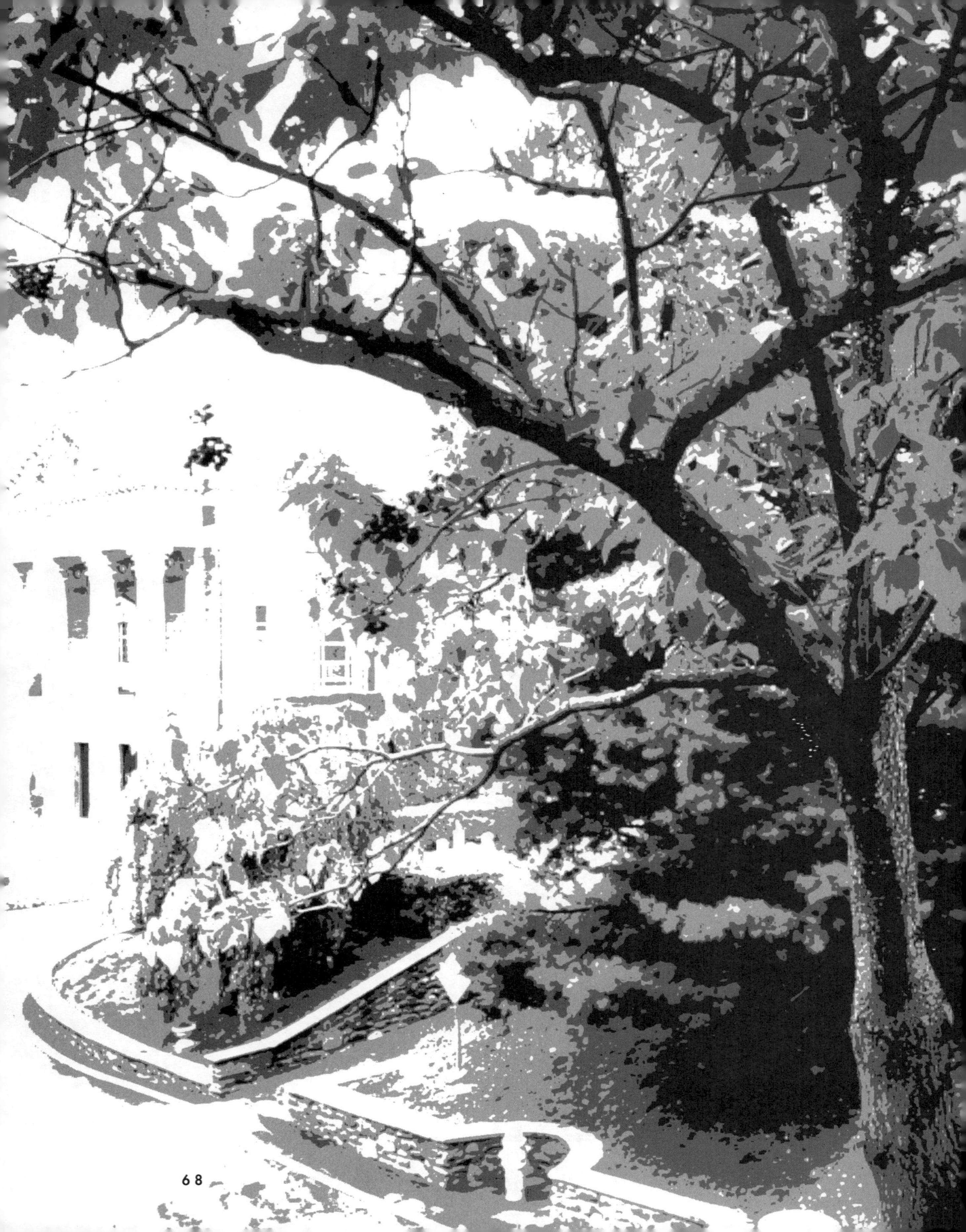

GREENING WORCESTER
Chapter Four

While the evening's turnout at Horticultural Hall was modest, Worcester was certainly greener for the day's work. Thanks largely to the Worcester Grange, nearly 500 trees had been planted in the city: 413 shade trees (mostly maples) and 80 fruit trees and ornamentals, to be precise. It was a good effort, this first Arbor Day in Massachusetts on April 30, 1885—no rival to the nation's first Arbor Day celebration in Nebraska ten years earlier, when 12 million trees were planted state wide in one day—but a respectable showing in Worcester and 35 other communities, nonetheless.[1]

Standing on a stage bedecked with flowers and potted plants, before a canvas inscribed, *Our first Arbor Day—may it take as firm and lasting a hold on the hearts of the people as the trees take root in the soil,* State Grange Master James Draper urged an enthusiastic audience to plant trees. Draper's concerns about dwindling timber resources and deforestation were echoed by Stephen Salisbury III, a member of Worcester's Parks Commission. "It was a matter of common knowledge . . . that the timberlands of the country were disappearing," reported the next day's *Worcester Daily Spy.* "Something more than Arbor Day was needed to prevent utter desolation in New England. Those who participated in its observance, however, would always be honored and their service would be appreciated."[2]

Though centuries of waste had ravaged the region's forests, celebrants noted that Worcester itself had much to be proud of. Trees shaded many streets and a once useless swamp had been transformed into popular Elm Park—thanks to the boundless efforts of Salisbury's colleague, Parks Commission Chairman Edward Winslow Lincoln. Unable to attend the Arbor Day ceremony, Lincoln penned a characteristic mix of classical analogies and acerbic wit for a crowd-pleasing Arbor Day message:

"Not until Lebanon had been stripped of its cedars, did the glory fade away from the City of God!" he wrote in a statement read by Draper to the assemblage. "Manhood and Godhood! Personal freedom and national development, alike trace their origin to the primeval forests, in whose dim recesses their infancy was nourished, and in whose falling foliage should be murmured their dying requiem." Those lofty sentiments were punctuated by a few choice barbs at one of Lincoln's favorite targets: boys who damage city trees. Softening an earlier public commentary that "all boys possessing jackknives should be shot at sight," Lincoln wrote, "Every boy in possession of a jackknife, caught within 400 feet of a shade tree, and not having a license as a common whittler, shall be doomed to confinement for one month in the city [dog] pound."[3]

Mischievous boys and unleashed dogs were anathema to Lincoln, who had spent much of the previous 15 years battling railroads, utilities, the Worcester Police Department, the Department of Public Works, various city administrations and public skepticism to ensure that Worcester, now a booming industrial railroad hub, would protect public health and uphold aesthetic ideals by planting and preserving trees. It was a battle that mirrored the times: a period in which rapid economic growth produced both great material rewards and urban blight, and civic leaders from New York to Chicago were struggling to counter the cost of slums, congestion and pollution with the newest British import—urban parks.

Curing the City with Country—The Urban Parks Movement

In England as in the United States, the urban parks movement was a response to industrialization's ills. Fifty years before factories transformed America's agrarian economy, England had begun its technological metamorphosis. As a result, by the turn of the 19th century, London was already marred with soot and slums. Though public squares broke up crowded blocks, the largest green spaces, such as Hyde Park and Kensington Gardens, were the perquisites of royalty. Evolved from the medieval "deer parks" of nobility and landed gentry—privately owned hunting grounds, stocked with game—these landscaped artifices of natural countryside, popularized by Humphry Repton and other leaders of the landscape gardening school, were confined to the wealthy West End, and public admission was at the Crown's pleasure.[4]

With the rise of factory reforms in the 1820s and 1830s, however, British social reformers began to push for public green spaces in London's congested East End slums. As early as 1803, prominent landscape gardener John Loudon had noted the connection between parks and public health, observing that London's open squares improved the city's air circulation. But it wasn't until the cholera epidemic of 1832 that reformers began a concerted push for a public park that would infuse the diseased East End with cleansing fresh air. Promoting parks as the "lungs of London," they ultimately succeeded in creating the city's first public green space, East London's Victoria Park, finished in 1846. One year later, 100-plus-acre Birkenhead Park was completed as part of a new community built just outside Liverpool.[5]

The public health benefits of London's parks were not lost on Americans. In the United States, too, cholera had ravaged congested cities, first in 1832 and again in 1849. Most communities maintained finite green spaces in the form of public squares, town commons or waterfront promenades, but these open areas were declared insufficient for maintaining public hygiene by the newly created American Medical Association (AMA) after the second cholera epidemic. In its 1849 sanitary survey of the nation's cities, modeled after a similar British survey conducted seven years earlier, the AMA advocated for planting trees and building parks to cleanse polluted air and moderate temperatures in overcrowded slums.[6]

That argument was supported by influential writers like William Cullen Bryant and Horace Greeley. Traveling to London in 1844, New York *Evening Post* editor Bryant praised the city's parks as key to "public health and happiness" and lamented New Yorkers' lack of foresight in setting aside comparable tracts of land for "parks and public gardens" in central Manhattan. Greeley, who edited the *New York Daily Tribune,* was equally impressed. Writing of London's parks after his 1851 trip to the Crystal Palace Exhibition, he urged his readers to make every effort "to secure breathing-space and grounds for healthful recreation to the millions who will ultimately inhabit New York."[7]

Aesthetics, too, defined the debate. According to the theory of "popular refinement," championed by landscape architect Andrew Jackson Downing, among others, public parks had the potential to elevate the nation's moral character by exposing common citizens to aesthetic ideals. Parks and other institutions of beauty and knowledge, such as art museums and libraries, were needed to supplement public schooling, which Downing deemed inadequate. By building these institutions, he wrote, the nation would "soften and humanize the rude, educate and enlighten the ignorant, and give continual enjoyment to the educated."[8]

Refining American culture was a sensitive issue for intellectuals like Downing, who were angered and shamed by endless snubs from European visitors who made sport of the young nation's coarseness. Among their criticisms, foreigners often cited the dearth of landscaped gardens and green spaces, and the ragged, deforested countryside—an embarrassment for American travelers who admired the European alternatives. No one, wrote American novelist Catharine Maria Sedgwick, could "enter the London parks without regretting the folly (call it not cupidity) of our people, who, when they had a whole continent at their disposal, have left such narrow spaces for what has so well been called the lungs of a city."[9]

But parks were more than just proving grounds for aesthetes or tools for social engineers and sanitarians. They were also important symbols. Like the rural cemeteries that inspired their design, these manmade rustic landscapes embodied the republic's agrarian past and romanticized notions of rural piety and purity. By creating curvilinear vistas that were the antithesis of urban gridiron, reformers believed they could cure the city with an injection of country: here was a place for play or respite from worldly pursuits, where trees cleansed not just the air but the soul as well—the crucial antidote for a society choking on mammonism.[10]

Here, too, was a common ground where citizens of all circumstances could meet on equal terms. This democratizing influence of parks was evident to American observers like Downing, who noted with some envy that Europeans, for all their aristocratic heritage, had created public landscapes (by midcentury, no longer the exclusive domain of royalty) more inherently democratic than anything in the United States. Of German parks he wrote, "all classes assemble under the shade of the same trees—the nobility, (even the king is often seen among them,) the wealthy citizens, the shopkeepers, and the artisans, etc." It was, he affirmed, a model "worth imitating."[11]

Visiting Liverpool in 1850, a 28-year-old American traveler named Frederick Law Olmsted was similarly impressed by the new public park at Birkenhead. "I was ready to admit that in democratic America there was nothing to be thought of as comparable with this People's garden," wrote Olmsted. "The poorest British peasant is as free to enjoy it in all its parts as the British queen.

SUGAR MAPLE
Acer saccharum

Aflame in glorious red, orange and gold, sugar maples are New England's autumnal splendor. Firing hillsides crimson, flickering across green lawns, they consume the October landscape in a blaze of color that lasts but a few short weeks, until chilling gusts strip their leaves with a wintry warning. Brilliant hues have made the sugar maple a popular street tree throughout the region, including Worcester, where 19th-century Parks Commission chairman Edward Winslow Lincoln favored them above all other shade trees for their beauty and vigor.

Lincoln's appreciation for sugar maples' hardiness and adaptability to an urban environment prompted their planting throughout the city; by century's end, the even hardier, though less colorful Norway maple *(A. platanoides)* was the favored species. As a result, a century later, a 1988 inventory revealed that 90 percent of Worcester's 20,000 street trees were maples—two-thirds were Norway maples—a risky situation should a disastrous disease like Dutch Elm blight ever emerge that threatens the species.

A new parasite, the Asian longhorn beetle *(Anoplophora glabripennis),* first reported in Brooklyn in 1996, favors maples among hardwoods, posing a serious potential threat to maple-dense cities like Worcester. Devouring host trees from the inside out, the inch-long, black-and-white beetles leave telltale piles of sawdust around the bases of trunks or branches. The 1996 beetle infestation in Greenpoint, Brooklyn, resulted in the removal of over 800 trees, of which about 200 have since been replanted.

At present, however, the greatest risk to sugar maples is a by-product of human activity—acid rain. The chemical fallout of fossil fuel power plants and car exhausts, acid rain laces the soil in forests and cities with sulfates and nitrates, leaching out valuable nutrients and releasing previously stable, poisonous heavy metals. For sugar maples, whose shallow root systems are sensitive to pollution, acid rain and even more damaging acid fog have spelled disaster in recent decades. A University of Vermont study of sugar maples showed a significant decline in saplings on Camel's Hump Mountain over two decades: from 140,000 maple saplings per acre in 1965 to 21,500 in 1983—a decline that researchers believe is most probably due to acid deposition.

Two centuries ago, humans were also a threat to sugar maples, burning acres of the trees for potash, a colonial cash crop used to make soap, glass and gunpowder. Valued for high yields, a cord of sugar maple could produce 140 pounds of ash, which, when reduced to potash, was worth at least $200 a ton in 1800.

The quality that made sugar maples a good source of potash—dense, strong wood—also made the species a favorite for furniture, kitchen tools, shoe lasts and gun stocks. Hard, durable, with a beautiful, straight grain that enhances cabinets and the striped backs of violins, the wood of a sugar maple has been known to outlast marble when used as flooring. The tree's sap, too, remains a valued commodity. From Native Americans, the European colonists learned to tap sugar maples during the spring snow melt, boiling down the sap to a precious amber liquid. Used to sweeten everything from candy to cigars, maple sugar has the added benefit of containing bone-fortifying phosphates that aid in calcium retention.

Reaching heights of 130 feet and diameters up to four feet, sugar maples are characterized by deeply furrowed, grayish bark and three- or five-lobed, bristle-tipped leaves, 3 to 6 inches wide. Growing in opposing pairs along each twig, the leaves are dark green above, pale beneath, splashes of orange, red and yellow in autumn. Like all maples, the sugar maple's fruit is a two-winged key, or double samara; its two ovoid seeds lie close to the stem, with papery wings extending downward. When released to the wind, the keys twirl like a helicopter's rotors as they drift earthward, a delight for children who enjoy a good chase.

More than that, the baker of Birkenhead has the pride of an OWNER in it . . . Is it not a grand good thing?"[12]

Aside from high-minded principles, there were also pragmatic considerations driving the urban parks movement. In particular, there was money—a lot of money—to be made from creating city parks. American capitalists were quick to realize that building a park created a windfall for abutting landowners, whose property values soared with the beautiful view. At the same time, by unloading midtown real estate, wealthy landowners could free themselves from burdensome property taxes and hefty assessments for sewers and other public improvements—costs that had skyrocketed with the accelerated pace of urban development.[13]

The Model—New York's Central Park

All these factors—capitalism, public health reform, aesthetic ideals, cultural chauvinism, the rhetoric of republic and democracy—converged in New York City during the 1850s. The nation's leading port and a major center for finance and industry, New York was swelling exponentially, from 90,000 residents in 1800 to a half-million by midcentury. To house all those people, the city had created some of the nation's worst slums, home primarily to immigrants who streamed through Ellis Island at the rate of more than 20,000 a year.[14]

Congestion bred disease and the nation's highest mortality rate. It also bred social upheaval. Political corruption, alcohol, crime, grime, sweatshops, slums—all became causes for reform. In the midst of this maelstrom, a handful of wealthy New Yorkers, led by merchant Robert Browne Minturn and his wife, Anna, decided the answer to New York's ills was a large public park. Such a project, they believed, would help rid the city of disease, civilize the unruly underclass, bolster commerce and prove that New York was the cultural equal to any European city.[15]

The park's supporters also believed the project would actualize the landscape aesthetics they so admired and promoted elsewhere—most notably in the design of Brooklyn's Greenwood Cemetery, opened in 1838, and the landscaped grounds of their Hudson River estates. Founders of the New York Horticultural Society, Minturn and his circle of merchants-cum-gentlemen-farmers hoped the park would be a source of moral uplift for their fellow New Yorkers, instilling in the masses a refined appreciation of nature and republican roots.[16]

Drawing on support from influential writers like Downing, Bryant and Greeley, park proponents initially staked their hopes on Jones Wood, a 150-acre uptown estate of landscaped grounds and woodlands that abutted land holdings of several wealthy New York families. Since the Jones family heirs had no interest in selling their land, the plan was to take the tract by eminent domain. But the proposal soon became embroiled in a heated political debate over how the park's development would be paid for. Minturn and his supporters argued for financing the project through general tax revenues, instead of assessments on abutting landowners. Outraged, those outside the elite circle countered that such an arrangement would essentially force the public to pay for land improvements that benefited only the new park's wealthy neighbors.

Instead, they proposed creating a park in central Manhattan, to be financed by assessments on abutters under the auspices of an independent commission.[17]

After three years of contentious debate in the state legislature, despite enthusiastic approval of the so-called Central Park plan in July of 1853, the Jones Wood proposal emerged victorious on a technicality, due to skillful political maneuvering by Jones Wood advocate and abutter Senator James Beekman. Infuriated, the Jones heirs sued to overturn the legislation; their position was upheld by a district supreme court justice in a January 1854 ruling that the Jones Wood bill basically transferred ownership of land from one "limited community to another," at the public's expense. Thus, by default, Central Park became the site of the city's—and the nation's—first urban public park.[18]

Beginning in 1856, New York City used its powers of eminent domain to acquire more than 800 acres of midtown real estate. Another year of political wrangling and court battles followed, but by the next autumn, most of the accounts were settled and the land was ready for development. Hired as the project's superintendent by the newly created, independent board of park commissioners was Frederick Law Olmsted, whose visits to public parks in London and Liverpool had inspired him to apply for the job.[19]

A widely traveled gentleman farmer and journalist who benefited from the financial support of his father, a successful Connecticut dry goods merchant, Olmsted had built a literary reputation as an expert on agriculture and a keen observer of social conditions in the antebellum South. When the publishing firm in which he was a partner fell victim to the 1857 depression, Olmsted decided to follow the advice of a family friend who sat on the Parks Commission and apply for the superintendence. With the backing of several prominent literary figures, including Washington Irving, Horace Greeley and William Cullen Bryant, he won the post—though not the respect of the park's chief engineer, who, on their first meeting, disparaged Olmsted's lack of "practical" experience.[20]

Initially content to oversee the creation of New York's massive public garden, Olmsted soon had higher ambitions. About a month after he was hired, the Park Commission decided to host a design competition for Central Park on the advice of a young British architect named Calvert Vaux. At first the new park superintendent had no plans to enter the competition, which offered a $2,000 first prize for the winning design. But when asked by Vaux, who admired his writings and whom he had met several years earlier at the Newburgh estate of Vaux's mentor and former partner, Andrew Jackson Downing, to combine their talents and submit a plan, Olmsted ultimately agreed.[21]

The result of that collaboration was the prize-winning Greensward plan. A rustic landscape of woodland and glade, field and lake, Olmsted and Vaux's ambitious design embodied their shared reverence for aesthetics and desire to create a self-contained, pastoral environment at the city's heart. For Vaux, who contributed his draftsman's skill and artistic talents to the project, the Greensward would enable New Yorkers to simply enjoy the pleasure of art and recreation in beautiful natural surroundings. For Olmsted, who brought familiarity with the parkland itself and extensive knowledge of horticulture, the design would provide a source of moral uplift and refinement to a city bent on material gain.[22]

It took eight years of power struggles, political skirmishes, and $4 million in cost overruns before the major landscaping and construction of Central Park was finally completed in 1866. Enthusiastically embraced by the public, the elegant grounds and structures were hailed as a national treasure, inspiring other cities to follow suit, and establishing Olmsted and Vaux as the nation's premier landscape designers.[23]

Central Park's Steward—Andrew Haswell Green

Central Park's success was of great interest to Worcesterites. For one thing, the project's completion was due in large part to a member of one of the city's leading families—Andrew Haswell Green. First cousin of the city's most prominent physician, Green had moved from Worcester to New York City in 1835 at the age of 15 to seek his fortune. After clerking for several merchants and spending a year on a sugar plantation in Trinidad, he returned to New York and took up real estate law; soon after, he became involved in school politics, and rose to president of the New York City School Board in 1855. Two years later, Green's achievements in public service earned him an appointment to the new commission overseeing the construction of Central Park.[24]

Cherishing childhood memories of his family's 200-plus-acre estate on Green Hill, overlooking Worcester's downtown, Green shared Olmsted and Vaux's aesthetic values and vision for Central Park. A frequent Sunday dinner guest at the Olmsteds' during his early years on the commission's finance committee, Green was often Olmsted's strongest defender against a board that increasingly challenged the superintendent's cost overruns and pressured for patronage appointments. But their friendship soured in 1859, when an exhausted Olmsted left for a six-

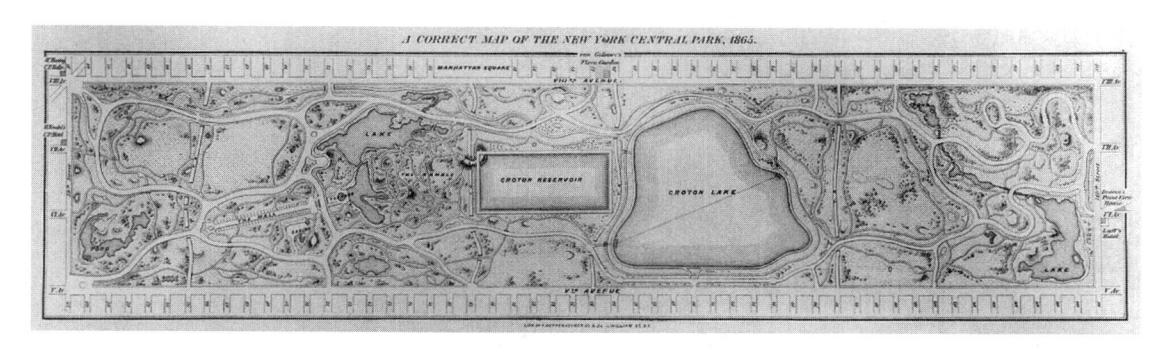

A Correct Map of New York Central Park.
Courtesey, American Antiquarian Society, Worcester, Massachusetts

week trip abroad to visit parks in Europe. Concerned about escalating expenditures, Green convinced the board to appoint him as comptroller, a new position that consolidated all supervisory responsibilities for the park's construction and preempted Olmsted's oversight.[25]

A tight-fisted, autocratic manager with a penchant for detail, Green slashed wages and reorganized the work force to rein in costs. In 1860, he became Park Commission president, wielding his additional power and reputation for honesty and parsimony to garner needed state appropriations for the project's completion. Green's belt tightening gained him the respect and support of wealthy New Yorkers, whose backing was key to funding; it also engendered Olmsted's deep resentment as Green and the board gradually stripped him of responsibilities. Angered and alienated by their former ally, Olmsted and Vaux resigned as landscape architects in 1863.[26]

Two years later, the two men rejoined the project to oversee its finishing touches. Green built on his success as commission president and expanded the board's planning authority to encompass the design of northern Manhattan's public squares and streets. In 1868, he suggested the idea of consolidating sections of surrounding counties with Manhattan under a shared municipal government—a concept actualized some 40 years later that earned Green a national reputation as "The Father of Greater New York." It was Green, too, as an executor for his former law partner Governor Samuel Tilden, who proposed consolidating the Tilden, Astor and Lenox foundations to create the New York Public Library. His tough-minded fiscal management style

Andrew Haswell Green
Courtesy,
American Antiquarian Society,
Worcester, Massachusetts

eventually won him an appointment as city comptroller; scrutinizing public expenditures, Green exposed the cost overruns that led to the downfall of Boss Tweed.[27]

His distinguished career of civic service ended tragically in 1903, when Green was murdered by an intruder in his New York home. "It may truthfully be said that to no one man who has labored in and for the city during the last 50 years is the city under greater and more lasting obligations than to Andrew H. Green," said New York Mayor Seth Low. "The city itself, in some of its most beautiful and enduring features is the monument of his love; and the city may well cherish his honored name with the undying gratitude that is due to a citizen who has made it both a greater and better city than it was."[28]

Street Trees and Public Parks—The Demand for Green Space in Worcester

Green's accomplishments in New York were more than just a matter of civic pride for Worcester. Central Park's success also bolstered the arguments of local leaders and horticulturists, who had been promoting the idea of a public park since the 1850s.

Like New York, Worcester was experiencing its own population explosion. With 17,000 residents by midcentury, the city had absorbed a fourfold population increase in just one generation. Much of that growth was spawned by railroads. A break-of-bulk point where goods were unloaded from one rail line and transferred to another, Worcester by midcentury was the hub for six railways radiating in all directions. Benefiting from that easy access to major markets throughout the country, and the fact that Worcester products could be shipped directly without expensive interrail transfers, factories and small shops multiplied. Boot and shoe manufacturing dominated a diversity of local industry, followed by artisans' tools and plows.[29]

Manufacturing jobs were quickly filled by Irish immigrants fleeing famine in the late 1840s and early 1850s, and farm laborers seeking a new life; factory employment swelled from about 1,900 in 1845 to just over 5,200 in 1855. To accommodate the influx, Worcester more than doubled its dwellings in a decade. The city's property valuation rose dramatically during the same period, from $4.2 million in 1840 to $11.1 million in 1850—a 158 percent increase.[30]

Bullish on the city's prosperity, Worcester's leaders were also mindful of congestion's consequences. In his 1850 inaugural address, Worcester Mayor Henry Chapin broached the need to acquire additional public grounds:

> Increasing as our city is in population, the time will soon come when the necessity for more extensive public grounds will press strongly upon us. With the exception of the common, which is by no means a large one, we are nearly destitute of them. It is unfortunate that in years gone by, when land could have been procured at a low price, tracts of land were not purchased, which would have been a most prolific source of health, comfort and ornament to the city . . .
>
> Year by year the hum of industry grows louder, and the footsteps of an increasing

population are more distinctly heard. . . . I know of nothing which would insure as valuable an income upon the outlay, as an investment of a reasonable sum in grounds, to be made public as the occasion should demand.[31]

Chapin's sentiments were echoed by his successor, Mayor Peter Bacon, in his 1851 inaugural address. Advocating for the purchase of public grounds, Bacon suggested "that lots and sites for their location should be selected and purchased at the same time in different, if not opposite, parts of the City, for the accommodation of different sections of it." Others, disparaging the deteriorated state and diminished size of the Common—now but nine acres, less than half its original area—argued for creating an ovoid, tree-lined mall to encircle the city.[32]

To begin to address the problem, that same year Worcester established a standing Committee on Shade Trees and Public Grounds. Comprised of two aldermen and three common councilors, the committee was responsible for overseeing the Common and municipal burial grounds, as well as planting and maintaining shade trees along city streets. In so doing, Worcester became one of the first communities in New England to designate the planting of street trees as a function of municipal government, rather than to continue relying solely on the volunteerism of private citizens.[33]

A Matter of Public Priorities—Worcester's Elm Park

Three years after Mayor Chapin articulated the need for additional public grounds, at the height of neighboring New York's legislative battle over Central Park, the city's most distinguished statesman presented a solution. Governor Levi Lincoln, formally retired from elected office but still active in local and state politics, and John Hammond, a farmer for Governor Lincoln who had purchased the family's Highland Street farm, offered to sell the city a 27-acre parcel of land abutting the Agricultural Society's fairground for use as a new public common. On March 17 and 20, 1854, the city closed the deal, purchasing the land for $11,257.50, and distinguishing itself as one of the first, if not the first, municipality in the nation to buy land for the explicit purpose of creating an urban public park.[34]

The public, however, was not impressed. Taxpayers felt the city had paid too much for what amounted to a piece of swampland, located far from the center of town, which required drainage before it could be used. They were also angered that the deed required the city to construct a new road on the parcel's western perimeter, or forfeit ownership to the grantors' heirs. Undoubtedly, their displeasure was also fueled by the fact that the Lincoln family, for all their civic-minded generosity, had nothing to lose and everything to gain from the parcel's development at taxpayers' expense, since the Lincolns had major land holdings in the new Common's vicinity.[35]

That public opposition to the purchase and development of the new Common was a clear reflection of the decade's antigovernment prejudices. Notwithstanding Worcester's recent shift to

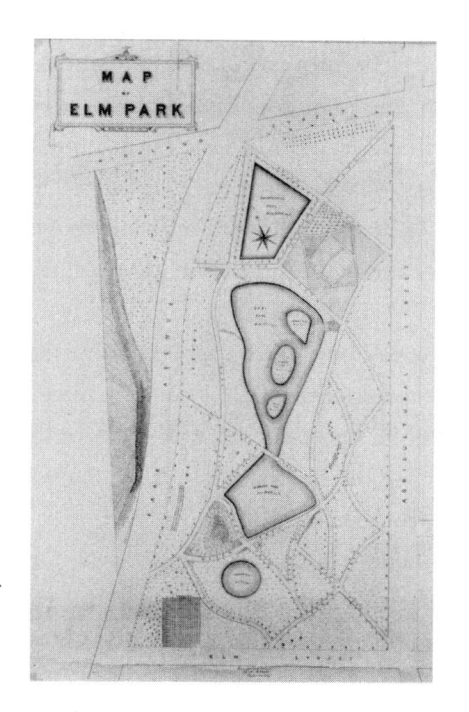

A map of the original plan for Elm Park. From the collections of WORCESTER HISTORICAL MUSEUM, *Worcester, Massachusetts*

a municipal form of government in 1848, most citizens wanted less, not more, action from their local officials. Despite significant population growth, voters opposed the idea of increasing government services, such as expanding the public water supply for domestic use, choosing instead to raise water rates to curb private demand and retire the city's debt. Throughout the 1850s, a suspicious electorate kept its new municipal government in check, voting in fiscal conservatives and discouraging government activism.[36]

As a result, although Worcester was several years ahead of New York City in acquiring land for a public park, the city fell well behind other communities at the forefront of the urban parks movement in realizing that goal. Nearly two years after the land's purchase, nothing had been done to improve the new Common. Hoping to spur his elected colleagues to action, Mayor Isaac Davis, in his 1856 inaugural address, warned that Governor Lincoln had reaffirmed his intent to reclaim the parcel for his heirs if the city continued to stall.[37]

Lincoln's ploy worked. By the following year, the city had complied with the deed by constructing a wide street bounding the parcel's western edge, done a modicum of grading, enriched the soil with street scrapings of horse manure, and planted some shade trees in and around the new Common. But once the basic requirements set out by Lincoln and Hammond were met, the city did little else to develop the park for the next 14 years. Other than gradually filling the swampy lowlands, the Joint Committee on Shade Trees and Public Grounds saw fit simply to collect income from apples and hay harvested on the new Common and rents from traveling carnivals and circuses. So deep was the resistance to spending money on developing public grounds that when Mayor Davis offered to donate 14 acres for a park along Lake Quinsigamond in 1861, the city rejected the gift because the deed required constructing a right of way through the property, and building and maintaining a fence or wall around it.[38]

Instead, the joint committee put its energy and limited budget into planting shade trees along city streets, repairing fencing around the Common, and fighting the losing battle of maintaining the dilapidated, often vandalized burial grounds at Pine Street and Mechanics Street. By 1861, as Worcester sent its sons off to war, city leaders decided the task of supervising Worcester's shade trees and public grounds had grown large enough to warrant a different form of oversight.

That November, with approval from the state legislature, Worcesterites voting for state officials also considered a ballot item to create a standing, three-member Commission on Shade Trees and Public Grounds. Of the 3,000 residents who participated in the election, only 451 bothered to vote on the commission, which was approved by a 57-vote margin, "such was their indifference to the subject."[39]

Commenting on the outcome in his 1862 inaugural address, Mayor P. Emory Aldrich observed, "There certainly is nothing in the external appearance of our city, during the spring, summer and autumn months, which adds more to its attractiveness than the great variety and beauty of the trees which border our streets and fill and beautify the public and private grounds of the city. . . . [Their care] can undoubtedly be much better accomplished by a permanent board, selected from the citizens at large, than by committees appointed every year from the city council, and at no greater expense."[40]

The following January, in accordance with enabling legislation, a three-member commission consisting of Edward Earle, James B. Blake and Henry Prentice was elected by the city council. Choosing Earle as chairman and Blake as secretary, the commissioners got down to business with the arrival of the spring planting season. Using $156.48 of their $500 appropriation, they bought 975 maples and elms from the nursery of S. H. Colton, planting 299 trees on 39 streets and the rest at the city almshouse to create a nursery for future use.[41]

In carrying out its mission, the new board had the backing of a powerful former member of the old joint committee, Mayor Daniel Waldo Lincoln. The third son of Governor Lincoln, lawyer, railroad director, banker and horticulturist, Mayor Lincoln guided Worcester into a new era of government activism. A Democrat who had the support of both Irish Democrats and elite Republicans, Lincoln capitalized on the war-induced growth of manufacturing to persuade skittish taxpayers of the need to improve city services, including an expanded city water supply and a new, franchised public transit system—the Worcester Horse Railroad. He also urged the commission to fulfill his father's dream and drain the swampy new common. "A very moderate expenditure in draining the lowest part of it into an adjoining meadow . . . would make it as fine a parade ground as the Agricultural Park opposite," said Lincoln in his 1863 inaugural. "No intelligent farmer owning the land would hesitate to make so obvious an improvement. The increased value of the crop would soon pay the cost."[42]

The new commissioners, however, chose to ignore the mayor's advice. Instead, they appealed to the public for help, proposing that the new Common would be named for anyone willing to donate $10,000 for its drainage and development. They also dispelled the popular misconception that now that the new board was in place, it would be solely responsible for maintaining the city's thousands of shade trees. Rather, wrote Chairman Edward Earle in the commission's first report, ". . . the commissioners hope that the more care the city takes of the public shade trees, the more willing individuals will be to start and nurse trees against their estates, that thus with the combined attention of the city and individuals, the increased growth of trees in all our streets and highways shall be such as to make the City of Worcester more and more noted for its beautiful shade trees." To encourage citizens to plant and care for shade trees along city streets, the commission recommended that the city pay a bounty of two dollars for any privately tended tree that was accepted by the commission 26 months after planting.[43]

While Earle and Prentice continued the new board's work for the next few years, James Blake had other ambitions. Superintendent of the Worcester Gas Light Company, trustee of the Five Cents Savings Bank and director of the City National Bank, Blake was elected in 1865 to the first of six terms as mayor. A republican champion of the city's business and financial interests, he was an outspoken government activist who believed that increasing the city's debt to finance public improvements was an investment in Worcester's future. His vision was shaped in part by his many business holdings, which depended on the city's growth for their financial success; also, Blake was motivated by the needs of Worcester's burgeoning population, which had jumped 21 percent in just the previous five years, from 24,960 to 30,055. Diverse new industries had attracted more factory workers. By the year Blake was elected, machinery and metals firms, many of which had supplied munitions to the Union forces, accounted for nearly 28 percent of the city's 9,232 manufacturing employees.[44]

Not all Republicans agreed with Blake's aggressive municipal agenda, however. In particular, the artisans and small-shop mechanics who accounted for Worcester's diverse industrial base comprised a powerful arm of the political party and were quite opposed to any outlays for projects that would increase the public debt and, as they saw it, promote business interests of the privileged at taxpayers' expense. That fiscal conservatism prevailed on the Commission for Shade Trees and Public Grounds, which, despite the proactive stance of their former colleague, continued to do and spend little on the new Common.[45]

Writing in 1867, at the start of Mayor Blake's second term, Commissioner George Jaques admitted that not much had changed at "'Elm Park,' as public spirited citizens more ambitiously style it." Other than basic maintenance—mowing, fence repair, filling low spots, and fertilizing—the parcel looked much as it had a decade ago. "Everything has been done," asserted Jaques. "If no throngs of gay visitors have transformed the solitary place into a fashionable resort, it would seem unreasonable to censure the commissioners, however great may be the provocation to blame the popular taste." Noting that total expenditures on the new Common since 1854, including the original purchase price, were about $25,000, Jaques added that the commissioners "look forward to a possible future when 50 or more years hence, the purchase of this now unneeded pleasure ground may be as much a subject of congratulation as it is to-day of regret. Who lives will see."[46]

A bachelor schoolteacher, Jaques was equally tight-fisted when it came to the city's shade trees. Noting that Worcester's debt had increased faster in the past five years than it had in the entire preceding period since the city's founding by Jonas Rice in 1713, he said the commission must rely on private donations for planting any new shade trees or ornamentals. The incentive for such donations, he noted, was the increased market value that beautiful sidewalk trees add to adjacent real estate.[47]

Apparently, that incentive wasn't great enough. In 1868, Jaques reported that the commission had finally gained approval for a modified version of its original proposal to established a tree bounty and was offering citizens one dollar for every street tree they planted. While the plan stimulated tree planting, however, it created some new problems. Amateur arborists, more interested in collecting their bounty than properly setting in trees, were planting either too close together or too far apart, setting trees on ungraded or remote streets, or simply planting trees that were too big for a given site. "Thus," wrote Jaques, "what was intended to grow into an ornament, becomes from the first an obstruction, and almost a nuisance." As a result, the commission modified its program, making bounties conditional on the board's approval of a given tree and site.[48]

Finding a means to encourage street tree planting was a significant issue for Jaques. A co-founder of the Worcester County Horticultural Society who himself had planted dozens of elms on Piedmont Street, Jaques was concerned about the impact of rapid urban development on the city's oldest trees. Already, as the Blake administration continued its aggressive program of street improvement, sewer and water main construction, and as private enterprise laid gas lines and erected office buildings, many "fine, large and beautiful trees" were disappearing from the city's densely populated core. Some of the city's "ancient trees," Jaques wrote in the commission's annual report, needed to be removed before they posed a safety hazard from decay. "Some, also, of the younger and still healthy trees, will have to be sacrificed to the bustling improvements of modern times," he added. "Indeed, it may be regarded as a sort of necessity, in the growth of American cities, that, where brick and mortar, pavements, and underground conduits steadily increase their encroachments, trees are doomed. The law of the future promises nothing more favorable that that of the past. And so it must be—wherever Business frowns, this Commission reverently bows its head and retires."[49]

Jaques's fiscal conservatism dominated the commission through the end of the decade. Despite a $1,000 bequest by Governor Lincoln to finance the drainage of Elm Park via a connection to the public sewer system, nothing was done to carry out the project. Jaques commended his fellow board members for their prudent accomplishments: pruning trees away from street lights, planting shade trees on public school grounds, erecting tree guards, and maintaining the common and Elm Park. In his 1869 report, he dreamed of enhancing the city's two public grounds with landscaping, gardens and fountains, and suggested the possibility of creating three other parks throughout the city—but fretted about the associated costs and risk of further escalating the municipal debt.[50]

The Relentless Visionary—Edward Winslow Lincoln

It would take a different kind of visionary to realize those dreams. In 1870, a new chairman was appointed to head the Commission on Shade Trees and Public Grounds: a respected horticulturist whose annual reports for the Worcester County Horticultural Society were widely read, Edward Winslow Lincoln assumed his new role with a tenacity and forcefulness that marked a complete break with the commission's reticent past and once again brought Worcester to the forefront of the urban parks movement.

In many ways, Lincoln was a natural for the job. The youngest child of Governor Levi Lincoln, nephew of Worcester County Horticultural Society co-founder William Lincoln and brother of activist Mayor Daniel Waldo Lincoln, Edward Lincoln had witnessed much of Worcester's industrial transformation and its social costs. Born John Waldo Lincoln in 1820 (he later changed his name to avoid confusion with the uncle for whom he was named), just eight months after the death of his venerable grandfather, Levi, Sr., Edward was a teenager when the railroads his father facilitated as governor first chugged into Worcester. Although he left his hometown briefly on two occasions, Lincoln always returned, eventually to blend his gift for persuasion, love of horticulture and sense of public duty in his effort to ensure that Worcester would not be buried under the trappings of progress.[51]

Born in the old family mansion at the bottom of Elm Street, Lincoln attended public school with classmate Andrew Haswell Green. Shortly after Green left for New York City, Lincoln went to Cambridge, Massachusetts, following the family tradition of studying at Harvard College. Graduating in 1839, he moved to Alton, Illinois, to practice law with his brother William and soon entered public service as the city's prosecuting attorney. But his midwestern legal career was short. Returning to Worcester in 1845, Lincoln found few opportunities for a young lawyer and chose instead to pursue his love of horticulture, as well as his passion for words as a journalist. By the fall of 1845, he became part-owner of the *Aegis,* the first New England newspaper to support Zachary Taylor's Whig presidential candidacy against Free Soiler Martin Van Buren, and was soon engaged in a barbed exchange with *Spy* editor John Milton Earle, a staunch Van Buren supporter.[52]

Lincoln's advocacy for Taylor earned him a four-year presidential appointment as Worcester's postmaster in 1849, the year after he married Sarah Rhodes. Completing his term, Lincoln moved his young family briefly to Illinois, but once again returned to Worcester. It was a tragic period in Lincoln's life: three of the couple's four children died in infancy, and Sarah died two weeks after the loss of her last baby in 1856. Picking up his career as journalist, Lincoln edited the short-

Edward Winslow Lincoln, Worcester's first Parks Commissioner, who "thought and wrought" Elm Park Courtesy, Worcester Parks Commission

lived *Bay State*, initially a daily, then a weekly before it folded. In 1858, he married Kate Von Weber and settled into a comfortable family life, eventually fathering seven children, all of whom lived to adulthood.[53]

A Democrat in national elections, Lincoln remained an independent in municipal politics, favoring those candidates he believed best suited for the job. An occasional candidate for public office, including county sheriff in 1856, he eventually veered away from electoral politics, turning down frequent requests to run for mayor and choosing instead to serve his community through volunteer activities.[54]

By the time Lincoln was appointed head of the Commission on Shade Trees and Public Grounds in 1870, he had already been secretary of the Worcester County Horticultural Society for 10 of the 36 years he would fill that role and was a dependable presence at the society's annual shows, checking in entries and handing out exhibition cards. A "sturdy-looking," robust man, with a long, gray beard and piercing eyes, Lincoln was well known for his sharp wit and "caustic pen," which he wielded freely in his annual society reports. He brought the same editorial zeal to his new commission role, quickly transforming the board's dry annual reports into popular polemics. Not one to mince words, he was kind and supportive to friends and respected colleagues but critical and direct to those he disdained. At his death, it was observed, "No one ever made the mistake of believing him his friend when he was not, for Mr. Lincoln was frank and outspoken. In fact, he was noted for making sharper criticisms to a man's face than behind his back."[55]

Lincoln's first two years on the commission set the tone for his next quarter-century as chairman. Joined by Stephen Salisbury II and Obadiah Hadwen, both avid horticulturists who served with Lincoln for much of his tenure, the chairman used his annual reports to advocate his agenda. Chastising his predecessors for only planting and protecting shade trees "in cases of absolute necessity," Lincoln took aim at the old board's parsimonious ways. "[T]he distinction between prudent thrift and a griping penuriousness is kept closely defined," he sniped in 1871. "And, among the monuments to their Civic Idols which they may erect, it is very certain that no Golden Calf will perpetuate the worship of the Official Skinflint."[56]

By contrast, Lincoln advocated for an aggressive tree-planting effort. In its first year, the commission set out or supervised the planting of nearly 100 trees and, by the following year, had established a new municipal nursery in the southwest corner of Elm Park, including 1,000 maples and 500 elms, for eventual transplanting along city streets. Urging developers to follow the board's lead and plant shade trees along new streets, "of their own volition," prior to petitioning the city council for acceptance of the new thoroughfares, Lincoln wrote, "The man who cannot perceive his private interest in the matter should have his wits sharpened by a refusal of the public to grind his axes."[57]

At the same time, Lincoln was no sentimentalist when it came to trees and derided those who were. To him, public health and safety took precedence, and he took full responsibility for an unpopular decision to fell an ancient, decaying giant at the foot of Elm Street—a venerated tree that stood in front of his father's mansion, one that Governor Lincoln himself had spared from destruction three years before Edward assumed responsibility for the city's trees:

Without wind or warning on July 4, 1867, the decaying elm had dropped a huge limb that spanned the entire street. When workmen gathered to cut down the tree soon after, however, Governor Lincoln ordered them to leave. The elm, which had graced the street longer than any resident could remember, continued to rot until the year Lincoln became commissioner. Then he took a firm stand for public safety and ordered it cut down. "Trees were made for man: not man for trees," wrote Lincoln. "Yet too many still stand, spared because of lingering associations, or on account of their age and massive proportions, whose removal would be a great public accommodation and appease an increasing popular demand."[58]

Nonetheless, the event, according to the June 3, 1870, *Worcester Daily Spy*, was marked with appropriate formalities: "It seems that the old tree on Elm Street will not be allowed to pass away without the proper rites; for we understand that around the spot will gather some of the old citizens, who remember it as a landmark in childhood, and listen to remarks by Judge Chapin and others, some time this forenoon."

Despite such sentimental attachments to aging public trees, Lincoln prevailed. In its first year, the commission removed 15 hazardous live trees, cut down 193 dead trees, ranging from two inches to two feet in diameter, erected 372 new box guards and repaired over 400 old ones. In addition, they surveyed which streets were in greatest need of new trees. To focus the commission's efforts more effectively, Lincoln also gained a ruling from the city solicitor that the board was no longer responsible for supervising the city's two old burial grounds. "The resort of juvenile gamblers and prostitutes," he noted, "almost any use to which they might be devoted would be an improvement."[59]

As for Elm Park, Lincoln supported the idea, first suggested publicly by George Jaques, of creating an artificial pond for ice skating to accommodate "the fast multiplying children of the vicinity." But the commission's efforts in 1870 to gain city council approval for draining the parcel via a connection to the Piedmont Street sewer had been "deemed inexpedient." Without such a connection, Lincoln argued, the ground remained too soft to work. Since the city had as yet failed to use his father's bequest for the project, he added with more than a hint of sarcasm, the council should pay interest on the fund "for which it has found convenient use."[60]

By the end of his second year, Lincoln floated two proposals that he would work hard for decades to realize: the acquisition of Newton Hill, next to the Elm Park parcel, for a fire-protection reservoir and additional public grounds, and the creation of a "broad boulevard, like those in Paris to encircle the city," to improve access to Lake Quinsigamond and traffic flow throughout Worcester, and to enhance the city's aesthetic appeal. The latter idea, he noted, was supported by his former classmate, Andrew Haswell Green, "whose signal merits have but just obtained fitting recognition, and whose long service as the virtual head of the New York Central Park Commission entitles his opinion to commanding influence."[61]

Lincoln's ambitious agenda, however, faced formidable political odds. In a tragic accident in late December of 1870, just two weeks after he was elected to a sixth term, Mayor James Blake was fatally injured in an explosion while conducting a routine inspection at the Worcester Gas Light Company. His death sent the elite business leaders of the Republican Party into free fall. Without a popular standard-bearer who could draw votes from both wealthy Republicans and Irish Democrats, party leaders could not muster support for a continuation of Blake's progressive policies. Instead, struggling to hold their party together, they eventually threw their support behind Clark Jillson, clerk of the police court and a former machinist who appealed to the city's large native-born middle class. A fiscal conservative who served as mayor in 1873, 1875 and 1876, Jillson not only slashed spending on public works but essentially returned municipal government to the conservative policies and values of the 1850s.[62]

For Lincoln and the commission, these events translated into reduced appropriations just as the new board was trying to breathe life into Elm Park. From a high of $5,000 in 1871, the commission's appropriation was sliced to a low of $3,000 during Jillson's third term in 1876. Funds were not restored until the end of the decade, when the newly formed Citizen's Coalition of elite Republicans and Irish Democrats—with the help of key business leaders like Stephen Salisbury III, son of Lincoln's fellow board member who served on the commission after his father's death in 1884—reasserted their agenda of municipal activism and reclaimed the mayoralty.[63]

The early years were challenging ones for Lincoln. First, there was the problem of the city's other public ground, the old Common. Bordered along Main Street by a noisy wood and hay market that filled the air with dust, sliced by the Norwich & Worcester's double railroad track, crisscrossed by myriad footpaths, cluttered by the town hall, dilapidated Front Street schoolhouse and aging Old South Church, the Common had been chiseled away over decades to just eight acres. Its grassy fields had long been popular for ball games and beating carpets; but those practices, as well as the firing of cannons, had been recently disallowed by Lincoln's predecessors. Now the Common was used for occasional carnivals, open-air concerts, public gatherings and military drills, and was widely appreciated as the sole green space in the city's congested downtown. Nicknamed "Central Park," it was the only recreational ground easily reached by all social classes—a place for a peaceful walk, provided one could ignore the intermittent clanging of a passing train. [64]

By the end of 1872, Lincoln had accomplished his first step—removing "the antique, shapeless and somewhat fragrant School-House" from the Common's northeast corner. His next goal was the removal of the Old South Church, a more controversial challenge that took several years, because it was the city's oldest Protestant house of worship. Grading had to be done, as well, using, among other things, the excavated remains of the cellar from the old homestead of former Mayor Isaac Davis. Then there was the matter of the railroad tracks, a battle that Lincoln waged for seven years, until the tracks were finally removed in November 1877, with help from Mayor Charles Pratt. Lincoln also hoped for a fountain at the Common's center—or, as he preferred to call it, a "jet d'eau"—but money was not forthcoming. "'Ask and it shall be given!' saith the Scripture: State what you need! writes the *Auditor*, and verily your appropriation shall be reduced," griped Lincoln. "The COMMISSION do not complain; they merely wish that the whole people would understand that they are no more capable than others of compelling one dollar to do the work of two."[65]

For all those improvements to the Common, however, including landscaping, graded and graveled pathways, and repaired fencing, the commission was criticized by local newspapers for neglecting the green. Vandalism was a perpetual problem. In addition, the Common's new "settees" were a popular spot for loafers. The settees were eventually removed, Lincoln noted in his 1879 report, "upon a general and intolerable complaint from ladies in every condition of life . . . that they could never pass those settees without having to listen to filthy language and ribald comment."[66]

Trees, too, presented a challenge, as the commission strove to keep up with new street construction. Meticulously recording the number and species of shade trees planted along city streets, Lincoln wrote passionately about the importance of selecting the proper tree for the proper location. Abhorring lindens for their vulnerability to parasites and foul-smelling blossoms that litter sidewalks, and horse chestnuts for their tendency to shed decayed foliage, Lincoln lauded several species that soon came to characterize Worcester's streets:

The Elm should be restricted to our longer and broader highways, where the far-reaching limbs that spread out from its massive boles may canopy a limitless vista, The ASH, too, if happily located as at the junction of Elm and Oak Streets, has a rugged beauty of its own. But, all things considered, hardiness, vitality under abuse, density of shade, cleanliness of foliage, and above all its tinted variegation, the Maple is fairly entitled to rank among Shade Trees *facile princeps*.[67]

Accordingly, the vast majority of trees planted during Lincoln's quarter-century as commission chairman were maples. Seeking to fill in barren streets, he placed a priority on the city's working-class East Side, noting that the mostly immigrant neighborhoods had a "greater need of Shade Trees than any other." Lincoln's civic and *noblesse oblige* sensibilities were echoed in letters to the editor of the *Worcester Evening Gazette*. In 1879, one writer bemoaned the lack of enough street trees throughout the city and emphasized the need to make tree plantings in Worcester's poorer neighborhoods a priority: "[S]urely it would be little for the city to set aside $2000 or so a year for simple tree-planting; beginning first with the great thoroughfares; next with the streets where the poorer people live. For as they can not afford to plant trees themselves, as richer citizens can, and can not hie away to monutain [sic] or sea to escape the heat, most certainly it is a Christian duty to help them—to surround them with what verdure and beauty we can."[68]

Elm Park pond
From the collections of
WORCESTER HISTORICAL MUSEUM,
Worcester, Massachusetts

The following day, another reader responded that, given current tax levels, civic-minded individuals should raise the necessary funds, following the example of neighboring Framingham, where the donation of 1,000 trees by a private citizen 40 years earlier had resulted in what were now beautiful, shaded streets: "No better monument could be erected to one man or to twenty than two thousand dollars properly invested in shade trees for the streets of this beautiful city of Worcester."[69]

Such sentiments notwithstanding, the commission relied on tax dollars for tree plantings and did the best it could within budget constraints. By decade's end, the commission was planting upwards of 700 street trees annually, replacing their old method of planting trees according to individual requests with a systematic approach of targeting a main street and its feeders. In so doing, Lincoln observed, the results were "not only obvious to the eye, but palpable to the sense of comfort."[70]

Not everyone appreciated the enhanced aesthetics, however. Vandalism was an insidious problem. Horses carelessly tethered to trees gnawed at trunks and low branches, mischievous youths carved bark with jackknives, and others cropped the treetops or simply stole newly planted saplings. During three days in May of 1877, Lincoln noted angrily in his annual report, 19 young trees just planted on Shrewsbury Street were stripped of their bark, and every other white ash on the north side of Elm Park was cut part way through its trunk and snapped in half. In response, the city council passed an ordinance offering a $50 reward to anyone who provided evidence leading to the conviction of those willfully mutilating or destroying shade trees on public grounds. But Lincoln was unimpressed, placing the blame on police who failed to enforce tree-protection ordinances already on the books.[71]

The police were more vigilant in tracking down vandals of trees and plants on private property. In one highly publicized case in 1876, a large crowd gathered in Worcester's Central District Court for the trial of Henry J. Chamberlin, accused of stealing 12 pear trees, 12 currant bushes, an ivy plant and flower pot, one fuchsia and eight different varieties of geraniums from the homes and grounds of his neighbors. Despite Chamberlin's claims that he bought the greenery from a New York nursery, bootprints near the site of the purloined plants matched his own, and he was convicted of theft and trespassing.[72]

Undaunted by the apparent lack of comparable protection for public trees, Lincoln continued to advocate. Much as he disdained the police, his greatest wrath was reserved for the telephone and telegraph companies that cut down or mutilated trees as they strung communications wires. "By suffrance of the *City Council*," growled Lincoln in 1881, "Telegraph and Telephone Companies have invaded the City, during the last year; lopping the limbs, or felling the trunks, of trees, indiscriminately, as best suited their immediate purpose."[73]

He also railed against highway department workers who "hack mercilessly at whatever impedes their way" when laying curbstones, including the roots of shade trees; road salt runoff from the Worcester Horse Railway Co.'s tramway, which "surely destroys the vitality of those patriarchal elms that adorn the northerly line of the COMMON"; and the practice of moving entire houses from the city into the more spacious suburbs, wrecking curbstones and street trees along the route.[74]

Sounding the clarion call in his annual reports, Lincoln fought all his battles with a barrage of personal visits, letters, testy appeals to the city council, endless queries to the city solicitor and fiery letters to the editor. He was relentless, year after year haranguing, cajoling and jabbing government officials, business leaders and the public to care for the planting and preservation of the city's shade trees. But the project he advocated for with unmatched ferocity was the creation of Elm Park.

A Swamp Transformed—The Development of Elm Park

Work finally began "in earnest" on the park in 1873, when the city council authorized $2,000 for the "unemployed and destitute" to excavate the first ornamental pool. Two years earlier, a severe summer drought had enabled the commissioners to examine the subsoil beneath a four-foot bed of peat in the tract's soggiest section, and determine that a sheet of ornamental water could be constructed; the plan was to tie a series of pools into the park's drainage system, both controlling the surface water problem and creating a focal point for the new public ground. The Oval Pool (later called the Elm Mere) and Diamond Pool (South Mere), excavated several years later, were purposely dug only a few feet deep, so that in winter, according to Lincoln, the ice "should nowhere be such as to imperil the life of a child old enough to be trusted in the park and smart enough to stand up straight should it unluckily break through."[75]

Soil from the excavations was used to level other sections of the park and to grade the old Common. Soon after the Oval Pool was created, workers also began laying out footpaths in Elm Park; by 1875, 2,500 yards of graveled footpaths were completed. Despite budget cuts during Mayor Jillson's tenure, the commission also began planting a variety of trees in Elm Park, including many donated by Lincoln and his fellow commissioners, Stephen Salisbury II and Obadiah Hadwen. The park also received several gifts from Harvard's Charles S. Sargent, the founding director of the Arnold Arboretum. Sargent's first gift in 1876, a Menzies Spruce, was among more than a dozen species the Arboretum eventually donated to the park, as part of its effort to test trees under different growing conditions.[76]

By 1877, a foundation for a fountain in the center of Diamond Pool was connected to new water mains on neighboring streets, and two islets were added to Oval Pool. The two ornamental pools were linked by a neck of water, and a cedar bridge, "slightly changed from a rustic design in an English Horticultural Magazine," according to Lincoln, was constructed over the channel between them. With financial support from a sympathetic municipal government, the commission was able to forge ahead with the park's completion over the next five years, adding a third and a fourth ornamental pool, more landscaping, plantings, gravel footpaths and, in 1881, the steeply arched, cast-iron bridge designed by Henry F. Edwards, which became Elm Park's landmark.

Several additional islets were completed, providing not only an attractive form to the ornamental ponds but also a habitat for wildlife and waterfowl, including three white China geese and three "Pekin ducks" donated by Lincoln, and a pair of white swans imported from Weymouth, England—a gift from the chairman's "old schoolmate," Andrew Haswell Green.[77]

Soon after the Oval Pool was constructed and first gravel paths laid, despite its lack of finish, Elm Park became a popular pleasure ground. In spring and summer, the paths were filled with nannies pushing baby carriages, and the water's edge was crowded with children sailing boats or feeding ducks; in winter, the ice was packed with skaters. During the leaner years, as he battled the close-fisted Clark Jillson, Lincoln quipped that the cost of re-seeding trampled grass should be financed by fees for marriage licenses and birth certificates: "One-half of the courting, in the City, is commenced or consummated upon the PUBLIC GROUNDS . . . why should not the profit enure to this COMMISSION of that relation which it has done so much to invite and render charming?"[78]

As it gained popularity, however, Elm Park also suffered from vandalism. Lincoln's rustic cedar bridge was soon stripped of its bark, trees were mutilated and plantings stolen. "Too many door-yards and gardens are stocked by their owners or lessees with plants that were but just set out by the COMMISSION," Lincoln chided in 1880. "This sort of larceny has grown so inveterate that it excites deep thankfulness when, from any cause, such depredations are less than ordinarily rapacious." He also groused at the anonymous individual who chose to mow the grass in Elm Park in order to feed his own animals: "Better far that the PARK should be depastured; since some manure would be left; than to suffer its aftermath to be skinned so closely." To help control the problem, police patrols were instituted that year on Sundays and holidays.[79]

Much of that vandalism was undoubtedly the result of adolescent mischief. But there were also those who vented their anger in the newspapers—and possibly in the park itself—about the amount of money being spent on Elm Park at the expense of the Common, which was more accessible to the city's working-class population. One writer to the *Worcester Evening Star* in 1879 claimed that park benches from the Common— "the people's seats"—had been removed to Elm Park, "a desolate spot where nobody will use them excepting the crows." Others criticized the amount of money being spent to design the pools and scenic gardens, and lambasted Elm Park as "Lincoln's Patch."[80]

Monitoring for signs of trouble, Lincoln made it a daily practice to tour Elm Park each morning before arriving at the Horticultural Society, where he made his office. Supervising and helping with plantings and pruning in warm months, shoveling snow off the ice for young skaters in winter, the chairman tended Elm Park as if it were his own garden. Deeply committed, he was also deeply offended by criticisms that the park paled in comparison to Boston's Public Garden, which had been acquired five years after Elm Park, in 1859, but was well under development by the end of the Civil War. "Our Citizens visit Boston and return vociferous in their praises of its Public Garden," said Lincoln in 1879. "But the people of Boston, when they made up their minds to dance, knew also that the piper must be paid." By contrast, he noted in a later report, lack of comparable resources for Elm Park meant that "the Chairman is crowded out from the garret and cellar of his house by the bulbs and tender plants belonging to the city, because nowhere else is there a place wherein to protect them from the severity of winter."[81]

For all the frustrations, financial roadblocks and public snipes—Lincoln was labeled "the Earle of the frog ponds" by those who favored the Common over the new public garden—the chairman, by 1882, was able to take some pride in Elm Park. Despite admitted mistakes, he wrote in his annual report, the commission had "pursued, consistently, the design proposed to themselves from the first, of securing and growing one specimen at least of every hardy Tree, Shrub, or Plant, that could be made to thrive away from its native habitat." The park had benefited from an unusual combination of soil types, including peat, fine sand, gravel and bog-iron ore, enabling a rich array of flora to thrive. Rhododendron, azalea and kalmia—by century's end, among the best collection in Massachusetts—flourished along the banks of the ornamental pools, while trees from as far away as England, France, Germany and Japan shaded the graveled walks. His work on the project largely complete, Lincoln inscribed the park's original plan, "Thought and wrought by Edward Winslow Lincoln, anno Domini 1874–1882."[82]

As Elm Park gradually took shape, Lincoln also took pleasure in a parallel accomplishment, the development of Park Avenue along the park's western edge. That, plus the construction of Lake Avenue on the city's east side, along Lake Quinsigamond, were the first two lengths of the broad boulevard loop he had proposed in 1871. "Built wide, for common convenience; thoroughly built for public comfort," wrote Lincoln in 1877, "built as flat as might be and allow the flow of surface water, nor spoiled, as are too many road-beds by the conceited ignorance which would substitute the hemisphere for its plane; [Park Avenue] stretches out along the western edge of the City—a constant pleasure to its original advocates and a singular fascination for its irrational foes."[83]

Lincoln's idea was to create an aesthetically pleasing, graceful and efficient thoroughfare; but Park Avenue's design was so successful that it soon became a favorite site for horse racing. By the summer of 1881, the problem had become so offensive—raising dust that damaged Elm Park's plantings and annoying the park's visitors—that Lincoln appealed to the city marshal to stop the practice. The marshal complied, much to the outrage of those who enjoyed the sport. With much "blowing of the 'hugag' and ringing of the 'loud hogannah' in the local newspapers," as Lincoln put it, about 400 people petitioned the mayor and aldermen to raise the speed limit on Park Avenue above eight miles per hour. Among the petitioners was none other than Lincoln's nemesis, the former Mayor Clark Jillson, who, ironically, during his first term of office had invoked the first veto by a Worcester mayor in an attempt to block appropriations for improving the road.[84]

The battle between horse-racing enthusiasts and those who preferred restricted use of Park Avenue continued for decades. Attractive as the road was, however, the city never saw fit to complete Lincoln's dream of an encircling boulevard, much to his frustration. Still, the chairman took pride in the avenue's success, declaring in 1884 that "PARK AVENUE is its own present justification. . . . Already has it more than repaid its cost, by the taxable value of edifices that would never even have been thought of but for its location and opening. It supplies an unrivalled thoroughfare from Northville to New Worcester, with a saving to the traveler of well-nigh a mile and a half. Once, along its route a house was scarcely to be seen. Now—you may look sharp before you discover unoccupied lots between frequent buildings."[85]

By the mid-1880s, Park Avenue was also the western boundary of Worcester's most elegant neighborhood. Gracious homes with fine trees and grounds stretched from Harvard Street, overlooking the city, west along Elm, Cedar, and part of William Streets toward Elm Park. Much of that land, originally the old Sever Farm, had come into the Lincoln family as a result of Governor Levi Lincoln's marriage to Penelope Winslow Sever. While Governor Lincoln developed parcels around his Elm Street mansion in the 1830s and 1840s, however, he held much of the property off the market during his lifetime. Following his death in 1868, his sons began to sell off large tracts of the remaining land to select buyers, during the same period that Elm Park and Park Avenue were being developed—no doubt, at significant profit.[86]

Parks for All—Worcester's Comprehensive Municipal Parks Plan

Edward Lincoln and his family surely prospered from the public projects he championed; yet the commission chairman did not confine his vision to that which benefited wealthy West-Siders. Early in the process of building Elm Park, he suggested that the city should purchase "one to two acres elsewhere" for baseball fields. Lincoln himself was no fan of the game, deriding it as "scarcely supplying the redeeming merit of a dreary amusement to the spectators," but he understood the need to create public playgrounds. Indeed, as forcefully as he opposed working-class recreation in his beloved Elm Park, Lincoln argued just as strongly for less restricted use of the old Common, endearing himself to the Irish immigrants living in nearby Washington Square, who relied on the common for their recreation. Lincoln's advocacy of public works projects further tightened his bonds with the city's Irish Democratic politicians, since Elm Park provided jobs for many of Worcester's Irish laborers. That political support was crucial when the commission—legally empowered to become the Worcester Parks Commission in 1884—proposed a comprehensive municipal parks system in 1886.[87]

Seeds for the plans were sown in 1882, when, inspired by the public's enthusiasm for Elm Park, Citizen's Coalition Mayor Elijah Stoddard took up the cause of his activist predecessors and called for the purchase of more land for public parks. The mayor's suggestion was welcomed by Lincoln, who for years had argued that the city should purchase Newton Hill, a drumlin with a panoramic view overlooking Elm Park, located on a tract of 61 acres. With the backing of over 200 prominent citizens in 1884, he presented a petition to the state legislature to empower the city council to take the property by eminent domain. The bill passed, only for its enabling period

WORCESTER'S OLMSTEAD LEGACY

Elm Park circa 1905 From the collections of WORCESTER HISTORICAL MUSEUM, Worcester, Massachusetts

Local lore attributes the design of Elm Park to Frederick Law Olmsted, but the famous landscape architect actually had no involvement with the park. Nonetheless, his influence was felt in Worcester. Olmsted's work in New York's Central Park inspired municipalities across the country to create gracious greenspaces; Elm Park, "thought and wrought" by Parks Commission chairman Edward Winslow Lincoln, reflected Olmsted's landscape aesthetic. His influence extended to Worcester in another, more direct way, as well—through the work of his son, Frederick Law Olmsted, Jr., and the Olmsted Firm, which provided landscape consulting services to the Worcester Parks Department through the first half of the 20th century.

The Olmsted Firm of Brookline, Massachusetts, was first engaged by the city in 1910 to assess Worcester's recreational spaces. From 1910 to 1918, the firm consulted extensively on Elm Park and guided improvements, including refinements to the shape of the South Mere and islands, new curbing for the ponds, modifications of bridges and rhododendron plantings, a new location for the playgound and the creation of paths for Newton Hill. From 1910 to 1913, the firm also consulted on Kendrick Field, Crompton Park and Washington Square. On and off for the next 30 years, the Olmsted architects reviewed various park projects in Worcester, making additional recommendations regarding improvements to Elm Park, as well as Burncoat, Green Hill, Institute and Morgan Parks, the Common, and Rockwood and Beaver Brook Playgrounds.

The firm's involvement with the city diminished during the 1920s and 1930s, a period when, according to Elm Park historian Rudy Favretti, "Worcester had the lowest per acre allotment for park maintenance of any major city in New England." At the Great Depression's end, in 1939, the Olmsted Firm was again engaged to do a comprehensive review of Worcester's parks. The result was the second phase of their involvement with Elm Park, from 1939 to 1941—landscaping the triangular plot of land at the base of Newton Hill, bordered by Highland Street and Park Avenue, that surrounded what was to become the site of the Rogers-Kennedy Memorial. The firm's work on this and other sections of Elm Park was the basis for funding in the 1980s from the Olmsted Historic Landscape Preservation Program for study, planning and historic restoration of the century-old landmark.

to expire while a committee of the city council wrangled with property owners over the terms of compensation.[88]

Exasperated, but far from defeated, Lincoln pressed on. That same year, another of his dreams—a park along Lake Quinsigamond—was finally taking shape, thanks to Horace H. Bigelow and Edward L. Davis. A former Democratic candidate for mayor and lakeside real estate investor who operated the city's only public transportation to the lake, Bigelow offered the city a 38-acre tract of land, including 1,000 feet of waterfront, in June of 1884. Unlike the city council that balked at Mayor Isaac Davis's offer in 1861, this time Worcester's municipal leaders gratefully accepted the gift of lakeside property. Bigelow's generosity was soon matched by former Mayor Edward Davis, son of Isaac Davis, who donated another 60 acres, including extended waterfront property. His gift prompted Bigelow to donate an additional 12 acres, plus an encircling strip for a driveway, bringing the combined gift to 110 acres. The land, plus $5,000 from Davis for its improvement, gave Worcester the basic ingredients for the city's second major public park. For Bigelow, who owned extensive property around the lake, including amusements and summer cottages, the development of Lake Park also meant a windfall in land values; from 1884 to 1886, prices reportedly soared from $35 per acre to as high as $500.[89]

For Edward Davis, Lake Park was just the beginning. Appointed to the Parks Commission in 1886, he quickly became immersed in a planning effort with Commissioner J. Evarts Greene to develop more public grounds. The results of that effort, presented to the city council on September 20, 1886, was a masterpiece of planning and politics—one of the nation's first proposals for a comprehensive municipal park system.[90]

Balancing East Side demands for recreational play spaces with West Side desires for gentile pleasure grounds, the plan recommended developing seven parks throughout the city, including much-needed recreation space in congested immigrant neighborhoods. The need for the latter, Lincoln argued forcefully, was "imperative and immediate." "Factories have covered much of what was once a hopeless swamp; and the remnant is being rapidly absorbed for dwellings or stores—often both under the same roof," he wrote of the so-called "Island" district. "Those dwellings are mostly tenement-houses, swarming with life, for whose conveniences the merest court-yard is reserved; and, not seldom, scarcely that much. . . . Into such crowded existence, against which this PARKS-COMMISSION will never cease to protest, if powerless to prevent…it seems desirable to introduce clear, open spaces for recreation, rest, and the quiet enjoyment of the air and earth."[91]

Lincoln's unyielding advocacy for recreational breathing space amid the city's tenements and the commission's careful effort to distribute public grounds throughout the city won key support for the Parks Plan. Despite Republican opposition to the Newton Hill purchase, the Citizen's Coalition of Irish Democrats and elite Republicans held. The commission's cause was furthered by Plan co-author Greene, who used his position as the *Spy*'s editorial writer to great advantage, and Commissioner Stephen Salisbury III, who donated land for the first of the proposed new parks across from Worcester Polytechnic Institute in 1887.[92]

Three years after the plan was proposed, in 1889, Worcester had acquired land for seven new parks: to the north, Fairmont Square and North (Burncoat) Park; to the east, East Park; to the south, Crompton Park; to the southwest, University Park; and to the west, Newton Hill and Institute Park. By this time, Lake Park was already a popular summer attraction and Elm Park continued to draw thousands of enthusiastic visitors to its flowered, shaded paths.[93]

Looking back over his accomplishments in 1895, 25 years after he first accepted the task of stewarding Worcester's trees and parks, Edward Winslow Lincoln was pleased and proud of the city's varied pleasure grounds. Even still, he reminded, "the City should, by no means, rest supinely content with what it has, so long as aught remains attainable for completer fruition."[94]

That challenge would remain for others to meet. The following year, at 1 A.M. on December 15, Lincoln died of complications from diabetes at age 76. His tireless service to the city over a quarter-century, eulogized the *Gazette*, would have cost $100,000 for a comparable hired professional; indeed, it took three years for the city to find an adequate, salaried replacement.[95]

Not one to leave details unattended, Lincoln had made clear, in writing, how his remains were to be disposed of: his body was to be placed in a pine box and, "without any form of priestcraft or rite, petition of clergy," reduced to ashes, under supervision of his friend and executor, Charles Aldrich. "[T]hereafter at sunset of some pleasant day," penned Lincoln, "I wish him to ascend to the top of Newton Hill and in the presence of my friends, Obadiah B. Hadwen and Edward L. Davis, to disperse my ashes to the four points of the compass from the flagstaff."[96]

His remains thus scattered over the soil he had guarded and beautified for a third of his lifetime, Lincoln had ensured that, even in death, he would continue to nurture the parks he had loved so well. Never again would Worcester know such a tenacious advocate for urban greenery, nor would its landscape be so passionately tended by one individual.

TREES OF WORCESTER

*Black pine
(Pinus nigra)
at Rural Cemetery*

*Color photos
©Robert Nash*

Weeping beech

(Fagus sylvatica)

Garden of the late

Helen Stoddard

Worcester, Massachusetts

*Sugar maples
(Acer saccharum),
Rural Cemetery
Worcester,
Massachusetts*

Magnolia accuminata blossom

Severely damaged city tree, corner of Elm and Hudson Streets

Autumn in Elm Park Worcester, Massachusetts

photo by John W. Trexler

*Rural Cemetery
Worcester,
Massachusetts*

*Rural Cemetery
Worcester,
Massachusetts*

*The Salisbury Mansion
Worcester, Massachusetts*

Close up of Common Horse Chestnut

(Aesculus hippocastanum)

Fern leaf beech
(Fagus sylvatica
'Asplenifolia')
Hadwen Arboretum,
Worcester,
Massachusetts

Rural Cemetery

Worcester, Massachusetts

Close up of Common Horse Chestnut (Aesculus hippocastanum), flowering

Norway maples, (Acer platanoides) line a Worcester Street

European beech
(Fagus sylvatica)

Honey locust
(Gleditsia triacanthos)

Hadwen Arboretum

Rhododendron

*Princess-tree
(Paulownia
tomentosa)
Holy Cross campus,
Worcester,
Massachusetts*

*Tulip tree
(Liriodendron
tulipifera)
Worcester,
Massachusetts*

Ginkgo tree
(Ginkgo biloba)

Elm Park
Worcester, Massachusetts

[1] *Worcester Daily Spy*, May 1, 1885.
[2] Ibid.
[3] *Report of Worcester Parks Commission*, November 1885; Ibid.
[4] Norman T. Newton, *Design on the Land: The Development of Landscape Architecture* (Cambridge, Mass.: Harvard University Press, 1971), pp. 220, 221–32; Roy Rosenzweig and Elizabeth Blackmar, *The Park and the People: A History of Central Park* (Ithaca, N.Y.: Cornell University Press, 1992), pp. 3–4.
[5] David Schuyler, *The New Urban Landscape: The Redefinition of City Form in Nineteenth-Century America* (Baltimore: The Johns Hopkins University Press, 1986), pp. 59–61; Newton, pp. 221–32.
[6] Schuyler, pp. 60–61.
[7] Ibid., pp. 63–64.
[8] Downing cited in Schuyler, pp. 65–66.
[9] Sedgwick cited in Schuyler, p. 63; Rosenzweig and Blackmar, pp. 23–24.
[10] Schuyler, pp. 59, 66–67.
[11] Downing cited in Schuyler, p. 65.
[12] from Frederick Law Olmsted, *Walks and Talks of an American Farmer in England* (London, 1852), cited in Newton, p. 232.
[13] Rosenzweig & Blackmar, pp. 32–33.
[14] Ibid., p. 22.
[15] Ibid., pp. 16–17, 23.
[16] Ibid., pp. 28–29.
[17] Ibid., pp. 18–22, 30–36, 52–53.
[18] Ibid., pp. 52–53.
[19] Ibid., p. 85; Newton, p. 270.
[20] Ibid., p. 128; Newton, p. 270.
[21] Ibid., pp. 123–24, 128–29; Newton, p. 271.
[22] Ibid., pp. 130–31.
[23] Ibid., pp. 180–205; Newton, p. 273.
[24] Charles Nutt, *History of Worcester and Its People,* Vol. I,(New York: Lewis Historical Publishing Co., 1919), pp. 134–36.
[25] Rosenzweig and Blackmar, p. 186.
[26] Ibid., pp. 180–205.
[27] Ibid., Nutt, pp. 134–36.
[28] Low cited in Nutt, pp. 135–36.
[29] *Worcester City Documents* #4 (1851) and #6 (1852); Robert J. Kolesar, *Urban Politics and Social Conflict: Worcester, Massachusetts, in the Nineteenth Century*, PhD dissertation, Clark University, 1987, pp. 35, 38.
[30] *City Documents* #4 and #6; Kolesar, p. 39, pp. 46–51.
[31] *Worcester City Documents* #3 (1850).
[32] *Worcester City Documents* #4 (1851); Rudy J. Favretti, *History of Elm Park, Worcester, Massachusetts* (Commonwealth of Massachusetts, Department of Environmental Management, 1985), pp. 2–3.
[33] Favretti, p. 2.
[34] Favretti, p. 3; *Worcester City Documents* #8 (Jan. 1, 1854) & #9 (Dec. 30, 1854); Nutt, p. 428; Waldo Lincoln, "Mrs. Penelope S. Canfield's Recollections of Worcester One Hundred Years Ago," *The Worcester Historical Society Publications*, Vol. I, No. 4., April 1931. Though Worcester has long claimed that Elm Park was the first piece of land purchased for a public park in the United States, other communities were engaged in acquiring park land during the same period. In particular, citizens in Hartford, Connecticut, voted to approve a plan by the Reverend Horace Bushnell to create a park in the center of town on January 5, 1854. The first contracts to acquire the land which became Bushnell Park were executed shortly thereafter: see Horace Bushnell, *The Beginnings of Bushnell Park* (Hartford, Conn., [s.n.], 1936), and John Alexopoulos, *The Nineteenth-Century Parks of Hartford: A Legacy to the Nation*, (Hartford, Conn.: The Hartford Architecture Conservancy, 1983). It should also be noted that other parks predate this period, such as Brooklyn's Washington Park, established in 1847. The distinction here is that Washington Park was created on land that was already publicly owned—in this case, the site of Fort Greene, a fortification during the Revolutionary War. Worcester's Elm Park was built on land purchased specifically for use as a park, from private owners. For background on Washington Park, see *The Papers of*

Frederick Law Olmsted, Vol. VI: The Years of Olmsted, Vaux & Co., 1865–1874, David Schuyler and J. T. Censer, eds. (Baltimore & London: The Johns Hopkins University Press, 1992), p. 207, n. 2.

[35] Favretti, pp. 3–5; Roy Rosenzweig, *Eight Hours for What We Will: Workers and Leisure in An Industrial City, 1870–1920* (Cambridge: [Cambridgeshire]; New York: Cambridge University Press, 1983), pp. 134–35.

[36] Kolesar, pp. 82–83.

[37] Favretti, pp. 5–6; *Worcester City Documents* #10 (1856).

[38] Favretti, pp. 6–7; Nutt, p. 433; *Worcester City Documents* #15 (1861).

[39] *Worcester City Documents* #17 (1863).

[40] *Worcester City Documents* #15 (1862).

[41] *Worcester City Documents* #13 (1864).

[42] *Worcester City Documents* #17 (1863); Kolesar, pp. 88–92; Nutt, pp. 176–77.

[43] *Worcester City Documents* #13 (1864).

[44] Kolesar, pp. 88–97.

[45] Ibid.

[46] *Worcester City Documents* #21 (1867).

[47] Ibid., Mildred McClary Tymeson, *Rural Retrospect: A Parallel History of Worcester and Its Rural Cemetery* (Worcester, Mass.: [s.n.] 1956), p. 94.

[48] *Worcester City Documents* #24 (1870).

[49] Ibid., *Worcester City Documents* #25 (1871); Tymeson, p. 94.

[50] *Worcester City Documents* #25.

[51] Waldo Lincoln, *History of the Lincoln Family* (Worcester, Mass.: Commonwealth Press, 1923), pp. 419–21 (collection of the American Antiquarian Society).

[52] Edward Winslow Lincoln Obituaries, Dec. 15, 1896 (collection of Worcester Historical Museum).

[53] Ibid.

[54] Ibid.

[55] Ibid.

[56] *Annual Report of the Commissioners of Shade Trees and Public Grounds*, 1870; *Commission Report*, 1884.

[57] *Commission Report*, 1870.

[58] Ibid, *Worcester Evening Gazette,* May 31, 1870, Collection of Worcester Historical Museum.

[59] Ibid.

[60] Ibid.

[61] *Commission Report*, 1871.

[62] Kolesar, pp. 98–109.

[63] Kolesar, pp. 118–127.

[64] *Worcester City Documents* #22 (1868) & #24 (1870).

[65] *Commission Reports*, 1872, 1873, 1875, 1877; Kolesar, p. 136.

[66] *Commission Report*, 1879.

[67] *Commission Report,* 1870.

[68] *Worcester Evening Gazette,* July 15, 1879.

[69] *Worcester Evening Gazette,* July 16, 1879.

[70] *Commission Reports,* 1873, 1877, 1880.

[71] *Commission Reports,* 1876, 1877.

[72] *Worcester Evening Gazette,* May 23, 1876.

[73] *Commission Report,* 1881.

[74] *Commission Reports,* 1881, 1882.

[75] *Commission Report,* 1875; Favretti, pp. 11–12; "What The Citizen Has Done For Our Public Parks," *Worcester Magazine,* Feb. 1904, Vol. 7, No. 2, pp. 37–40.

[76] Favretti, pp. 15–16; *Commission Reports,* 1876, 1875; The Arnold Arboretum was not formally established until 1881.

[77] *Commission Reports,* 1879, 1881; Favretti, pp. 16–18.

[78] *Commission Report,* 1875.

[79] *Commission Reports,* 1877, 1880.
[80] Discussion and quotes follow Rosenzweig, *Eight Hours,* p. 132.
[81] *Commission Reports,* 1879, 1883; Schulyer, pp. 138–39; EWL Obituary.
[82] Rosenzweig, *Eight Hours,* p. 132; *Commission Report,* 1882; *Worcester Magazine,* Feb. 1904.
[83] *Commission Report,* 1877.
[84] *Commission Report,* 1881; Evelyn Herwitz, "Park Avenue: Some Call It 'The New Main Street' ; Others Describe It As Example of Unplanned Growth," *Business Digest/Central Massachusetts,* Nov. 1985.
[85] Herwitz, *Business Digest*; *Commission Report,* 1884.
[86] Edwin T. Weiss, Jr., *Patterns and Processes of High Value Residential Districts: The Case of Worcester, 1713*–1970 (PhD dissertation Clark University, 1973), pp. 100–1.
[87] Kolesar, p. 136; *Commission Report,* 1873.
[88] Kolesar, p. 136; *Commission Report,* 1884.
[89] Rosenzweig, *Eight Hours,* pp. 134–35; Nutt, pp. 433–35; Kolesar, pp. 136–37.
[90] Nutt, p. 435; Rosenzweig, *Eight Hours,* p. 135.
[91] *Commission Report,* 1887.
[92] Kolesar, pp. 138–39; *Worcester Magazine,* Feb. 1904, pp. 37–40, Mar. 1904, pp. 46–48.
[93] *Commission Report,* 1888.
[94] E. W. Lincoln, "The Public Grounds of Worcester," in Elbridge Kingsley & Frederick Knab, *Picturesque Worcester*, Part I (Springfield, Mass.: W. F. Adams Co., 1895), pp. 18–20.
[95] EWL Obituary; "Worcester Horticultural Society To Observe 100th Anniversary In April," *Worcester Sunday Telegram,* Mar. 29, 1942; Favretti, p. 25.
[96] "100th Anniversary."

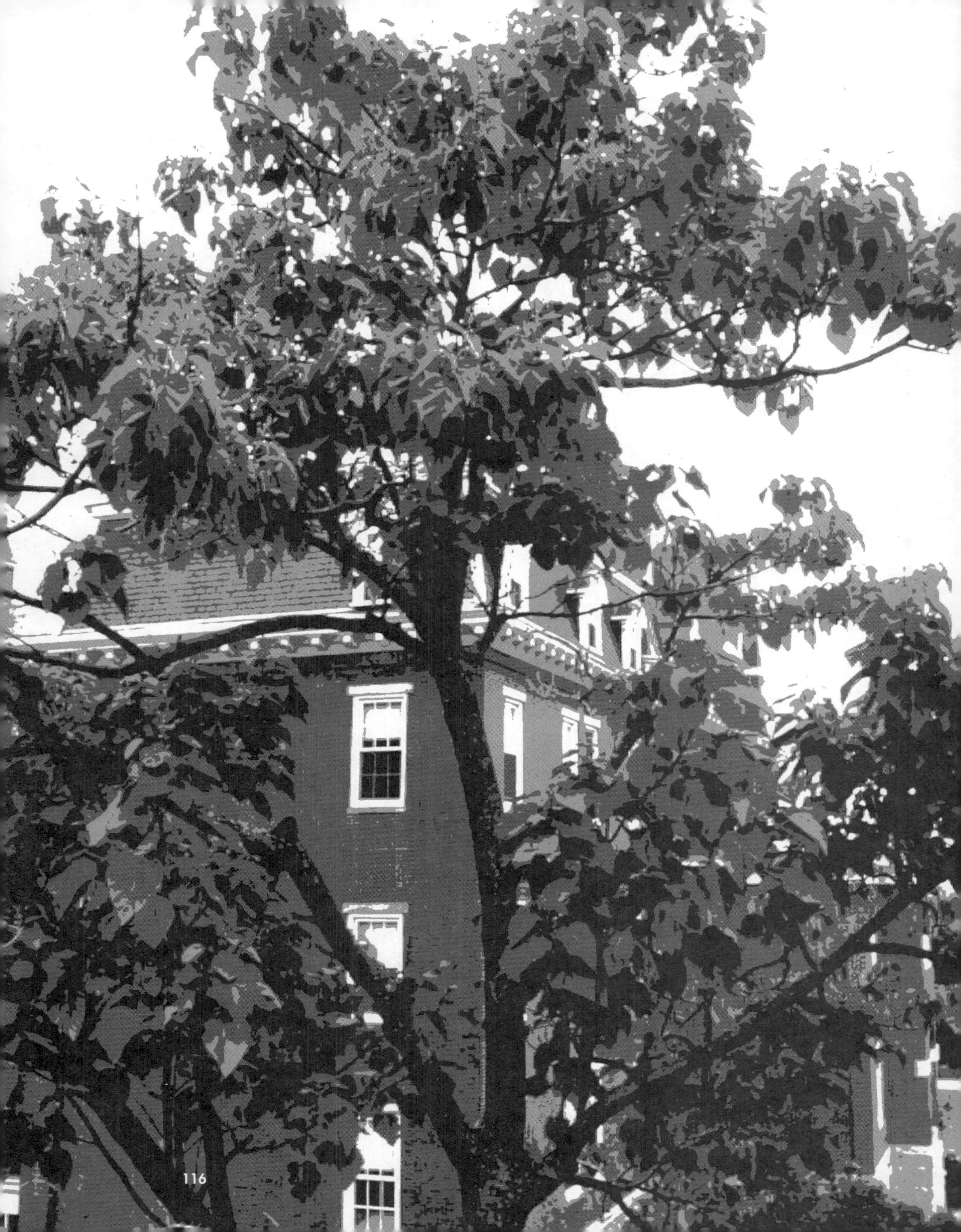

END OF AN ERA
Chapter Five

Leaden skies and a steady drizzle couldn't deter the crowd that had been waiting for more than an hour in Washington Square, and when the train pulled into Union Station at 9:28 A.M., two minutes ahead of schedule, they weren't disappointed. Stepping onto the platform as a military band thumped marches, President Theodore Roosevelt flashed his famous grin and hailed the cheering throng, then bounded into a waiting carriage. Through Worcester's bunting-draped streets, flanked by secret service men in silk hats and topcoats, Roosevelt led a triumphal procession, raising his hat and bowing to the "thousands upon thousands" of people who waved handkerchiefs, tossed hats and roses, and strained for a glimpse of the charismatic president.

It was June 21, 1905, and the nation's 26th chief executive was in Worcester to deliver two commencement addresses—one to the first graduating class of Clark College, and the second to graduates at the College of the Holy Cross. By the time Roosevelt reached Holy Cross, rain drenched the grandstands at Fitton Field. Undaunted, he regaled the record crowd of nearly 8,000 and awarded diplomas on a sheltered platform draped in red, white and blue, and the college's royal purple and white. His duties completed in less than an hour, the president strode back to his carriage, stopping just long enough to "toss a shovelful of earth about the roots of [an] elm tree," before leaving for a luncheon reception with Worcester notables.[1]

That Scotch elm was the first of two trees that Roosevelt planted in Worcester. Eleven years later, escorted by another marching band and 28 representatives of different countries carrying a 40-by-60-foot American flag, the former president stormed Indian Hill, a planned residential community built by the Norton Company. Pumping hands, touring the development and making an impromptu dash through one of the model company-built homes—where he paused momentarily to pet the family cat and wolf down a slice of freshly baked apple pie—Roosevelt pleased a cheering crowd of 800 with words of patriotism. As Norton Company children sang "My Country 'Tis of Thee," he shoveled a few ceremonial clods of dirt at the base of a pin oak in a small park named in his honor.[2]

Though perfunctory, those tree-planting ceremonies—where mature trees still stand—were fitting gestures by a man whose name would become synonymous with the nation's fledgling conservation movement. An avid outdoorsman who valued forays into natural wilderness as a means to build strength and character, Roosevelt, during his eight years as president, protected millions of acres of trees from uncontrolled lumbering. His administration's efforts to conserve wilderness, in response to rampant deforestation across the country, were just gaining momentum the year he visited Worcester for the Clark and Holy Cross graduation ceremonies. By his return in 1916, the former president could look back on accomplishments that included not only the preservation of vast tracts of forest but also the protection of natural wonders such as the Grand Canyon.

Even as the ceremonial plantings of elm and oak framed a period of growing awareness of the need to replenish the nation's ravaged forests, the timing of Roosevelt's visits to Worcester also marked a transition in the stewardship of city trees and parks—and a shift in outlook about the best use of public green spaces. For much of the 19th century, Worcester's street trees and parks had been developed, tended and preserved by men much like Roosevelt, an elite class of civic leaders with a strong sense of public duty, born into wealth and steeped in *noblesse oblige*. But in 1905, their era of influence was coming to an end. In November, Worcester's leading citizen, Stephen Salisbury III—who as president of Clark's board of trustees was among those riding in Roosevelt's carriage—died of pneumonia. Within two years of his death, the few remaining gentlemen farmers who had helped the Salisburys and Lincolns cultivate Worcester's parks and street trees had passed on, as well. Replacing them on the Parks Commission were businessmen and industrialists who valued parks less as manicured gardens for uplifting the soul, more as recreation spaces for building strong bodies and public spirit. Thus, by Roosevelt's 1916 visit, the same year the National Park Service was created, on the eve of World War I, the city's 19th-century aesthetic vision of its landscape gave way to 20th-century pragmatism.

Wilderness Squandered—The Rise of the National Conservation Movement

Worcester's turn-of-the-century transition came at a time when the nation was redefining the proper use and management of natural resources. By the end of the 19th century, the sylvan devastation documented by George Emerson in Massachusetts during the 1840s was evident across the continent. The giant white pines and spruces of Maine, the swamp-loving cypresses of Georgia, the oaks, elms and tupelos of the Mississippi basin, the dense pineries of the Great Lakes and dark evergreen forests of the Rockies, the Douglas firs and 4,000-year-old sequoias of the Pacific coast—all had felt the bite of the lumberman's crosscut saw. Not just privately owned forests were clear-cut for quick profit. Government lands, too, were routinely plundered without consequence. While vandals axed public trees with abandon, lumber companies and mill owners used bribery and exploited legal loopholes to acquire millions of acres of underpriced, government-owned prime timber, robbing resources behind a veneer of respectability. Beguiled by the same delusions of infinite abundance that had blinded New England's early colonists, lumbermen felled forests in a mad rush to meet the burgeoning nation's insatiable demand for houses, furniture, shingles, tools, wagons, railroad ties, fuel, paper, ships and matchsticks.[3]

Then there were fires. Thundering transcontinental locomotives showered sparks along newly laid steel tracks, igniting the felled trees left to rot on either side of the right-of-way, kindling vast forest fires. Prospectors, too, burned the forests, clearing patches of dense woods

AMERICAN CHESTNUT
Castanea dentata

A smattering of American chestnuts can still be found in Worcester's hardwood forests. But the giant shade trees that so impressed Daniel Gookin centuries ago are today merely shrubs. Devastated by the chestnut blight that entered the country around the turn of the 20th century, the tree once prized from Maine to Georgia for its versatile timber and annual crop of tasty nuts now rarely grows larger than an inch in diameter before new sprouts are choked off by the virulent fungus.

A member of the Beech family, American chestnut was so common in Gookin's day that it made up about a fourth of native eastern hardwood forests. Soaring as tall as 100 feet, the trees were distinguished by their massive trunks—up to seven feet in diameter—dark grayish-brown, furrowed bark, and sweeping, dense crowns. American chestnut produces narrow, oblong leaves that turn yellow-gold in autumn; each leaf has many straight parallel side veins emanating from a central vein, its edges frilled with curved teeth. The chestnut's sweet fruit is 2 to 2 1/2 inches in diameter; the spine-covered burs split open to reveal two or three egg-shaped chestnuts that flatten and turn a shiny dark brown as they ripen.

Those nuts were a valued cash crop for the colonists and an important protein source for Native Americans as well as poorer settlers who couldn't afford meat. The annual chestnut crop, more reliable than the yearly acorn crop, also supported an abundance of wildlife, including gray squirrels, black bear, wild turkey and deer.

The tree's timber, too, was valued for its straight grain and high tannin content, which rendered it rot-resistant. Easily split, American chestnut was used for fence rails, telegraph and telephone poles, railroad ties and ship masts. The wood, with its beautiful grain, was also used to make fine furniture, paneling and musical instruments. Tannin from chestnut bark and heartwood was considered the best substance for tanning heavy leather and became an industry essential.

But the tree once immortalized in Henry Wordsworth Longfellow's poem became nearly as extinct as the village smithy with the rapid spread of the fungus *Cryphonectria parasitica* during the first half of the 20th century. Probably imported with a shipment of chestnut species from Asia around the turn of the century, *C. parasitica* was first observed in 1904 when chestnuts at New York's Bronx Zoo developed cankers. Within a few decades, the chestnut blight had killed between three and four billion mature American chestnuts throughout the species' entire natural range.

Entering bark through wounds or holes, the fungus infects the cambium—the growing part of the tree trunk that makes annual rings—creating sunken cankers. As the infection spreads, the cankers encircle the trunk, essentially strangling the tree by cutting off its supply of water and nutrients. The section above the cankers eventually dies; however, the roots of the American chestnut can still live. As a result, the shrub-like *C. dentata* found in eastern hardwood forests are actually sprouts from the bases of trees long dead.

Those sprouts never get much taller than 20 feet before the fungus reemerges to choke off the young tree. But some promising research raises hope that American chestnut may someday experience a revival. Four main paths of inquiry include isolating the blight-resistant gene in the Chinese chestnut to create a new, disease-fighting variant of American chestnut; irradiating nuts to create mutations that might produce a disease-resistant strain; injecting cankers with a hypovirulent strain of *C. parasitica* that converts the fungus to a benign form; and seeking out survivors—native, disease-resistant trees. Progress is slow, but researchers are optimistic that American chestnuts may once again grace the nation's eastern hardwood forests.

to ease their search for rich mineral veins, while shepherds set fires to clear land for pastures even as their sheep devoured saplings. Lightning also scorched the land, aided by human wastefulness. Where lumbermen littered the forest floor with less-than-perfect trees, favoring only the biggest and straightest specimens for maximum profit at the sawmills, forest fires consumed rotting trunks and raged out of control. In one of the worst disasters of the period, the 1871 Peshtigo Fire of Wisconsin claimed more than 1,500 lives and 1,280,000 acres of timber.[4]

Around the world, such wasteful ways were being curbed by government edict. During the second half of the 19th century, France, Switzerland, Russia, Japan and India all passed laws protecting forests and regulating the felling of trees. But the United States was slow to curb its profligate habits. Writing at the turn of the century, wilderness advocate John Muir urged the nation to preserve its dwindling bounty:[5]

> So far our government has done nothing effective with its forests, though the best in the world, but is like a rich and foolish spendthrift who has inherited a magnificent estate in perfect order, and then has left his fields and meadows, forests and parks, to be sold and plundered and wasted at will, depending on their inexhaustible abundance. Now it is plain that the forests are not inexhaustible, and that quick measures must be taken if ruin is to be avoided. Year by year the remnant is growing smaller before the axe and fire, while the laws in existence provide neither for the protection of the timber from destruction nor for its use where it is most needed.[6]

Muir was not the first to sound the alarm. In 1864, George Perkins Marsh published *Man and Nature,* a seminal analysis of the cost of environmental destruction. A renaissance man who was at once a naturalist, linguist, lawyer, politician, historian, folklorist, diplomat and architect, Marsh forcefully argued that the decline of ancient civilizations was integrally linked to their rape of the natural environment. The prolific cultures of the Fertile Crescent, ancient Greece and Rome, early Chinese dynasties—all, according to Marsh, had spelled their own doom by stripping their forests bare and depleting other natural resources. America, he warned, was treading the same dangerous course: "[We] are, even now, breaking up the floor and wainscoting and doors and window frames of our dwelling, for fuel to warm our bodies and seethe our pottage, and the world cannot afford to wait till the slow and sure progress of exact science has taught it a better economy."[7]

Promoting the need to balance economic growth against nature's limits, Marsh made a persuasive case for environmental stewardship that resonated with a growing number of amateur foresters who were alarmed by the rate of timber cutting. In 1875, a year after Marsh's book was reissued, those advocates formed the American Forestry Association to push for federal protection of remaining forests. The next year, Congress created a forestry division within the Department of Agriculture. Heading the new division was Franklin B. Hough, a physician and amateur forester. Hough's studies of forest depletion in privately held timberlands, along with an 1880 government study by Harvard botanist Charles Sargent, documented a disastrous rate of deforestation. In just a few short decades, the nation had lost an area of forests equal to the European continent; if present timber-cutting practices prevailed, Sargent warned gloomily, America's forests would be depleted in another ten years.[8]

The rate of deforestation was noted with alarm in Worcester. Commenting on the 1883 Forestry Congress in St. Louis, the August 16 *Worcester Evening Gazette* editorialized, "The forests of America are disappearing, under the blows of the pioneer and the lumberman, with alarming rapidity, and with serious results to the water supply and the agricultural interests of the country. Efforts for re-clothing the denuded districts with some part of the natural covering of which they have been so wantonly stripped, must be vigorous and general."

Local public concern was particularly great regarding the pillaging of trees in New Hampshire's White Mountains, a popular pleasure spot. Throughout the 1890s, editorials in the *Worcester Evening Gazette* decried the destruction of the majestic New Hampshire forest by timber companies and emphasized the need for "scientific forestry" throughout the United States. Arguing that stripping the forests increases soil erosion and flooding, and diminishes the public water supply, an 1896 editorial added that New Hampshire legislators, disinterested in aesthetics, might at least consider the loss of tax revenues resulting from a drop in tourism: "The beauty of the White Mountains is . . . a source of wealth to New Hampshire, and the Legislature should see that to destroy that beauty is to kill the goose that lays the golden egg."[9]

To staunch the bleeding of America's forest, in 1891 Interior Secretary John W. Noble managed to slip a revolutionary piece of land-use legislation through Congress as a rider on another bill. The Forest Reserve Act, as it was later known, authorized the president to set aside any forested areas within government lands as public reservations, thus side-stepping the need for approval from a reluctant Congress. Presidents Benjamin Harrison and Grover Cleveland used the act to reserve 33 million acres of government-owned forest; but as the public argued over resulting restrictions to economic development, Cleveland balked at any further set-asides until Congress defined a purpose for the reserves. Congress met Cleveland's request with the Forest Organic Act of 1897, which stated that the reserves were essentially created to control flooding and soil erosion and to preserve the nation's timber supply. In addition, the act defined how and what kinds of timber could be taken and placed authority for administering the reserves under Interior's General Land Office. It also granted authority to the secretary of interior to "regulate the occupancy and use" of the forest reserves—an ambiguous power that later proved crucial to conservation policy under Theodore Roosevelt's administration.[10]

Preserving Nature's Grandeur—The First National Parks

As forestry advocates argued for preservation of the nation's trees on pragmatic grounds, others, like John Muir, who valued forests and wilderness for their aesthetic appeal, fought to save natural wonders by a different means—as national parks. Much as the urban parks movement had evolved in response both to urban ills and a yearning for European culture, so the uniquely American concept of national parks emerged as a reaction both to the perils of economic development and the desire to prove, once and for all, that the United States could outclass, in natural grandeur, any human-built monument in Europe.

Prior to the Civil War, the nation's preservation track record was nothing to be proud of. By the 1830s, the spectacular scenery of Niagara Falls was already plagued by hucksters charging exorbitant fees for access to the best views. The profit motive also figured in the creation of the country's first natural federal preserve in 1832—Hot Springs, Arkansas—valued not simply for its uniqueness but for the medicinal benefits of its waters. Toward the Civil War's end in 1864, the same year that Marsh first published *Man and Nature,* the federal government under President Abraham Lincoln ceded the Yosemite Valley and Marioposa Big Tree Grove to California as a state park, the nation's first; but Congress's failure to impose protective restrictions on the land and the state's encouragement of commercial use soon brought grazing, logging and other environmental degradation to the once pristine valley.[11]

Despite those failures, Yosemite's grandeur still inspired. Among those moved by its vistas was Frederick Law Olmsted, who came to work for the Yosemite Commission during the first of his several breaks with the New York City Central Park Commission. In his preliminary report to the Yosemite Commission in 1865, just one year after the new state park's creation, Olmsted

California redwoods
© *PhotoSphere Images Ltd.*

articulated both the grandeur of Yosemite and significance of developing the nation's majestic scenic areas as public reservations:[12]

> There are falls of water elsewhere finer, there are more stupendous rocks, more beetling cliffs, there are deeper and more awful chasms, there may be as beautiful streams, as lovely meadows, there are larger trees. It is in no scene or scenes the charm consists, but in the miles of scenery where cliffs of awful height and rocks of vast magnitude and of varied and exquisite coloring, are banked and fringed and draped and shadowed by the tender foliage of noble and lovely trees and bushes, reflected from the most placid pools, and associated with the most tranquil meadows, the most playful streams, and every variety of soft and peaceful pastoral beauty.
>
> This union of the deepest sublimity with the deepest beauty of nature, not in one feature or another, not in one part or one scene or another, not any landscape that can be framed by itself, but all around and wherever the visitor goes, constitutes the Yo Semite the greatest glory of nature . . .
>
> It is the will of the Nation as embodied in the act of Congress that this scenery shall never be private property, but that like certain defensive points upon our coast it shall be held solely for public purposes.[13]

Sadly, Olmsted's vision failed to stem the wave of commercial exploitation that defiled the Yosemite Valley. Similar troubles plagued the first national park, as well. Eight years after California acquired the Yosemite Valley, and a good 65 years after word first traveled east of magnificent falls, steaming springs and 100-foot water spouts in the Wyoming Territory, Congress created Yellowstone National Park for the public's "benefit and enjoyment" in 1872. But lawmakers chose not to appropriate funds for the new park's protection, assuming instead that park receipts would cover those costs. Such was not the case. Those who managed the arduous, expensive, monthlong round trip by riverboat and overland coach from Bismark, North Dakota, were quick to scrawl their names on boulders and toss debris into Old Faithful for sport. Poachers raided the park's unguarded buffalo, one of the nation's only remaining wild herds; before Congress finally stepped in to protect the animals, the herd had been reduced by 95 percent, from 541 to only 22. Not until 1886, when the secretary of the interior finally turned to the secretary of war for help, did the park's siege of vandalism end with the arrival of the U.S. Cavalry.[14]

Army troops patrolled the nation's next three parks, as well. Yosemite—initially a doughnut-shaped park surrounding the state-owned valley, until the two were merged under federal control in 1905—and Sequoia and General Grant national parks, both established in California to protect the giant redwoods, were all created within a few days of one another in 1890. John Muir was instrumental in the preservation of Yosemite, located at the heart of the Sierra Nevada mountain range, about 140 miles from San Francisco. "Benevolent, solemn, fateful, pervaded with divine light," wrote Muir of the region, "every landscape glows like a countenance hallowed in eternal repose; and every one of its living creatures, clad in flesh and leaves, and every crystal of its rocks, whether on the surface shining in the sun or buried miles deep in what we call darkness, is throbbing and pulsing with the heartbeats of God."[15]

Such beauty failed to inspire systematic federal oversight for Yosemite or any of the other national parks and monuments created in the new century's early years, however. Not until 1914, after Muir and his followers failed to save the Hetch Hetchy Valley, in Yosemite's northwest corner, from being flooded to meet San Francisco's demand for hydroelectricity, did pressure mount for more federal protection of national parks. Two years later, President Woodrow Wilson took the first step toward ensuring centralized oversight and protection of the nation's grandest lands by signing the bill that created the National Park Service. Over the next 13 years—under the leadership of Stephen Mather, a millionaire who had made his fortune in borax before devoting his talents to public office—the Park Service expanded its holdings from 15 to 22 national parks and added 13 national monuments to its initial 20, more than doubling protected areas from 7,500 to 15,846 square miles.[16]

Championing Forest Conservation—Theodore Roosevelt

Such accomplishments were only distant dreams when Vice President Theodore Roosevelt, just 43 years old, assumed the presidency in 1901 following the assassination of William McKinley. A man of firm principles, with a profound appreciation and love of nature, Roosevelt held strong views about the need to conserve and protect the nation's vast resources. "When I hear of the destruction of a species," he wrote prior to becoming president, "I feel just as if all the works of some great writer had perished."[17]

An amateur naturalist and ornithologist who had reveled in wilderness adventure since his teens, Roosevelt was, at the same time, no wilderness romantic when it came to conservation. His struggle to overcome asthma by conquering the outdoors—hiking through the dense pine forests of Maine, climbing the Matterhorn, stalking big game out West, cowpunching in the Dakota Badlands—had confirmed his belief that grappling with nature toughened character. While he advocated for wildlife refuges and the protection of certain pristine wilderness areas, Roosevelt believed that public lands should be preserved for public use, and he argued for opening forest reserves for camping and recreational activities, so that the public could enjoy the healthful and rejuvenating benefits of America's majestic outdoors.[18]

His conservation policies were strongly influenced by Gifford Pinchot, Bureau of Forestry chief for the Department of Agriculture. A pioneer of American forestry, Pinchot based his forceful campaign for forest preservation not on aesthetics but on the pragmatic conviction that the nation must maintain a supply of timber to foster economic development. Like Roosevelt, he believed that stewardship of the nation's forests could not be entrusted to state and local governments but should be centralized in Washington under the executive branch. This belief

Yosemite
© *PhotoSphere Images Ltd.*

was underscored by the Oregon land scandals that surfaced during Roosevelt's first term, in which several prominent state and local officials were convicted for accepting bribes from lumber and mining companies to grease acquisitions of forest lands in Oregon and California. In addition, Pinchot was a determined and shrewd administrator who sought to consolidate control of forestry resources under his office.[19]

Disdained by Muir as one who "never hesitates to sacrifice anything or anybody in his way," Pinchot nonetheless gained the trust of Roosevelt and Secretary of Agriculture James Wilson to push his agenda. A Yale graduate who had studied European sylviculture in France, with its emphasis on crop-like forestry management, Pinchot had served as the bureau's chief forester since 1898. Under Roosevelt, he earned the admiration and loyalty of his staff by raising professional standards and expanding the bureau's reach. He used his position on the president's Public Lands Commission to engineer a transfer of several agencies, including the Interior Department's General Land Office—whose commissioner was implicated in the Oregon land scandals—to the Forestry Bureau in 1905. Renamed the U.S. Forestry Service that year, Pinchot's expanding division also gained authority to collect revenues from timber sales and use of national forest lands, including grazing rights and water-power leases. By 1906, that arrangement, combined with the administration's successful effort to increase forest preserves—from about 43 million acres in 1905 to almost 107 million acres the following year—netted the Forestry Service $800,000 in revenues from grazing fees and timber sales, an amount that nearly matched the agency's congressional appropriation.[20]

Backed by Pinchot, Roosevelt continued his push for conserving forest lands throughout much of his second term. His success rested largely on support from the lumber industry, which had a vested interest in Pinchot's efforts to maintain a consistent timber supply. In addition, Roosevelt, himself a former cattle rancher, garnered political support from cattle corporations that benefited from favorable federal grazing fees. Riding on the momentum of his conservation policy, the president also persuaded Congress to pass the National Monuments Act in 1906. Empowered by that legislation, Roosevelt swiftly designated four monuments, including Devil's Tower National Monument in Wyoming, the first of 18 monuments named during his administration. Other legislation passed that year established the Grand Canyon as a game preserve; two years later, Roosevelt declared the site a national monument, effectively protecting the land until it was designated a national park in 1919.[21]

As more and more land was set aside for forest preserves and other uses, however, political opposition to the administration's conservation policies mounted. Small lumber companies and cattle ranchers who despised Pinchot for controlling Western lands from Washington joined forces with Republican Senator Charles W. Fulton of Oregon, who was angered that he had been implicated in the land fraud scandals, to sabotage the Agriculture Department's appropriation during the 1907 budget debate. Fulton engineered passage of an amendment that would prevent the creation of additional forest preserves in his home state and five others; rather than jeopardize the Agriculture Department, Roosevelt and Pinchot countered by designating 21 new national forest reserves, encompassing 16 million acres in the affected states, just days before the bill became law.[22]

During the remaining years of his presidency, Roosevelt found other means to end-run growing congressional disapproval of his conservation policies, including convening a meeting of the nation's governors in 1908 to discuss the issue; that first-ever assemblage produced the National Governor's Conference. Nonetheless, the Roosevelt-Pinchot strategy of defining national land-use policy via centralized, professional management rather than democratic process ultimately undercut the administration's long-range goals, as Congress disassembled decisions that were opposed by special interests. In addition, their pragmatic allegiance with the lumber and cattle industries would set the stage for a public debate over conservation and management of public lands that rages to the present day. Despite those flaws, Roosevelt succeeded in making conservation a national priority. With his mastery of the media, political acumen and unbounded energy, he alerted the country to the cost of exploiting natural resources and set aside 80 million acres of forest lands—nearly half of the country's national forests—for generations to come.[23]

Developing Worcester's West Side—The Salisbury Imprint

Roosevelt was flush with his early conservation successes, still idolized for his Rough Rider exploits, when he traveled to Worcester in 1905. Among the dignitaries who shared his triumphant ride down Main Street, fellow Republican Stephen Salisbury III had much in common with the popular president. He was old enough to be Roosevelt's father—Salisbury was 70 that year and the president, 47—but the two men had been shaped by similar influences. Both were sons of influential, wealthy scions who could trace their roots to the nation's first European colonists. Both had graduated from Harvard and traveled extensively abroad as part of their informal education. The two men shared a deep interest in reading and writing history, and an appreciation of nature, as well as a devotion to fathers who were committed to upright living and public duty to those less fortunate. Though their social circles were of a different order, the Salisburys were to Worcester what the Roosevelts were to New York City—leading citizens, influential because of their wealth, lineage, political connections, community involvement and moral character.

Doubtless there was little opportunity for the two men to share their common interests during Roosevelt's whirlwind visit that rainy June day. But had the president more time to tour the city, now a thriving metropolis of more than 120,000, he probably would have complimented Salisbury on some of Worcester's more striking landscapes and significant institutions. In particular, on the opposite side of town from Clark and Holy Cross, Salisbury's father had helped to build Worcester Polytechnic Institute, which was landscaped by Olmsted's partner, Calvert Vaux. Across the street from the engineering college, Salisbury had donated land for Institute Park to help the city realize its dream of a metropolitan park system, and personally overseen every planting and embellishment. Kitty-corner to Institute Park, on land given by Salisbury's father, stood the elegant brick and granite edifice of the American Antiquarian Society, a national repository of early-American and 19th-century historic documents, of which Salisbury was the current president. Just beyond the Antiquarian Society, a road wound up a hill to a fieldstone turret; one of

Stephen Salisbury III
Courtesy,
Worcester County Horticultural Society

Salisbury's favorite places to ride, his Bancroft Tower offered a stunning vista of Worcester—and an excellent view of his vast land holdings.

A Secret Deal with John Hancock—Stephen Salisbury I

Much of that land had been in the family since colonial times, purchased by Salisbury's grandfather, Stephen Salisbury I, in a secret business transaction with revolutionary leader John Hancock. Actually, the land had initially belonged to the first Stephen's in-law, Joseph Waldo, whose brother and business partner, Daniel, was married to Stephen's sister. A prosperous Boston merchant, Joseph Waldo had inherited a 150-acre tract of farmland from his father, Cornelius, one of Worcester's first proprietors. Joseph managed his frontier property from Boston, renting the land to tenant farmers. He also rented a store on the tract to Stephen, who moved to Worcester in 1767 to develop a new market for the Salisbury brothers' successful Boston importing business. But some unknown conflict between the two in-laws kept Joseph from selling the land to Stephen, despite his prospering venture.[24]

Jealousy may have been a factor, given Stephen's rapid rise. With the financial backing of his older brother and partner, Samuel, and a clever business plan to capitalize on trade at the centrally located county seat, he had quickly established himself as the region's leading merchant—capturing the rural market that Joseph's brother Daniel had also targeted. Buying wholesale from Boston merchant ships, Samuel would send hardware and other goods to Stephen's Worcester store without any markup, enabling the brothers to undercut local prices. That early success, enhanced by Stephen's skill at pleasing both individual and retail customers, no doubt prompted his desire to establish himself as a property owner. But Joseph wasn't interested in selling to the younger Salisbury. Instead, he decided to sell his land for £550 to John Hancock, who lived in Boston but often summered in Worcester with an uncle. The transaction devastated Stephen. "It is such an unpardonable breach of friendship as never will be forgot," he complained to Samuel in a letter dated April 29, 1771. "It has, I acknowledge, struck such a damp upon my spirits that I seem almost unable to do any business."[25]

Fortunately for Stephen, Hancock had no real interest in the property. "Mr. Hancock says he has no use for the place and has no intention to turn you out of business, and would sooner give up the place than do it," reassured Samuel in a same-day reply to Stephen's lament. "For my part I look upon it very sinful to be so cast down when you are in so good circumstances." Rebuffing his younger brother's anger at Daniel for any complicity in the transaction, Samuel wrote that the deal was all Joseph's doing, conducted in secret from Daniel "for fear he should inform you." To undo the damage, Samuel added that he and Daniel were conducting their own secret dealings with Hancock to arrange for a sale of the land to Stephen, after all. So it was in November, with the help of his brother and sister's husband, for £550, that Stephen finally acquired title to the land that would establish his personal fortune.[26]

During the War for Independence, Stephen continued to build his business. Siding with the patriots' cause, he traveled to Boston, Marblehead and Providence to find supplies for his Worcester customers after signing an agreement not to import goods from Britain. By the war's end, when the import bans were lifted, Stephen's business was flourishing and he began to focus on real estate investment. Already during the war, he had purchased a few farms in surrounding towns, which he later sold. In 1784, he acquired 25 acres adjacent to the initial 150-acre tract, and for several years continued adding parcels in the same vicinity at the north end of Main Street, buying from neighbors Timothy Bigelow and Levi Lincoln, Sr., among others.[27]

Investing all his efforts in his financial dealings, Stephen remained a bachelor during his first 30 years in Worcester. But in 1797, now a well-established, 51-year-old gentleman, he married Boston socialite Elizabeth Tuckerman. Twenty-five years his junior and a member of Boston's upper crust, Elizabeth found the move to Worcester hard and isolating. But she settled into a quiet domestic life with the birth of the Salisburys' first child, a son, the year after their marriage. The couple's only child to survive infancy, named Stephen for his father, the boy was "very carefully and delicately bred," educated in public elementary school, then prep school at Leicester Academy. Attending Harvard with childhood playmate George Bancroft, who would later distinguish himself as a U.S. historian and statesman, and George Emerson, future author of the Massachusetts tree survey, young Stephen graduated in 1817. He initially planned a career in law and was admitted to the bar, but his future changed suddenly with the death of his father in 1829. Eighty-three years old, the elder Salisbury died the richest man in Worcester County. His

The Salisbury Mansion.
From the collections of
WORCESTER HISTORICAL MUSEUM,
Worcester, Massachusetts

Lincoln Square, with the Salisbury Mansion on the left, 1912. From the collections of WORCESTER HISTORICAL MUSEUM, *Worcester, Massachusetts*

extensive land holdings anchored the family fortune, and young Stephen soon realized that managing the estate would require his full attention. Thus, one year shy of his 30th birthday, the would-be lawyer became a real estate baron.[28]

Land for Factories, Railroads and a College—Stephen Salisbury II

For the rest of his life, Stephen Salisbury II devoted his energy to developing and expanding those properties. He built factories and leased space to new ventures, damming Mill Brook to provide a source of waterpower for his Grove Street mill complex at the city's north end. He invested in railroads, selling a tract of land near Lincoln Square, not far from the old Salisbury estate, for a right-of-way to the Worcester & Nashua Railroad, of which he was a founding director (this despite the fact that his aging mother, by then in her late seventies, still lived in the estate and could hardly have benefited from the noise and belching of passing trains). He also became a leading banker in the city, assuming the helm of the Worcester Bank when his first cousin, bank president Daniel Waldo, died in 1845. The year before, Salisbury had succeeded Waldo as president of the Worcester County Institute for Savings.[29]

Salisbury's civic achievements were equally hefty. A selectman, city alderman, state legislator and two-time presidential elector, Stephen also distinguished himself as a director of colleges, museums and learned societies, including Harvard College, the American Antiquarian Society, the Peabody Museum of Archaeology and Worcester Polytechnic Institute (WPI).[30]

The latter was his particular passion. Built on a hill overlooking the mill pond Salisbury had created to serve his factory complex, on five acres of land he had donated, WPI was founded in 1865 as the Worcester County Free Institute of Industrial Science, with a $100,000 challenge grant to the city by tinware magnate John Boynton. If the city could come up with the land and buildings, Boynton offered to anonymously donate the seed money for a "scientific school" to train young men. With the gift of a machine shop from Ichabod Washburn, whose wire-drawing factory was Salisbury's main Grove Street tenant, plus Salisbury's donation of land and substantive contributions for teachers' salaries, one of the nation's first engineering schools was born.[31]

President of the board of trustees from the institute's inception until his death, Salisbury was involved at every level, from selecting faculty to corresponding with prospective students. Over his nearly 20 years in office, he donated more than three times Boynton's original gift but never wavered from the founder's original plans for the school. Meticulous in all his dealings, whether for profit or philanthropy, he also took responsibility for developing the grounds of the new college—in part, no doubt, because the land had been his to begin with. Inspired by reports of New York City's Central Park, the newly formed building committee hired landscape architect Calvert Vaux in 1865 to design the Institute's grounds. As he did in New York, Vaux strove to preserve a sense of natural scenery and harmonious groupings of buildings and greenery. Using techniques such as planting groups of trees at curves in the road, retaining natural plantings, and balancing buildings made of local granite with rounded trees such as oaks and ashes, he created picturesque scenes with clearly defined focal points.[32]

Salisbury's interest in landscape design and horticulture was not limited to the Institute campus. Founding vice president of the Worcester County Horticultural Society and the Society's president from 1851 to 1857, he was that organization's main benefactor, as well, rescuing it from financial demise on at least one occasion. Salisbury also served as one of the city's three commissioners for Shade Trees and Public Grounds from 1869 to 1885. For 15 of those 16 years, he worked closely with Edward Winslow Lincoln to plant shade trees, build Elm Park and foster Worcester's municipal parks plan. A gentleman farmer in his spare time, with a great knowledge and love of fruits and flowers, Salisbury maintained a large orchard next to his Highland Street estate that stretched all the way down the hill to Lincoln Square, where his father had built the first Salisbury mansion and tilled his own soil.[33]

For all the success and accolades in his public life, Salisbury's private life was marred by tragedy. Three times he married, only to lose each wife within a few years. His first marriage, to Rebecca Scott in 1833, lasted the longest—ten years—and produced his only child, Stephen Salisbury III, in 1835. Alone for seven years after Rebecca's death in 1843, Salisbury remarried in 1850 to Nancy Hoard, who died just two years later. In 1855 he tried one last time, marrying Mary Grosvenor, widow of Massachusetts Secretary of State Edward D. Bangs. Mary died in 1864, and Salisbury chose to live out the rest of his life with only his son as a companion.[34]

Institute Park and the New West Side—Stephen Salisbury III

A lifelong bachelor, Stephen Salisbury III cared for his father at the Highland Street estate for 20 years. Twenty-nine when Mary Grosvenor died, young Stephen was the one constant in his father's life, a dutiful son born to wealth and privilege, sheltered in childhood to the point of being nearly stifled. "We see how easily he might have become a prig, or a mollycoddle, or a platitudinous ego, or a daredevil by reaction," recalled one associate. "That he escaped these pitfalls is significant of much in him. The springs of his individuality had not been choked, though their happy murmur was rarely heard."[35]

As a young adult, Salisbury was spared antebellum unrest and Civil War service by well-timed studies and travel abroad. Schooled at Harvard—a period he described as "uneventful, save that he did not succeed in winning any college honors"—Salisbury graduated in 1856, then immediately left for two years of study and travel through Europe and the Near East, including a one-month horseback tour of archeological sites in Turkey, Asia Minor and Greece. During the Civil War, he studied law at Harvard and was admitted to the Worcester bar in 1861, then again left the country, this time to see a classmate on the Yucatán Peninsula—the first of two visits to Central America that inspired a lifelong fascination with Mayan artifacts. Back in Worcester, he was elected to the common council in 1863. The following year, his second stepmother died, and Salisbury was drawn closer to his thrice-widowed father and the family business.[36]

The elder Salisbury's death in 1884, at 86, following months of deteriorating health and a painful seven-week illness, evoked an outpouring of public sentiment. The mountain of eulogies and condolences were bound into a hardcover volume by Stephen III, now an established businessman in his own right, who wrote a memorial biographical note. Recalling his father's cheerful, even-tempered disposition, his decisiveness in business matters and exacting sense of responsibility, his openness to new ideas and his patience for anyone who asked for a moment of his time, Salisbury expressed his respect for the man who had been his lifelong mentor. He lived, wrote Salisbury, "a sincere and earnest life."[37]

Although the loss was painful, Salisbury's transition to head of the family business was a smooth one, thanks to his father's connections and tutelage in the fine points of real estate investment, banking and insurance. A director of the State Mutual Life Assurance Co., since 1863, Salisbury had been named a director of the Worcester National Bank in 1865, succeeding his father as president upon his death. Like the elder Salisbury, he was also a member of the board of investment for the Worcester County Institute for Savings and served as its president from 1877 until 1905, when federal law precluded one individual from serving simultaneously as president of a national bank and a savings and loan institution.[38]

Salisbury learned about financial investments from his father, too, and became a major shareholder in local utilities, railroads and manufacturing firms, including New England Telephone and Telegraph, the Worcester Electric Light Co., Worcester Gas Light Co., the Boston & Albany Railroad, Norwich & Worcester Railroad and U.S. Corset Co. Selective and shrewd in his investments, he could sway annual meetings with a few choice words. A newspaper retrospective at the time of his death recounted "more than one instance in which favorable words were spoken for a company at a stockholders' meeting by Mr. Salisbury has been directly the means of making possible an increase of the capital stock and of working capital."[39]

Like his cousins, the Lincolns and Waldos, Salisbury extended his influence through leadership positions on the most significant social, cultural and educational institutions in Worcester. Carrying on his father's commitment to Worcester Polytechnic Institute, the American Antiquarian Society and the Worcester County Horticultural Society, he was also a trustee of Clark University, as well as Memorial Hospital, St. Vincent Hospital, Worcester City Hospital, the Natural History Association, the Worcester Lyceum, the Worcester Society of Antiquity, the Worcester County Agricultural Society and his greatest pride, the Worcester Art Museum, among others. A member of one of the city's oldest elite social clubs, the Worcester Fire Society, Salisbury was quickly nominated to its most prestigious society, the Worcester Club, when it was founded in 1888.[40]

Despite those social and business connections, Salisbury chose not to follow the Lincoln's path to politics. A Republican who donated generously to local, state and national election campaigns, Salisbury served briefly as a common councilor and state senator but preferred to work behind the scenes. As a major force in the Citizen's Coalition, which strove to counter the penurious politics of rank-and-file Republicans, Salisbury willingly crossed party lines to support mayoral candidates sympathetic to municipal growth and his development interests. Indeed, his use of political influence to garner public improvements for his own gain often mired him in controversy. Clashes over who should finance repair of his privately owned dam at North Pond, whether a sidewalk outside Salisbury's new building at Union and Market Streets should have been constructed with unauthorized city funds, whether Salisbury's estate had been undervalued on local tax rolls, and whether a new city hall should be located on land he offered near his estate, all fueled tensions between Worcester's Republican elite and native-born working class—tensions that played out in the dispute over funding for the city's parks.[41]

Such controversies didn't sway Salisbury from pursuing his own interests. The city's wealthiest citizen, he was accustomed to getting his own way. But as shrewd as he was in business and politics, Salisbury was restrained and even awkward in manners. A tall, handsome man with a Roman nose, meticulously trimmed mustache and pensive eyes, he was not given to easy expression, but often halted mid-thought in search of the right word. Sober and ever the gentleman, he relaxed only with his closest associates, laughing and joking when musicians or friends from Central America would visit for a Sunday evening. Then Salisbury would let loose, joining in the revelry on his castanets or bones, delighting in gay melodies and "music of the harp."[42]

For all his wealth and social status, however, Salisbury never married. His one love, Susan Lawton, was estranged from her husband, who had abandoned her for the companionship of another man but never granted her a divorce. Childless, Salisbury willed Lawton $100,000 and the use of a home he built for her at the corner of Institute Road and Tuckerman Streets, kitty-corner from his own mansion, which she would inherit after 20 years if still alive, for her to enjoy the comforts he could never fully provide. He expressed his paternal instincts in other ways, as well, opening his gates to make a shortcut through his estate for local schoolchildren, and caring for his loyal servants like family, rising in the middle of the night to help them if they were ill. When friends took sick, he would always send a bouquet of fresh flowers, cut from his extensive greenhouse collection. Salisbury was also fond of indulging his small black-and-tan dog, which would sit at a side table in the dining room when he ate.[43]

Salisbury's compassion extended to those less fortunate, as well. Schooled by his father's example in the fine points of *noblesse oblige*, he donated to the many charities and needy individuals who besieged him with requests for financial assistance. The volume of private pleas was so great that he would first have an investigator verify the details of those appeals that interested him before sending food or fuel to families he deemed in genuine need. Often this was done anonymously, more to protect Salisbury's interests than to embellish his act of charity. "So overwhelmed was Mr. Salisbury with applications for assistance, after a large gift was announced," recalled an associate, "that he made . . . many important gifts quietly and with the injunction that they should not be spoken of." He was also instrumental in helping to form the Associated Charities, a precursor of groups like United Way, and gave generously to the Worcester Children's Friend Society, the Home for Aged Men and various city hospitals.[44]

Institute Park circa 1909.
From the collections of
WORCESTER HISTORICAL MUSEUM,
Worcester, Massachusetts

Among his most prized benefactions was his gift of 18 acres to the city for the creation of Institute Park. A member of the Parks Commission when the municipal parks plan was drafted, Salisbury gave tacit approval to the proposal to create a park out of his land across from WPI. The original plan, presented to the commission in September 1886, called for purchasing 31 acres of Salisbury's property—the undeveloped area bordering his Grove Street mill complex, Salisbury Pond, Park Avenue and the Institute. Salisbury abstained from voting on the proposal, though he supported the concept. The following June, he offered to donate 18 acres across from WPI, with three stipulations: that the land would be named Institute Park in recognition of the college his family had helped to found, that part of the tract would be reserved for WPI to build dormitories, and—a bonus for Salisbury's real estate investments as well as the park—that the city would grade the section of Salisbury Street running between WPI and the new park, from Grove Street to Park Avenue, taking land as necessary from the donated parcel.[45]

In his June 20th letter to Mayor Samuel Winslow offering the land, Salisbury explained his desire to complement Edward Davis and Horace Bigelow's earlier donation of Lake Park with a gift of a smaller, more accessible park within the city: "Through the wise forethought and generosity of two of our citizens, we now possess at Lake Quinsigamond a park of one hundred acres, which is destined to be more used and more fully appreciated as the years roll by, when the population of our city increases and advances to meet this outlying district. While large parks accessible by conveyance are important, smaller parks easily reached on foot in different parts of the city are equally desirable, and these smaller parks, if not properly secured, can never be obtained within easy distance from the business portion of our growing city. With a view of promoting to some extent the accomplishment of what is desired by many of our citizens, I offer to give to the city a tract of land situated on the southerly side of Salisbury pond. . . . "[46]

The city council graciously accepted his offer a month later. In a resolution dated July 11, 1887, local officials praised Salisbury for his "great contribution to the growing beauty and attractiveness of our city, a growth as essential to the happiness of its inhabitants as the more often vaunted increase in business prosperity and convenience."[47]

Salisbury's gift turned out to be a major windfall for the city. Like his father, who closely tended the design of WPI's campus, Salisbury supervised every step of the park's development, paying for much of the work and plantings with his own money. Collaborating with Parks Commission Chairman Edward Winslow Lincoln on the landscape design, he specified that the tract should be shaded with trees and include an inviting waterfront drive. In contrast with nearby Elm Park, however, Salisbury wanted no gardens, flowering shrubs or signs reading "Keep Off the Grass." Rather, he favored a park where visitors could wander at will, enjoying the breeze off the pond and a chance to relax under the cool, green trees.[48]

Work began in 1888, with defining the park's boundaries around Salisbury Pond and building a stone embankment, as well as filling in some of the low lands. Though city park employees performed some of this labor, most was done by Salisbury's own employees, at his expense. Frustrated by the slow, phased pace of work dictated by city budget constraints, Salisbury assumed the full cost of park development the following year, supervising the project himself. Over the next five years, from 1889 to 1894, he poured about $50,000 into landscaping and construction, including a bandstand, boat and summer houses, sanitary facilities and a granite tower modeled after one in Newport, Rhode Island. Adding his own notion of public art, Salisbury rescued the granite columns from Boston's Tremont House when the hostelry was slated for demolition and placed one in a corner of the park, topping it with a huge, polished granite sphere. Resembling an inverted exclamation point, the enigmatic monument still stands as a memorial to Salisbury's total absorption in the project. "[D]uring the park's formative period," wrote a *Telegram* reporter in 1905, "Mr. Salisbury might be found there almost every morning giving the improvement of the park his personal attention, even to designating the location of the different trees and shrubs dotting the broad green lawn."[49]

As he became more invested in Institute Park, Salisbury came up with a new project—to build a tower on Bancroft Hill. Located on the outskirts of his West-Side land holdings, accessible by a newly constructed road off Salisbury Street, the wooded drumlin afforded a fine vista of the city, WPI and the elegant properties Salisbury was developing west of Park Avenue. To see over the treetops, he constructed a small fieldstone castle complete with rook-like turret, surrounded by trees and shrubs. Though Bancroft Tower remained Salisbury's until it was ceded to the city as part of Salisbury Park after his death, he opened his castle to the public and, like a proud nobleman, often rode there to enjoy the view.[50]

On his way to Bancroft Tower, Salisbury would pass the fine, large homes along Massachusetts Avenue, the exclusive neighborhood he was creating off Salisbury Street. Just as Elm Park had defined adjacent properties east of Park Avenue as one of Worcester's most desirable residential areas in the 1870s and 1880s, so Institute Park and Salisbury's development of Massachusetts Avenue were defining the 20th-century locus of fine homes in the city—west of Park Avenue, on old, treeless farmland abutting Salisbury Street. The high-value development was anchored by the American Antiquarian Society at the corner of Salisbury and Park, a graceful library and grounds built with generous donations from Salisbury's father. Other Salisbury Street landmarks built with Stephen III's support near his Highland Street estate, including the Worcester Society for Antiquities (later the Worcester Historical Society) and the Worcester Art Museum, which he founded, further transformed what had once been the old road to Holden—renamed Salisbury Street in 1824 to honor the first Stephen Salisbury—into a shaded thoroughfare lined with some of the city's preeminent cultural institutions and best homes.[51]

By the turn of the century, according to one newspaper account, the neighborhoods near Bancroft Tower were "dotted with some of Worcester's handsomest and most expensive residences, with the grove of chestnut trees and the slopes of Bancroft hill forming the background." That elegance was no accident. Salisbury kept a tight rein on both the style of new homes and "the character of the occupants." Prospective buyers had to submit their construction plans as part of their real estate transaction; if Salisbury didn't approve, the sale was canceled. The same held true of other properties Salisbury developed near the Art Museum and WPI's campus, around Lancaster, Highland, Tuckerman and Dean Streets, the latter two named for his mother and grandmother.[52]

In restricting development to select families, Salisbury was catering to the growing demand for exclusive neighborhoods. As Worcester's economy boomed with industries that he and his father had helped to build and finance, Salisbury profited not only from his investments but also from *nouveau riche* industrialists who were scrambling to establish their place among Worcester's elite by building impressive homes on the right streets. Location and the size and style of a home were such important factors in defining social status that turn-of-the-century real estate advertisements openly emphasized neighborhood restrictions. Such specifications for buildings and grounds, written into deeds of sale or understood via informal agreements among neighbors, ensured both that the elegant streets with their shaded lawns would conform to high standards and that Worcester's wealthy would not be overrun by the poor immigrants whose labor had brought them such good fortune.[53]

So it was that land first purchased in a secret deal with John Hancock became Worcester's prized real estate. An appraisal of Salisbury's land holdings shortly after his death in 1905 placed the value of his factories, tenements, office buildings, apartment houses, undeveloped pastures and private estate at just under $1.3 million. Speculation over his total net worth, including stocks and personal property, ranged from $5 to $20 million—but the estate was ultimately valued at about $4 million. Around $3 million in cash and property went to the Worcester Art Museum, Salisbury's residuary legatee; just under $200,000 went to various relatives and his companion, Susan Lawton, and another half-million was split among WPI, the American Antiquarian Society and several other cultural institutions.[54]

News of Salisbury's death on November 16, 1905, spread quickly throughout the city. Ailing for several months, he had caught cold waiting for a carriage after attending evening services for All Saints' Day. Several days later he took to his bed with what developed into pneumonia. Surrounded by his grieving house staff, many of whom had served him for over 30 years, Worcester's leading citizen, then 70 years old, died at 9:15 A.M. By afternoon, flags on all city schools, city hall, the courthouse, WPI and the Worcester Club were lowered to half-mast.[55]

At his funeral on November 20, the list of pallbearers read like a who's who of culture and finance. Among them were three university presidents—Harvard's Charles Elliot, Clark's G. Stanley Hall and WPI's Edmund Engler; presidents or officers of Worcester National Bank, Worcester County Institute for Savings, the Worcester Trust Co., and State Mutual Life Assurance Co.; former mayor Edward Davis, who had given the land for Lake Park and was now chair of the Worcester sinking fund commission; Francis Dewey, the president of Worcester Consolidated Street Railroad Co.; Massachusetts Historical Society president Charles Francis Adams; American Antiquarian Society vice president Samuel A. Green; Worcester librarian Samuel S. Green; and Salisbury's childhood friend Nathaniel Paine. "Mr. Salisbury loved Worcester; he loved its past perhaps more than its discordant and uncouth present," wrote a colleague for the annals of the Worcester Fire Society. "He wished to see it happy, prosperous, intelligent and beautiful. . . . To it he left his fortunes, and the greater legacy of an unsullied name, and an imperishable ideal of a noble life."[56]

A Park for the Common Folk—Green Hill

The same year that Stephen Salisbury died, ending more than a century of control over Worcester's landscape, the heirs of another prominent family facilitated the purchase of what was to become the city's largest urban park—and a park, unlike Elm and Institute, for Worcester's working class. High on a hill to the east of Lincoln Square, on the opposite side of the tracks from the Salisbury family's holdings, the Green family estate encompassed nearly 550 acres of rolling pastures and woods, including some of Worcester's most scenic views. Originally a 100-acre tract purchased by Thomas Green, one of the region's first physicians, for £333 in 1754, the hilltop estate became the family homestead. Three more generations of Greens—including Thomas's son John, the first of three physicians by the same name who ministered to Worcester's sick through the mid-19th century—tended the estate, ending with Thomas's great-grandson, Andrew Haswell Green, whose boyhood years at Green Hill inspired his involvement with New York's Central Park. He lived in New York City, but Andrew still prized the estate as a refuge and family gathering place, adding 312 acres and expanding the Green mansion with a fine addition during his 50 years of ownership. When Andrew was murdered outside his New York home in 1903, Green Hill passed to his five nephews and nieces, none of whom lived in Worcester.[57]

Not wanting to relocate, the heirs decided to sell the vast estate to the city for a public park in 1905. To sweeten the sale, they contributed $50,000 toward the land's assessed valuation of $104,000, charging the city only $54,000 for the valuable property, a fraction of its true market value. Restrictions in the deed allowed the city to sell no more than 100 acres for other purposes, with the caveat that any proceeds from such transactions be used to benefit the park itself. In short, a grateful Parks Commission concluded, the Greens had donated land equivalent to a $250,000 real estate investment, including a 30-acre spring-fed pond, mansion house, gardens, pastureland, granite quarry, panoramic vistas, forests and glades—a bucolic respite from urban stress, easily accessible by streetcar. It was, without doubt, the most generous gift of land the city ever received.[58]

Among its scenic attractions, the new park was home to one of the city's largest and oldest trees, a locust planted by the first Dr. John Green around the time of the War for Independence. Standing over 100 feet tall in its prime, with a circumference of 13 feet, the deeply furrowed yellow locust was obtained by Green from Aaron Lopez, leader of Leicester's short-lived colonial Jewish community. According to family legend, Lopez, himself an accomplished horticulturist, gave Green a locust branch for a horsewhip after the doctor had paid him a medical call. Upon

A view from Greenhill Park. From the collections of WORCESTER HISTORICAL MUSEUM, *Worcester, Massachusetts*

his return to Green Hill, the physician stuck the branch in the ground in front of the family mansion, where it took root and flourished. As such, the tree was one of the region's first locusts, since it was Lopez who had introduced the species—then native to the Ohio and northern Mississippi River banks—to Central Massachusetts.[59]

Soon after the land was donated, the mansion house became a popular meeting place for clubs and organizations to hold parties and dances. Unlike Elm Park, Green Hill was a place for picnicking and play, a welcome oasis for the city's many immigrants who gathered with their ethnic churches or fraternal groups for a weekend frolic. It was not, however, a place for ethnic groups to mingle. Large enough to accommodate a variety of picnic facilities, Green Hill was a public play space where ethnic church and fraternal organizations kept to their own.[60]

Indeed, for all the civic-minded language and public-spirited intent of the elite families who donated so much land and time to create Worcester's parks to enhance the life of the community, there were also clear expectations about appropriate behavior and who belonged where. Not much was said publicly about conduct in playgrounds within immigrant neighborhoods, such as Crompton Park and East Park. But regarding the larger, scenic parks that were shared by immigrants and gentry alike, such as Green Hill and Lake Parks, proper behavior was a constant source of concern among the elite who oversaw their use. Unlike Olmsted, who had marveled at the democratizing effect of public parks in Europe, Worcester's gentry worried that the uncouth manners, drinking and loafing of their working-class brethren would pervade the very spaces that were intended to teach refinement and an appreciation of nature.[61]

For all that fretting over proper park comportment, however, the truly brazen behavior of Worcester's working class was confined to undeveloped wooded areas outside the parks system.

Precisely because they were hidden, woodlands were the favored spot for turn-of-the-century illegal speak easies and cockfights. In one particularly detailed account, "Hot Gamecock Blood Spilled," the April 27, 1896, *Worcester Telegram* reported incredulously that police were oblivious to a daylong cockfighting contest in a wooded section of Shrewsbury, despite the fact that "teams were driving to and from the place all day. Any one seeing the procession would have jumped to the conclusion that the Methodist camp meeting season had begun."[62]

Woodlands were also a haven for hoboes who used Worcester's excellent rail system for free transportation. In 1894, the *Telegram* reported that an "organized gang of hoboes" was terrorizing the village of Lake View, next to Lake Park. Sleeping in the woods beyond the park's borders, near the Boston & Albany Railroad tracks, the hoboes allegedly canvassed the village during the day, begging for food and stealing whatever they could find: "A gang of from 6 to 10 do the begging, always going in pairs. One takes one side of the street, and his companion the other. They stop at every house and even after their own hunger is satisfied they keep on begging. What they obtain then they cram into their pockets to take back to the gang."[63]

Similar complaints about beggars and bums taking over the Common prevailed during the same period. Letters to the editor criticized "idlers" who loitered on park benches and slept off a night of drinking. Reflecting the sentiments of the emerging temperance movement, the public controversy was also a reaction to the many workers who found themselves with nothing to do and nowhere to go when they lost their jobs during the 1893 economic depression.[64]

The Arboretum's Keeper—Obadiah Hadwen

Despite those pervasive social conflicts, the gentry elite and gentlemen farmers who managed Worcester's park system through much of the late 19th and beginning of the 20th centuries tried to maintain their focus on horticulture and aesthetics. In particular, for the 1905 Parks Commission's elder statesman, Obadiah B. Hadwen, cultivating trees was his first love. A nationally recognized expert in scientific agriculture, horticulture and pomology, Hadwen had spent the better part of the past 50 years growing more than 100 different species of trees on his Lovell Street farm to test their ability to survive Worcester's climate. Among the 1,000 trees on his 18 acres of pastureland were a small Siberian maple known as a ginnale, magnolias from Germany and a black walnut from Japan.[65]

Hadwen's interest in trees grew from his boyhood life on the family farm. Born in Providence, Rhode Island, in 1824, he moved with his family to Worcester when he turned 11. Though his father was a leading Providence merchant and manufacturer, Hadwen was fascinated by farm life and eventually took over part of his parent's farm when he was 20. His experience with raising garden produce and dairy cows paid off in adulthood: not only was Hadwen one of the city's leading milk producers for 40 years but he also honed his skill for growing things to a science, proving that certain trees and other plants formerly thought too frail for New England could grow locally. His work earned him appointments to prestigious organizations, including president of the Massachusetts Horticultural Society and the Massachusetts Agricultural Club, and chairman of the executive board of Amherst Agricultural College. In addition, he served for many years as an officer of the Worcester County Horticultural Society and the Worcester County Agricultural Society, and was an active member of the American Pomological Society.[66]

In Worcester, Hadwen was most closely associated with his work on the Parks Commission. Appointed in 1867, he served for four decades, many of those years helping Edward Winslow Lincoln and Stephen Salisbury III develop the city's metropolitan park system. Just as Lincoln nurtured Elm Park and Salisbury birthed Institute Park, so Hadwen stewarded University Park, a 13-acre parcel across from Clark University. Many of the trees and flowers he planted himself, closely monitoring the park's design and management. In addition, Hadwen gave a 50-acre parcel near Curtis Pond to the city for Hadwen Park, after the city refused to purchase the land from him. Here, too, he set out many of the trees. "The only condition which I annex to the gift," he wrote in the 1892 deed for the land, "is the single one that it shall be forever devoted to the purposes of a public park. I make this gift out of the affection which I bear to the city of Worcester, and the interest that I have in her system of parks, tending to promote rural and healthy enjoyment to her citizens for all time."[67]

For all his civic commitment to beautifying Worcester, Hadwen's first love was his Lovell Street farm, where he explored growing conditions and adaptability of a vast range of imported trees. Named Magnolia after the 15 different varieties planted there, the grounds included trees from China, Japan, Germany, Norway, England, Scotland and throughout the United States. More than 20 varieties of maples, a stately fern leaf beech, sweet gum, walnuts, birches, lindens, ashes, horse chestnuts, a Kentucky coffee tree, ginkgo, poplars, elms and spruces shaded the

Obadiah Hadwen
Courtesy,
Worcester County Horticultural Society

rolling farm. Among Hadwen's most prized plantings was a cork tree from Spain that was imported with Spanish soil packed around its roots, to ease its transition when the tree was transplanted. In addition, there were fruit orchards patrolled by a collection of guinea hens and peacocks, and a parrot named Pedro who occasionally escaped from the farmhouse and had to be retrieved, with some difficulty, from the tall maple branches. Upon Hadwen's death in 1907, he willed Magnolia to Clark University "to be forever kept for the purpose of educating students in agricultural, horticultural and arboreal knowledge, scientific and practical."[68]

Unfortunately, Hadwen's dream of preserving his life's work as an arboretum and outdoor classroom was not to be realized. A gardener hired to care for the trees didn't work out and was never replaced; recommendations by Clark's biology department in 1921 to restore the arboretum were accepted and subsequently ignored; and a bequest of eight abutting acres to Clark ten years later by Hadwen's daughter, Annie Coes, failed to spur any additional action by the university to fulfill the conditions of Hadwen's will. During the 1950s, the university discussed the possibility of selling the land but decided against it. Several ideas were put on the table, including using the site for dormitories or faculty housing. None of those plans was pursued as the university fended off pressure from the city in the 1960s to acquire the land by eminent domain for a new high school. Nine decades after Hadwen's death, the fern leaf beech and cork are among the few original trees remaining in the forested plot, now crowded with native hardwoods and other vegetation that have choked out many of the rare plantings.[69]

Last of the Gentlemen Farmers—James Draper

Seven months before Hadwen's death, in March 1907, Worcester lost its other surviving gentleman farmer, James Draper. A nurseryman and nationally recognized expert in pomology, Draper also served four decades on the Parks Commission. Tending the development of Lake, Crompton and East Parks, he emphasized the importance of building pools and playgrounds for the immigrant children who crowded surrounding neighborhoods. He also took a special interest in maintaining the city's shade trees. An active member of the local, state and national grange organizations, Draper was instrumental in helping to establish Arbor Day in Massachusetts, and presided over the city's first Arbor Day Celebration in 1885.[70]

His devotion to the city's shade trees and the tireless efforts of those who had come before were readily apparent to anyone strolling Worcester's streets. According to a 1912 account by city forester Harold J. Neale, Worcester had 30,000 street trees, mostly Norway, sugar, silver or red maple. There were also elms, ashes and horse chestnuts. Nearly 20 years earlier, a teacher at the Worcester normal school named Arabella Tucker had counted 161 species of trees growing throughout the city on private and public property, including 70 species introduced from foreign countries, 35 species indigenous to the United States but not native to Worcester and 56 native species. Noting the toll of new construction and expansion on older plantings, Tucker wryly observed, "Although the march of improvement is constantly demanding fresh victims, the generous provision made by the Parks-Commission for setting out young trees in the streets, resulting already in the planting of more than twelve thousand, will in time more than make up for all these losses."[71]

She was right. Though the deaths of Salisbury, Draper and Hadwen within two years of one another marked the passing of the Parks Commission's old guard at the end of 1907, their legacy to the city was a lush urban forest of well-tended street trees and a diverse network of cool, green parks and playgrounds.

Soon, however, priorities began to shift. With the loss of Hadwen and Draper, the Parks Commission was no longer guided by devoted horticulturists who strove to create aesthetically pleasing, green oases. Instead, headed by *nouveau riche* manufacturers rather than landed gentry, the commission shifted its emphasis to more pragmatic concerns—creating safe, contained, controlled play spaces. The new emphasis on parks for play and sports was clinched with the appointment of Harry Worcester Smith to the commission in 1916. One of the city's emerging elite, a specialist in corporate mergers whose family fortune was built on cotton manufacturing, Smith had helped to found the Grafton Country Club in 1895 to introduce Worcester to the pleasures of the English fox hunt. A vocal advocate for public playgrounds and recreation spaces, he argued effectively to create a public golf course and to institute Sunday baseball.[72]

It was Smith who hosted Theodore Roosevelt during his visit to Indian Hill in 1916. Both shared a conviction that athletics developed character and a healthy, competitive spirit, the key to "true national greatness." So in Worcester, as in other cities across the country, urban parks took on a new symbolism as the training grounds for future leaders. Their role as contemplative oases was soon revised by playgrounds and ball fields, and their significance as urban refuges was diminished with the coming of the automobile, which eased escape from city stress. As 20th-century pragmatism erased the pastoral ideals of the 19th century, those same automobiles would become the lifeline between city dwellers and the country's new version of natural artifice—the great and grand vistas of the national parks and forests—and the link between city workers and their greener, suburban pastures.[73]

---

[1] *Worcester Telegram*, June 22, 1905; *Worcester Evening Gazette*, June 21, 1905; *Worcester Evening Gazette*, "Teddy Tree Found," June 4, 1964.

[2] "Roosevelt Visits Indian Hill," *The Norton Spirit*, Vol. 3, No. 2., September 1916 (WHM); Mildred McClary Tymeson, *The Norton Story* (Worcester, Mass.: Norton Co., 1953), pp. 140–1 (WHM); "College of the Holy Cross Campus Arboretum," 2nd ed.

[3] John Muir, "The American Forests," in *Our National Parks* (New York: Ames Press, 1970), pp. 331–65.

[4] Muir, pp. 331–365; Dyan Zaslowsky and the Wilderness Society, *These American Lands: Parks, Wilderness and the Public Lands,* (New York: Henry Holt & Co., 1986), p. 73.

[5] Muir, pp. 331–365.

[6] Muir, pp. 338–40.

[7] cited in Zaslowsky, pp. 70–72.

[8] Zaslowsky, pp. 70–71.

[9] *Worcester Evening Gazette*, Oct. 23, 1896; Oct. 25, 1892; Feb. 28, 1895; see also Nov. 17, 1883, on deforestation in Canada.

[10] Zaslowsky, pp. 74–75.

[11] Zaslowsky, pp. 11–13; Norman T. Newton, *Designs on the Land: The Development of Landscape Architecture* (Cambridge, Mass.: Harvard University Press, 1971), p. 555.

[12] Newton, pp. 274–75.

[13] "Preliminary Report Upon the Yosemite and Big Tree Grove," *The Papers of Frederick Law Olmsted, Vol. V, The California Frontier 1863–1865*, Victoria Post Ranney, ed., (Baltimore and London: The Johns Hopkins University Press, 1990), pp. 488–516.

[14] Zaslowsky, pp. 13–18.

[15] Muir, p. 76; Zaslowsky, p. 18.

[16] Zaslowsky, pp. 20–22.

[17] Lewis L. Gould, *The Presidency of Theodore Roosevelt* (Lawrence, Kans.: University Press of Kansas, 1991), p. 40.

[18] Gould, pp. 4, 40; Edmund Morris, *The Rise of Theodore Roosevelt* (New York: Coward, McCann & Geoghegan, Inc., 1979).

[19] Gould, pp. 112, 40–41.

[20] Gould, pp. 112, 200–4; Zaslowsky, pp. 75–79.

[21] Gould, Ibid.; Newton, pp. 517–554.

[22] Gould, pp. 203–4; Zaslowsky, pp. 80–81.

[23] Gould, pp. 205–7; Zaslowsky, pp. 63–65, 81.

[24] I am indebted to Holly Izard, the Worcester Historical Museum's curator for the Salisbury Mansion, for her help in interpreting the early Salisbury family land transactions. The following discussion of Stephen Salisbury I's land purchase from John Hancock is based on her unpublished research into deeds, based on family records at the American Antiquarian Society.

[25] Izard research; Salisbury family papers, (Collection of American Antiquarian Society).

[26] Ibid. Note: Though the deed was in Stephen's name, Samuel apparently co-signed it. In 1799, he signed a quitclaim agreement with Stephen, selling his claim to the Hancock land for 5 shillings to his brother.

[27] Izard research; Salisbury family real estate ledger, (Collection of American Antiquarian Society).

[28] Izard research; *Memorial of Stephen Salisbury, LLD* (Worcester: 1885) AAS; quote is from George Bancroft in letter to Reverend Peabody, Salisbury family papers, (Collection of American Antiquarian Society).

[29] Izard research; *Memorial*.

[30] *Memorial*.

[31] Mildred McClary Tymeson, *Two Towers: The Story of Worcester Tech, 1865–1965*, (Worcester Polytechnic Institute, 1965).

[32] *Memorial*, pp. 101, 140–41; John Grimm and Paul Halloran, "A Picturesque Analysis of WPI and Institute Park," American Studies Seminar, 1986, AAS; According to Frank Kowsky's history, *Country, Park & City: The Architecture and Life of Calvert Vaux* (New York: Oxford University Press, 1998), p. 198, Vaux was invited to design the Institute's campus grounds by D. Waldo Lincoln, whom he had met while preparing a report to the trustees of the new Massachusetts Agricultural College. My thanks to David Schuyler for this clarification.

[33] Charles Nutt, *History of Worcester and Its People*, Vol. II (New York: Lewis Historical Publishing Co., 1919), p. 1051; 1884 Worcester Parks Commission Report; *Memorial*, p. 69; Frances Herron, "Worcester County Horticultural Society: A Look at the Early Years," p. 11.

[34] *Memorial*.

[35] Worcester Fire Society, *Reminiscences and Biographical Notes of Past Members*, 7th series (Worcester: Commonwealth Press, 1916), p. 67.

[36] Salisbury family papers, (Collection of the American Antiquarian Society).

[37] *Memorial*.

[38] *Worcester Telegram*, Nov., 1905.

[39] Ibid.

[40] Robert J. Kolesar, "Urban Politics & Social Conflict: Worcester, Massachusetts in the Nineteenth Century," Unpublished Ms., p. 61; Salisbury family papers, (Collection of the American Antiquarian Society).

[41] Kolesar, pp. 123–24; Salisbury family papers, (Collection of the American Antiquarian Society).

[42] Worcester Fire Society, p. 69.

[43] *WT*, Nov. 17, 1905; Will of Stephen Salisbury III, (Collection of the American Antiquarian Society); Albert B. Southwick, *More Once-Told Tales of Worcester County*, (Worcester: Databooks, 1994), pp. 51–59.

[44] *WT*, Nov. 17, 1905.

[45] Ibid; Worcester Parks Commission Report, 1886.

[46] "What the Citizen Has Done for Our Public Parks," *Worcester Magazine*, Vol. VII, No. 2., Feb. 1904, pp. 37–40.

[47] Salisbury family papers, (Collection of the American Antiquarian Society).

[48] *WM*, Feb. 1904.

[49] *WT*, Nov. 17, 1905; *WM*, Feb. 1904, p. 39; Elbridge Kingsley & Frederick Knab, *Picturesque Worcester*, Part I, (Springfield, Mass.: W. F. Adams Co., 1895), p. 21.

[50] *WT*, Nov. 17, 1905; Nutt, Vol. I, p. 433; *WM*, Feb. 1904.

[51] *WT*, Nov. 17, 1905; Edwin T. Weiss, Jr., "Patterns and Processes of High Value Residential Districts: The Case of Worcester, 1713–1970, PhD dissertation, Clark University, 1973, pp. 109–11; Ivan Sandrof, *Your Worcester Street* (Worcester: Franklin Publishing Co., 1948), p. 123.

[52] *WT*, Nov. 17, 1905.

[53] Weiss, pp. 127–29, 145–46.

[54] *WT*, Nov. 17, 1905; Southwick, p. 52; Salisbury family papers, (Collection of the American Antiquarian Society).

[55] *WT*, Nov. 17, 1905; *Worcester Evening Gazette*, Nov. 16, 1905.

[56] Worcester Fire Society, 1916; *WT*, Nov. 17, 1905; *WEG*, Nov. 20, 1905.

[57] Nutt, Vol. I, pp. 436–37; *Green Hill* (Worcester, Mass.: 1906).

[58] Nutt, Vol. I, pp. 437–38; *Green Hill*.

[59] *Green Hill*; Arabella H. Tucker, *Trees of Worcester: A List of Trees Both Native and Introduced*, (Worcester: Putnam, Davis & Co., 1894), p. 27; Unpublished manuscript from 1906 cornerstone of Sha'arai Torah Synagogue, 32 Providence St., Worcester, (collection of the Worcester Historical Museum).

[60] Nutt, Vol. I, p. 438; Roy Rosenzweig, *Eight Hours for What We Will: Workers and Leisure in an Industrial City, 1870–1920* (Cambridge [Cambridgeshire]; New York: Cambridge University Press, 1983), p. 139.

[61] Rosenzweig, *Eight Hours*, p. 137.

[62] See also "Sold Beer in the Woods," *Worcester Telegram*, July 24, 1895.

[63] "Infested with Tramps, Lakeview in the clutches of an Organized gang of Hoboes," *Worcester Telegram*, Sept. 13, 1894.

[64] Rosenzweig, *Eight Hours*, p. 137.

[65] "Trees of Many Climes on Farm," circa 1902, (Collection of the Worcester County Horticultural Society); "The Art of Arboriculture—A Gentleman Farmer's Legacy," *Clark Now*, Spring 1981, pp. 14–15.

[66] "Mr. Obadiah Brown Hadwen," *Worcester Magazine*, Vol. 10, No. 11., Nov. 1907, pp. 229–32.

[67] "What the Citizen Has Done for Our Public Parks," Part II, *Worcester Magazine*, Vol. 7, No. 3, Mar. 1904, pp. 46–48; Nutt, Vol. I, p. 440.

[68] WCHS files; *The Evening Gazette*, "Obadiah Hadwen, We Salute You," Jan. 31, 1963; Margaret Parsons, "The Fate or Fortune of Some Famous Trees That Grew Up with Our History," *Sunday Telegram*, Oct. 23, 1938, (Collection of the Worcester Historical Museum).

[69] Brad Calloway, et al., "Preliminary Report on the Status of Hadwen Arboretum," Dec. 1971, (Collection of the Worcester County Horticultural Society).

[70] Nutt, Vol. III, pp. 222–23; Franklin P. Rice, ed., *Eighteen Hundred and Ninety-Eight: Fifty Years a City, A Graphic Presentation of Its Institutions, Industries and Leaders* (Worcester: F. S. Blanchard & Co., 1899), pp. 607–8.

[71] Nutt, Vol. I, pp. 439–40; Tucker, pp. 93–94.

[72] Rosenzweig, pp. 144–45.

[73] Ibid., p. 142.

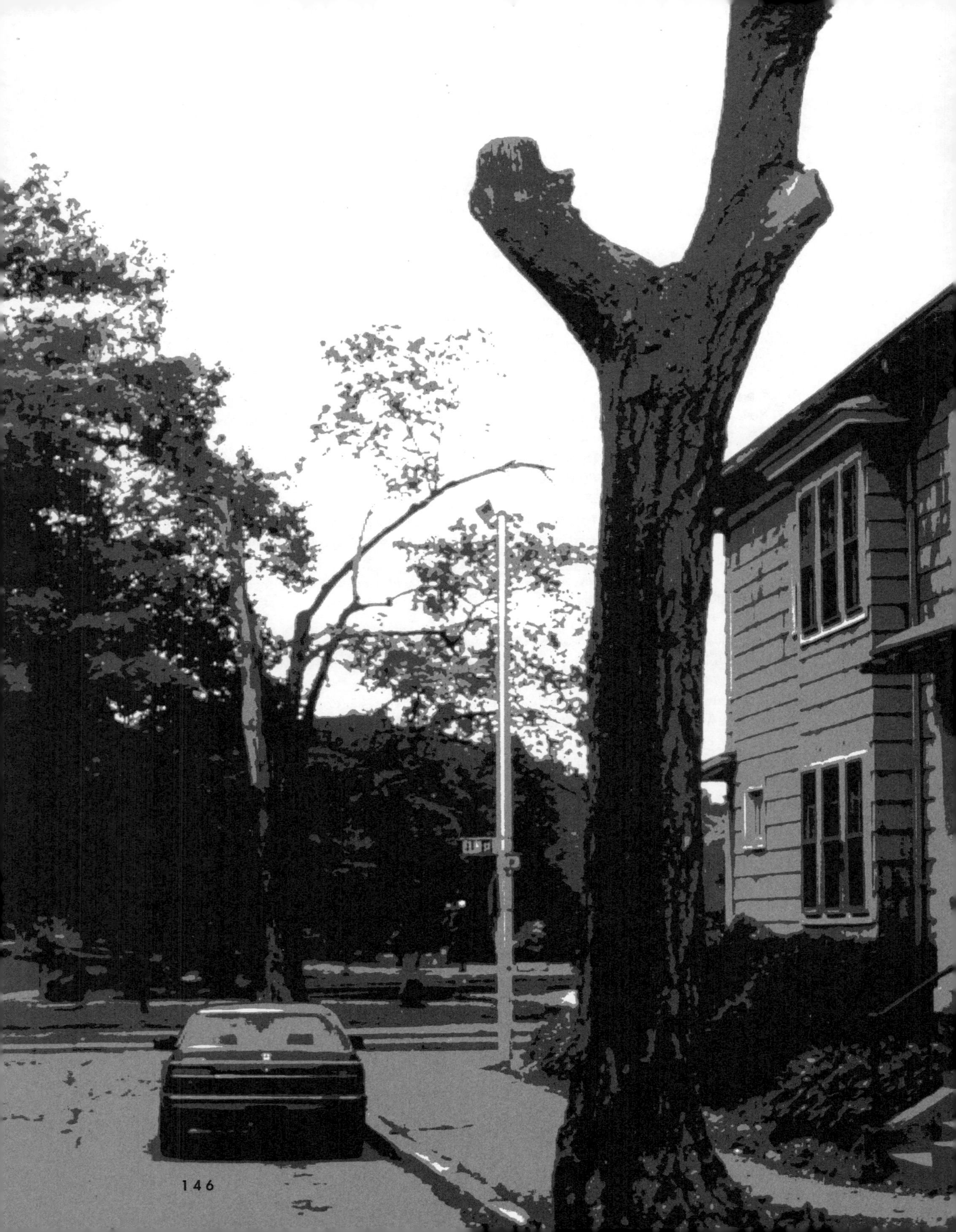

UNDER SIEGE
Chapter Six

It had been raining hard since Saturday, so hard that the road to Barre was under five feet of water. Throughout western Worcester County, flooding had cut off rural towns from food supplies and emergency assistance, leaving hundreds of families homeless. But the front-page story in the *Worcester Evening Gazette* on Wednesday, September 21, 1938, was reassuring: according to chief meteorologist G. Harold Noyes of Boston, the endless rain would finally ease by evening, and the tropical hurricane heading up the Atlantic coast would spare New England and veer out to sea south of Nantucket.[1]

Noyes was wrong. Shortly after the *Gazette* hit the streets, a devastating hurricane with gusts up to 100 miles per hour smashed into New England, wreaking death and destruction as it tore through Worcester and raged up the border between New Hampshire and Vermont. By the weekend, the New England death toll from the hurricane neared 500, parts of Rhode Island were under martial law and Worcester was struggling to recover from an estimated $5 million in property damage. Two enterprising *Telegram* reporters hired a private plane to view the devastation:

> Houses, barns and factory buildings, reduced to kindling wood. Forests of trees leveled. Structures along the coastline demolished. Boats driven a quarter of a mile inland, and left stranded as the tide raced back to sea. . . . From the air, Southeastern Massachusetts, Rhode Island, the Blackstone Valley and Central Massachusetts were alternate scenes of desolation and calm, undisturbed New England and communities. Some sections appeared to have escaped the severe ravages of the storm. Others were destroyed.
>
> Even in the wooded sections large areas of trees appeared undisturbed, only to give way to areas where the great trees had been uprooted and hurled about as if they were matches.[2]

In Worcester, the scene was utter chaos. "Buildings were partially collapsed," reported the *Gazette*, "roofs ripped off, church steeples toppled, store fronts blown out, trees uprooted, chimneys leveled, signs torn down and the streets littered with glass, tree branches and other debris. There were dangling live wires in many sections. Telephone and electric service, affecting lighting and radio went out of commission."[3]

With Worcester's trees, the hurricane was ruthless. In just three hours, the storm downed

3,931 street trees and 11,189 trees in city parks and playgrounds—roughly a third of an estimated 50,000 public trees throughout the city. Thousands of others suffered torn and broken limbs. Working day and night, men from the federal Works Progress Administration helped clear homes and public buildings of dangerous branches and fallen trees, but the full repairs would take years. Overwhelmed by the arduous task of recovering from the storm's damage, Parks and Recreation Executive Director Thomas E. Holland had a "breakdown" and took a six-month leave of absence.[4]

For Holland, the Hurricane of '38 came as a crushing blow after two decades of defending city trees from nature's fury. First there had been the chestnut blight that claimed all of Worcester's chestnuts during the 1910s and early 1920s. Then there was the ice storm of 1921 that had sheathed trees in glistening casts for three days, fracturing so many thousands of limbs that it took three years to repair the damage. In the meantime there were elm leaf beetles, brown tail moths and gypsy moths to contend with, and then in the 1930s, word of a new blight, Dutch Elm disease, which was spreading relentlessly throughout the Northeast, destroying the nation's most popular shade tree, the graceful American elm. And the hurricane had struck at the worst of possible times, during the Great Depression that had decimated the city's parks and recreation budget and rendered Worcester dependent on the federal WPA.[5]

Manmade stresses were also creating new challenges for the urban forest. In addition to the soot and grime from Worcester's factories and railroads, there were now automobiles to deal with. In Holland's opinion, they were even more destructive than the horses who had gnawed bark off street trees for centuries; cars and trucks commandeered by careless drivers, backing up or dodging traffic, could strip bark, break limbs or down young trees in a single skid.[6]

Even as cars and nature were bearing down on city trees, changing community values were revising the way trees were incorporated into the urban landscape. The turn-of-the-century shift from an aesthetic vision of parks as the spiritual cure for urban ills to a patriotic dream of playgrounds as wellsprings for strong, young leaders spelled an end to ornamental public plantings. By the early 1910s, gardenesque sites like Elm Park were deemed "old-fashioned" and of far less value than playgrounds. That shift in priorities was promoted by the Parks and Playgrounds Commission, which consolidated management of the city's recreation spaces in 1917. Headed by *Worcester Evening Gazette* publisher George F. Booth, the commission trumpeted the cause of healthy play. In place of Edward Winslow Lincoln's florid descriptions of the sugar maple's superior beauty as a street tree, or self-congratulatory praise of park beautification, annual commission reports boasted of toboggan runs, beach attendance and municipal golf.[7]

Municipal tree plantings, so long an emblem of civic refinement, were now primarily utilitarian. The city forestry department tended several thousand saplings of a few select species in the Green Hill Park nursery, but these were set out as shade trees for streets, parks and playgrounds, rather than ornament. Though Worcester retained the services of the Olmsted Brothers landscape architecture firm in Brookline, their work was confined largely to remodeling

AMERICAN ELM
Ulmus americana

Inspiring poetry and creation myth, the elm has graced landscape land literature for millennia before nearly disappearing from North America in the past century following the arrival of Dutch Elm disease around 1930. Called "the lady of the forest" by early settlers who discovered the towering, fountain-of-a-tree growing wild throughout the eastern continent, the elm averaged 100 feet tall and four feet in diameter, its sweeping, dark-green crown often broader than its height. The elm's classic, vase-like silhouette and hardy nature—prior to the Dutch Elm blight, the trees were known to live up to 300 years—have earned elms a place in American and local history. From Boston's Liberty Elm, sight of revolutionary speeches and protests, to the Washington Elm, beneath whose boughs General George Washington first took command of the Continental Army, these magnificent shade trees are part of America's earliest memories. At the turn of the century, Lancaster, Massachusetts, boasted the Commonwealth's champion American elm—95 feet high, with a crown spreading 114 feet and a trunk measuring 24 feet in circumference. Though Worcester's elms never rivaled that record, the city was proud of the graceful giants that lined streets and the Common, including the "Elephant Elm" near City Hall, whose unusual trunk protuberance resembled an elephant's head. There was also the much-revered Lafayette Elm near the corner of Elm and Main Streets, under which Governor Levi Lincoln greeted General Lafayette when he visited Worcester in 1824.

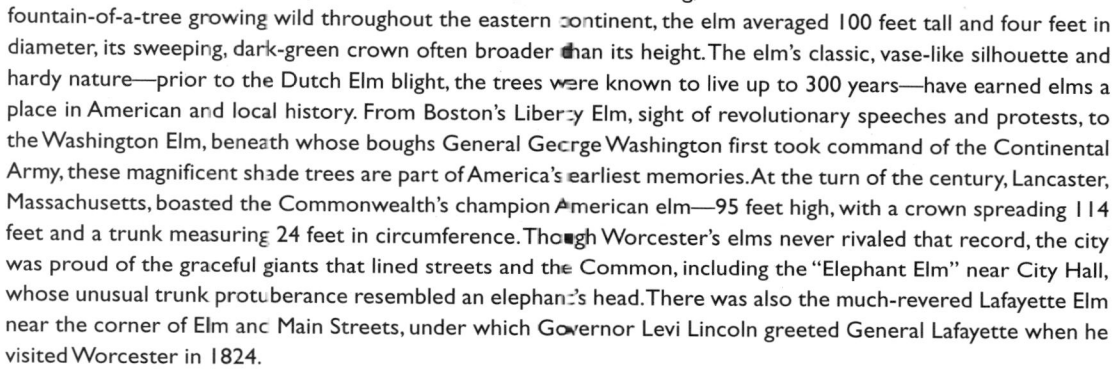

The Lafayette Elm was cut down in 1869 to much hue and cry by the public, but no hand wringing by Governor Lincoln's son Edward Winslow, who soon after assumed his position as Chairman of the Commission on Shade Trees and Public Grounds. A respected horticulturist, Lincoln well understood the characteristic weakness of aging elms—their innate tendency to drop large branches with no warning. Indeed, that deadly quality, and the fact that elm wood was often used for coffins, once prompted an English wit to write, "Elem haiteth man/And waiteth."

Such risks to unwary pedestrians notwithstanding, elms became one of the nation's most popular street trees and were planted, often as monocultures, in small towns and large cities throughout the United States. Across the rural countryside, the hardy giants, difficult to fell due to the toughness of their interlocking wood grain, were often left standing amidst fields, offering welcome shade to cattle and farmers alike.

Those elms felled by the lumberman's ax were converted to objects that last, from wagon-wheel hubs to oxen yokes. In addition, sturdy elm wood was used for trunks, dressers, Windsor chair seats, rat traps and shuffleboard tables. The elm's ability to resist rot when left in water also made it ideal for ships' keels, bridge pilings, canal-lock gates and even underground water pipes. Indeed, elm water pipes laid beneath the streets of London in 1613, when unearthed three centuries later, were found to be still sound.

Venerated in Mongol wedding ceremony and Germanic creation myth as the source of ancient gods and humans, elms have been immortalized by poets from Ovid to Robert Frost for their beauty, longevity and as a familiar vision in the landscape of heart and mind. In his poem *"To A Fallen Elm,"* John Clare (1793–1864) described one elm thus:

> Old favourite tree thoust seen times change
> But change till now did never come to thee
> For time beheld thee as his sacred dower
> And nature claimed thee her domestic tree.[1]

Tragically, Clare's eulogy for one beloved elm resonates through the centuries for millions of American elms, so devasted over the past 70 years by the fungus known as Dutch Elm disease. First identified in France in 1918, the

AMERICAN ELM
Ulmus americana

developed in the United States and spread back to Europe. Transported by the tiny elm bark beetle, *Ceratocystis ulmi* generates rapidly reproducing spores that spew toxins into the elm's vascular system—the vessels that transport water and minerals from roots to leaves. The tree responds by blocking the diseased vessels, effectively choking off its source of nutrients and eventually starving to death. Since 1930, Dutch Elm disease has killed an estimated 100 million elms throughout the United States.

Once treated with copper sulfate and, in the 1950s, with DDT, Dutch Elm disease is now managed with the herbicide cacodylic acid and with a synthetic pheromone that lures the fungus-carrying beetles to eat poisoned bark. In addition, sick or dying elms are best removed from the vicinity of other elms, to prevent the disease's spread. Most promising is a treatment developed by researchers at the University of Toronto that stimulates the tree's immune system to develop defenses against Dutch Elm disease. Not unlike a vaccination, a natural protein is injected annually into the tree's cambium and absorbed into the vascular system, triggering the production of mansonones, which help boost the tree's ability to fight Dutch Elm and other diseases.

Despite the virulent nature of the disease, isolated elms can still be found in many communities, survivors by chance or genetic makeup. In Worcester, two beautiful, well-tended American elms shade the grounds of Holy Cross College. Elms that have survived the blight are easily recognized by their tall trunks and sweeping boughs. Brown at its tips, the American elm's bark is light gray, scaled and deeply furrowed. Elliptical, pointed, doubly saw-toothed leaves grow in two rows, each leaf with one side larger than the other and many straight, parallel side veins. Clusters of small, maroon flowers appear in early spring, producing hairy, ovoid, one-seeded samaras. Elms are dark green in summer, bright yellow in fall.

Surviving elms are key to preservation research at centers including the United States National Arboretum, the Elm Research Institute in Westmoreland, New Hampshire, the University of Wisconsin and Princeton Nurseries in Princeton, New Jersey, which have created elm hybrids or cloned survivors that are genetically resistant to Dutch Elm disease. Among these hardy varieties now being planted in communities throughout the country are the Patriot, Princeton, American Liberty, Valley Forge and New Harmony elms. Typically smaller than the American elm, they nonetheless bring hope for the return of this once grand and adored urban shade tree.

[1] Geoffrey Summerfield, ed., *John Claire, Selected Poetry* (New York: Penguin Poetry Library, 1990), p.16.

Elm Park's South Mere and designing a small, triangular pocket of land across from Elm Park, at the base of Newton Hill.[8]

In turn, private plantings reflected the profit motives of Worcester's new breed of industrial leaders. Unlike Worcester's landed gentry, who had tended city trees and parks out of a sense of *noblesse oblige,* men like Norton Company's George Jeppson viewed investments in the city's landscape through the lens of corporate rather than civic priorities. With an eye to securing employee loyalty, Jeppson commissioned architect Grosvenor Atterbury, who had designed Forest Hills, New York, to devise a plan for a complex of employee-owned homes near the abrasives manufacturer's Greendale factory. The result, Indian Hill, incorporated Atterbury's preference for trees amidst the modest single-family houses. But the inviting landscape was designed specifically to retain Norton workers and build a corporate community, rather than simply to enhance the city for all to enjoy.[9]

The economy, too, bode ill for the city's trees. From 1929, when the Parks and Recreation Commission's budget reached an all-time high of $238,200 and Worcester's pride was its new municipal golf course in Green Hill Park, funding plummeted to $115,132 four years later, in the depths of the Depression. Grants from the WPA helped make up some of the difference and enabled the city to make some permanent park improvements in addition to keeping up with basic maintenance. But removals of dead and dying trees far outnumbered new plantings as resources shriveled.[10]

Thus it was as Worcester began to pick up the pieces after the Hurricane of '38. Across the Atlantic, the day the storm hurled through New England, Czechoslovakia gave in to British and French pressure to surrender Sudetenland to Adolf Hitler. Four days later, on Sunday, as Worcester rested from long days of clearing streets of tree limbs and broken glass, the Czech army was mobilizing to resist the German invasion. The maelstrom that followed would eventually draw thousands of Worcester men and women to distant shores, leaving the city's trees untended until the war's end.[11]

The Struggle to Manage Land Use—Growth Versus Zoning

Though the Great Depression was a sobering wake-up call, the 1920s had been a heady time in Worcester. Indeed, by the decade's start, civic boosters had plenty to brag about. Thanks to the city's diverse manufacturing base, Worcester had rebounded from the Depression of 1893 with steady growth since the century's turn. Now the census neared 180,000, a 54 percent increase in two decades, placing Worcester among the fastest growing cities in New England. Jobs were the city's big draw, and economic stability. Six hundred major industries, including metal working, rolling mills, textiles, leather goods and shoes, abrasives, envelopes, skates and clothing manufacturers, employed nearly 42,000 workers in 1922; retail stores and other businesses employed another 25,000. Encouraged by stories of opportunity, immigrants from Sweden, Ireland, Italy, Quebec, Lithuania and other parts of Eastern Europe streamed to Worcester, seeking work

Damage to Elm Park trees during an ice storm in 1923. From the collections of WORCESTER HISTORICAL MUSEUM, Worcester, Massachusetts

and finding strong ethnic communities. Their numbers meant an ample supply of cheap labor for the industrialists who were capitalizing on Worcester's strong economy. Touting their profits, those same industrialists continued to build fine homes along Salisbury Street, with the finest located at the city's newest status address—the elegant private development of Westwood Hills.[12]

As always, however, growth came at a price. Railroad tracks crisscrossed the city, knitting together a jumble of red-brick factories in a haphazard pattern. Living nearby, immigrant workers crowded into tenements. Though the number of new single-family homes far outpaced new apartment buildings by the early 1920s, civic leaders fretted that the factories and tenements—and by association, their ethnic occupants—were spilling into residential neighborhoods. They also worried about neighborhood invasions by stores, public and private garages, and the random placement of a new scourge, billboards. A 1924 master plan commissioned by the city's planning board summarized the problem: "The city has a distinct personality which unfortunately is rapidly disappearing through the unwarranted diffusion of factories and the spread of the unattractive houses."[13]

The plan's solution to rescue Worcester's character was essentially to preserve the city's best neighborhoods and contain factories along railroad corridors in the valleys "where they belong even in their own interest." That goal was to be accomplished through zoning, a new municipal land-use tool first considered by the city council just two years earlier. In 1922, empowered by the 1920 Massachusetts Zoning Enabling Act, Worcester had passed an interim zoning ordinance to protect existing property uses until such time as a master zoning plan could be approved. The following year, the city planning board submitted a comprehensive zoning ordinance and map to the city council; but when the 1924 City Plan was published 13 months later, the ordinance was still under review. As the debate dragged on, Worcester's industry bulged at the seams. Only the wealthy few could afford to insulate themselves from the ravages of growth they had fueled with their capital—either by purchasing abutting properties to create a buffer zone around their homes, or by buying a lot in an exclusive private development. For the rest of Worcester, wrote the planners, "The harmonious character of districts is rapidly being broken down and the orderly development of property is gradually disappearing."[14]

It would soon become readily apparent in Worcester and other American cities that zoning was no panacea—locking in land-use restrictions for the privileged at the expense of those who most needed protection—but it offered a powerful means to mitigate urban ills with more than just trees and parks. Prior to zoning's introduction at the century's turn, landowners could use their property for any lawful purpose they chose, and governments could do little but stand by and watch. A handful of local public health and fire ordinances regulated the location of offensive industries, such as animal slaughterhouses. But these were the only limits on the sacrosanct rights of property owners, other than restrictive covenants on deeds. Any conflicts over land use were resolved on a case-by-case basis in the courts.[15]

As cities became more congested, however, the courts alone could no longer manage growth by default. Los Angeles was the first municipality to adopt district zoning in 1909, followed

Headline from the Worcester Telegram, the Hurricane of 1938

Courtesy, Worcester Telegram and Gazette

by New York City, which passed the nation's first comprehensive zoning ordinance in 1916 to insulate downtown Manhattan from further overcrowding in response to planned transportation improvements. In Massachusetts, overcrowding in Boston was the impetus for a series of state laws empowering cities and towns to regulate specific land uses, culminating in the state Zoning Enabling Act of 1920. Four years later, the same year Worcester was debating its own comprehensive zoning ordinance, the U.S. Commerce Department under Secretary Herbert Hoover produced the Standard State Zoning Enabling Act, which was soon adopted by 19 states. Modifications followed after Supreme Court challenges; by 1930, the model zoning legislation had been adopted in some form by 35 states.[16]

Zoning was not the only response to urban growing pains. Planning, too, was gaining acceptance as an important tool of municipal government. Whereas zoning, at its inception, primarily addressed the problems of growth after the fact, town and city planning was a means to prevent such problems from happening in the first place. Often, the two approaches were used in tandem. Worcester's 1924 City Plan was thick with charts and graphs of population growth and land-use patterns to back up zoning proposals. Though the analysis was rudimentary—a 50-year projection of the city's population optimistically assumed that growth would continue unabated and pegged the figure at 300,000, nearly double the actual 1974 census—efforts to take a comprehensive look at how best to meet current and anticipated needs were noteworthy.[17]

Precursors to Land-Use Controls—Planned Communities

That scientific approach to city planning was a 20th-century invention; but the notion of devising plans to manage urban congestion, explicitly incorporating "rural" amenities such as parks and trees to ensure livable space, dated back nearly a century. In England, planned communities for factory workers began appearing around the mid-19th century, when enlightened industrialists like textile manufacturer Sir Titus Salt, chocolate baron George Cadbury and soap magnate W. H. Lever built new factory-centered rural towns for their employees. Lever Brothers' 56-acre development of Port Sunlight, opened in 1887 near Birkenhead and Liverpool, exemplified the trend: half of the tract was set aside for a new soap manufacturing plant and the rest for an employee village, including homes, schools, stores, parks and other amenities. Five years later, Port Sunlight had expanded to include 230 acres. Employee rents covered taxes and property upkeep, while Lever Brothers covered all construction costs, hoping to reap improved productivity from a loyal workforce in return.[18]

In the United States, urban planning also caught on by the mid-19th century, but with a different focus. Whereas English reformers had used planning as a means to improve the lot of factory workers by removing them from urban ills, American planners designed suburban towns to blend the best of urban and rural amenities for the emerging industrial elite. Inspired by the rural landscape movement that so influenced rural cemetery and urban parks design during the same period, their work was also fueled by new forms of transportation that stretched the distance between home and work, making it possible to benefit from urban commerce by day and return to fresh air and greenery at night.[19]

The move to the suburbs began in the 1830s, as first the wealthy and then the middle class began to move away from congested northeastern city centers to peripheral towns. In Boston, Philadelphia and New York, the street omnibus and then the horse-drawn streetcar carved the route to outlying communities like Roxbury, Germantown and northern Manhattan, all prosperous suburbs by midcentury. Railroads soon became the preferred mode of transportation; by 1850, Boston was surrounded by 83 commuter rail stations, all within a 15-mile radius.[20]

For landscape designers like Andrew Jackson Downing, however, the new suburbs were fatally flawed. Mimicking the cities from which they provided escape, outlying towns grew in a pattern of right-angled streets that locked the land in urban gridiron. Downing deemed the gridiron too restrictive and dreamed of suburbs centered on a park or common, surrounded by fine homes. Throughout this ideal town, instead of lock-step blocks of houses and street trees, he envisioned a design that allowed air to circulate around "broad, well-planted avenues of shade trees."[21]

One of the first American suburbs to incorporate Downing's vision was Llewellyn Park, New Jersey, built by pharmaceuticals importer Llewellyn S. Haskell on scenic Orange Mountain, 12 miles west of New York City. Haskell himself had moved to Orange Mountain in 1853, seeking a cure for poor health on his new 40-acre estate, Eagle Rock. Within 13 years, Haskell had bought up 750 acres of adjacent farmland and created a suburban village. At its center was a 50-acre park called the Ramble, jointly held and maintained by all property owners. A network of curving roads and walks wound around lots of one to 20 acres; no fences were allowed to separate properties, creating the impression of a vast, rolling estate for even the smallest lot owner.[22]

Many other planned communities were started during the same period but aborted during the Civil War, when the wartime economy drove thousands of businesses into bankruptcy and diverted capital from real estate investment to martial industry. But postwar prosperity inspired new interest in suburban development. In 1868, fresh from their success with Central Park, Frederick Law Olmsted and Calvin Vaux were commissioned by Emery E. Childs of Chicago to design a 1,600 acre "suburban village" along the Des Plaines River, nine miles from Chicago's core. The result—Riverside, Illinois—soon became a national model. A lacy design of curvilinear streets, parkways and promenades, Olmsted and Vaux's plan included a 160-acre riverside park and a landscaped commuter rail station. Trees were essential to the design; dense plantings were specified along roadways and throughout the park. In addition, the designers recommended that homeowners plant one or two fine trees in front of their houses to enhance a sense of peacefulness and domestic privacy.[23]

Although the plan was adopted, conflicts between the designers and promoters undermined the partnership, and Olmsted and Vaux left the project in 1870. Despite that falling-out and two

Early 20th century Worcester street scene. From the collections of
WORCESTER HISTORICAL MUSEUM, *Worcester, Massachusetts*

major catastrophes—the great Chicago fire of 1871 and the economic panic of 1873—Riverside was eventually completed along the lines that Olmsted and Vaux had conceived. Though modern critics fault the curvilinear street pattern as hopelessly confusing, Riverside's graceful, tree-lined streets made a strong imprint on suburban design well into the 20th century.[24]

While the nation's earliest planned suburban developments catered to the wealthy, in 1907 the philanthropic Russell Sage Foundation of New York ventured in a new direction with a plan for a middle class suburb. Located on 142 acres in Queens, about a half-hour train ride from newly completed Pennsylvania Station in midtown Manhattan, Forest Hills Gardens was designed by the Olmsted Brothers and architect Grosvenor Atterbury. With a picturesque railroad station at its heart, the design placed brick and stone homes and apartment buildings along curving, tree-lined streets and greenways. Six small parks and a village green were strategically located throughout the town, although the smaller green spaces were ultimately deemed unworkable. Unfortunately, like Riverside, Forest Hills was plagued by financial difficulties, and the Russell Sage Foundation eventually sold its interest in the development to cut its losses. Still, the experiment made real the notion that attractive suburban homes with shaded lawns and ample breathing space could be owned by those of modest means.[25]

Working-class suburbs, inspired by the British factory model, also began to appear in the United States around the turn of the century. Apollo Iron and Steel Company, north of Pittsburgh, and the Goodyear Company in Akron, Ohio, were among the early pioneers, as was the Postum Cereal Company in Battle Creek, Michigan. Conceived in 1898, Battle Creek's Postumville included

375 employee-owned cottages by 1914. Ranging in price from $800 to $3,000, the homes were built by the cereal manufacturer's Post Land Company and sold to workers on a modest monthly payment schedule. According to company president C. W. Post, the goal of the development was to encourage self-reliance, responsibility and stability—all the ingredients for an ideal, loyal employee. "The welfare work that I believe in is that which makes it possible for the man to help himself, but it does not include the holding of a milk bottle to his lips after he is weaned," wrote Post for a 1914 article in *Worcester Magazine*. "If the manufacturer esteems intelligent, high-grade employees with peace and content in his works, he will strive to carry out a program which includes good wages, fair terms, and freehold homes for his people."[26]

Norton Company's Planned Village—Indian Hill

Post's words were of more than passing interest to the businessmen who subscribed to *Worcester Magazine*. George Jeppson, who had taken the reins of Norton Company from his father, John, in 1911, was seriously considering creating just such a company village near the abrasive manufacturer's Greendale plant on the north side of Worcester. Corporate paternalism to foster worker loyalty—dubbed "the Norton Spirit"—was key to the company's creed, a value George had learned from his father, who had transplanted it from his native Sweden.[27]

John Jeppson had grown up in Höganäs, a small fishing village on the southeast tip of Sweden that became a mining town and, later, a center of pottery manufacturing when veins of coal and clay deposits were discovered in the 19th century. As early as 1801, the mining company, Höganäs AB, lured workers to the town with promises of cash and free housing for any who married and moved there. That successful experiment prompted the company in 1802 to build a new town, Ryd, to accommodate more workers. By 1864, when Jeppson was 20, Höganäs AB had converted to pottery making and constructed the town of Bruket, which included a factory, company-built Lutheran church, cemetery, park, ball fields, entertainment hall and schools. That same year Höganäs AB also began offering company financing to workers who wanted to buy their own homes.

Five years later, Jeppson moved to Worcester to work as a skilled potter for F. B. Norton. The depression of the 1870s cost him his job, but by 1880 Jeppson was back at Norton's, working with his brother-in-law Sven Pulson, who had devised a way to make ceramic grinding wheels. That formula became Norton's future. In 1885, Jeppson and several partners bought the company from F. B. Norton and established the Norton Emery Wheel Company; when Jeppson died in 1920, Norton had grown into the world's largest abrasives manufacturer and the city's leading employer.

Stories of Jeppson's concern for his mostly Swedish workforce became legend. If an employee needed a character witness for naturalization, a place to stay when he or she first came to the city, or bail and a ride home from the drunk tank, Jeppson was there. He was the stern disciplinarian for the worker who drank too much and beat his wife, and the benevolent father figure who presided over company Christmas dinners. In return, Norton employees were fiercely loyal.

When George Jeppson took over for his ailing father, the company had grown to 1,100 employees, far too many for one executive to know intimately. Instead, George instituted other means to foster loyalty, including more than a half-dozen sports teams, a glee club, drama group, band and orchestra. He also introduced a company folk festival, an agricultural society and a monthly corporate newsletter. Building housing for workers was the logical next step: if workers lived closer to the plant, Jeppson reasoned, they would be more likely to join clubs and catch the "Norton Spirit." In turn, the company would continue to benefit from a stable workforce and high productivity.

To design the company village, Jeppson hired Grosvernor Atterbury, who had earned national acclaim for his recent work on Forest Hills Gardens. Located on Indian Hill, behind Norton's Greendale abrasives factory, the development was to include several types of housing, financed by Norton's Indian Hill Company, to accommodate workers' varying incomes. Single-family homes and duplexes for skilled workers were to be sited on top of the hill, multi-family homes for semi-skilled workers midway up, and boardinghouses at the bottom for unskilled laborers. Not coincidentally, that stratified arrangement afforded Norton's Swedes, who dominated the skilled workforce, the best homes and views.

Starting at the top, the company began building in 1915. Atterbury designed small, high-quality homes ranging from $2,800 to $3,500 and placed them at varying angles and positions on each lot. He laid out roads to follow the hill's natural contours and strove to avoid a gridiron pattern. He also made careful use of trees, incorporating existing shade trees into his plans, as well as new plantings, to form natural boundaries between lots. In addition, Atterbury created small playgrounds and parks, including the site of Theodore Roosevelt's 1916 tree planting, throughout the development.

John Jeppson I *George N. Jeppson* *Courtesy of Ingrid Jeppson Mach*

Jeppson saw to it that the new homeowners kept their properties in order. He often visited the hill and would chastise any owner who let his property run down—even to the point of threatening to repossess the house if the owner could not maintain "Indian Hill Standards." To build civic pride among homeowners in what Jeppson hoped would be Worcester's finest working-class neighborhood, he created the Indian Hill Improvement Association in 1917. In addition to providing guidance on the best way to plant lawns and maintain hedges, the association also encouraged tree planting in common areas. On one Saturday, armed with trowels and thousands of pine seedlings that Norton had bought from the state, residents lined up along the hill, six feet apart, and proceeded to march up the hillside, three feet at a time, planting seedlings on signal. According to plants engineer Clarence Daniels, "It looked like a battle line advancing."[28]

Though World War I stymied Jeppson and Atterbury's plans to build boardinghouses for the company's Italian laborers, Norton directors did approve the construction of a second single-family home complex on Indian Hill. Started in 1920, Norton Village was promoted as a "Garden Village" that promised the serenity and freedom of country living with all the benefits of nearby Worcester. As with the original Indian Hill homes, Norton Village was soon populated by Swedes. Both developments earned Atterbury and Norton Company national accolades; though limited to the manufacturer's upper echelon Swedes, the housing improved the lot of hundreds of employees and their families.

On another hill in Worcester, on the city's West Side, wealthy residents were creating a different kind of planned neighborhood. Laid out in the 1920s, Westwood Hills was the city's first elite residential development to break from the gridiron design of the old West Side and incorporate the curvilinear streets and "natural" landscaping popularized by Riverside. Feeding into Salisbury Street, Westwood Drive and its winding connector roads were home to three residences in 1930; a decade later, the tony neighborhood had 39 families and the city's densest concentration of high-value homes.[29]

To ensure the quality of those homes and pedigree of their homeowners, Westwood Hills was organized as the Westwood Hills Improvement Association, a trusteeship that controlled development and maintenance of all lots—much in the same way that wealthy landowners, like Stephen Salisbury III, had controlled the appearance of upscale neighborhoods during the 19th century. As trustees, individual lot owners were also part owners of the development and had voting privileges to determine the outcome of any land-use decisions affecting their section. This arrangement enabled the Improvement Association to keep a close eye on housing styles, landscape design and the type of people who moved into the neighborhood.[30]

With its generous colonials and tudors, its exquisitely manicured lawns, lush gardens and handsome trees, Westwood Hills soon became the city's finest address—and its most exclusive. No Jews or other minorities were encouraged to apply to the Improvement Association: this was a development primarily for names like Coes, Smith and Higgins, the city's Yankee elite.[31]

The Political Landscape—Ethnic Politics and Public Parks

The ethnic divisions that defined Worcester's neighborhoods—Yankees dominating West Side developments along Salisbury Street; Swedes bordering Norton's Greendale factory to the north and wire-manufacturing plants in Quinsigamond Village to the south; French Canadians near the factories in Main South; Irish Catholics to the southeast atop Vernon Hill, Jews toward the bottom; Italians along Shrewsbury Street to the east; Poles, Greeks and Syrians in between—also defined city politics. Each new wave of immigrants exacerbated tensions between Yankee Brahmins, who had aligned themselves with Irish Catholics to bolster their progressive municipal agenda, and nativist Yankee mechanics, who feared losing control of their city to foreigners. But even as the city's undulating geography reinforced divisions, separating ethnic groups by hills and valleys, a new coalition between Swedes and the Yankee mechanics helped indirectly to mitigate some of the extreme anti-immigrant backlash that other American cities experienced during the first quarter of the new century.[32]

The new alignment also dissolved the decades-old Citizen's Coalition between Brahmin Yankee Republicans and Irish Catholic Democrats, which had been so crucial to the creation of Worcester's municipal parks system. Though their mutual interest in civic improvements had united Brahmins and immigrant laborers against the anti-tax, anti-big-government politics of working- and middle-class Yankees who controlled the Republican Party caucuses, the Citizen's Coalition fell apart in the 1890s, when the temperance movement and a clash over the school superintendent's alleged favoritism of Irish Catholics prompted Swedes—a growing political force with the rise of Norton Co., and the city's wireworking industry—to choose sides.

On both issues, the new ethnic voting block sided with nativist Republicans who advocated temperance (a movement adamantly opposed by Irish Catholics but strongly supported by Swedes

Garden of the late Helen Stoddard, Westwood Hills, Worcester, Massachusetts
© *Robert Nash*

who had broken away from the traditional Lutheran Church) and the superintendent's removal. As a result, the superintendent was fired, the local temperance movement gained momentum, and the local Republican Party was significantly strengthened. The Swedes' support of temperance was more a reflection of divisions within the Lutheran Church than any overtly anti-Catholic agenda; ironically, however, their moderating influence weakened the grasp of organized nativist groups such as the American Protective Association, which were thriving on xenophobia elsewhere in the United States, but could not make gains from anti-foreigner doggerel in a city where a dominant immigrant group had helped working-class Yankees regain control of their party.

With the coalition's collapse, Irish Democrats found their own voice. No longer dependent on the city's industrial elite for defining their candidate, Democrats beat Yankee Republicans in the mayoral race five times between 1901 and 1915. Ethnic rivalries remained vigorous, but the new party alignments channeled those tensions into partisan political fights over issues of concern to the whole city, such as the annual battle over liquor license renewals—rather than hate-mongering. The political balance was reinforced by the local economy: as Worcester recovered from the mid-1890s depression, local shops and factories favored Yankees, Swedes and British immigrants for skilled positions, strengthening their interdependence as the new core of the Republican Party.

That ethnic alignment held for a generation. Alienated by the Prohibition amendment that was soon to become law and congressional debate over federal immigration restrictions, in 1919 Worcester Democrats vented their anger by ousting three-term Swedish Republican Pehr Holmes from the mayoralty and replaced him with an Irish democrat, Peter F. Sullivan. Relations between Swedes and Catholics continued to deteriorate, erupting in violence in 1923, when the largely Irish police force and Knights of Columbus drove the Ku Klux Klan, whose local membership was disproportionately Swedish, out of Worcester. The political dominance of Irish Catholics over Swedes was confirmed that same year when Mayor Sullivan was defeated by another Irish politician, Michael J. O'Hara—a Catholic Republican. O'Hara's election in a tumultuous decade of ethnic hostility signaled Worcester's return, full circle, to the Brahmin Yankee-Irish Catholic coalition.[33]

As it had in the 1880s, that coalition bode well for Worcester's parks and trees. From an appropriation of $48,500 in 1917 during the first year of the Holmes administration, the Parks and Recreation Commission's budget grew to $146,500 by 1923, Sullivan's last year in office. Under the O'Hara administration, the Parks and Recreation appropriation expanded most years through the end of the decade, reaching an all-time high of $238,200 in 1929. Most of that money went toward city parks and playgrounds, but the increase benefited public trees, as well. Funding for city forestry under the Holmes administration averaged $8,000 annually; during the Sullivan and O'Hara eras, forestry appropriations ranged between $16,000 and $26,000 a year.[34]

For Mayor Sullivan, city trees proved a special concern. A few weeks after he won reelection to his second term, Worcester was paralyzed by a devastating ice storm. Over the course of three days—November 28 to 30, 1921—the city's trees were frozen inside heavy crystalline shrouds that bowed their limbs like weeping willows. "Thousands of branches were fractured, and large limbs torn from the trunks of the trees," reported Parks and Recreation chairman George Booth. The task of repairing all the damage to an estimated 30,000 street trees and tens of thousands of park trees, he added, was "truly a stupendous one."[35]

Maples and elms were the most hard-hit. Parks and Recreation executive director Thomas Holland said it would take three years to heal all the wounds and trim all the broken limbs—one year for each day of the storm. The need was reflected in the 1922 budget: the city forestry department appropriation was nearly tripled from $8,000 to $20,000, and an additional $10,000 was allocated just to fund the cleanup. Still, wrote Holland in his year-end report, $30,000 was barely enough. Over his protests, forestry funding remained at $20,000 in 1923 and dropped to $16,000 in 1924, the year the repairs were finally completed. The following year, forestry appropriations again increased, averaging in the low twenties for the rest of the decade; but even with that additional funding, it still took another three years for the city's trees to fully recover from the storm. "It is gratifying to be able to state," wrote commission chairman George Sumner Barton in 1928, "that the trees on public streets and parks, having received more than the usual amount of care and attention, are in better condition at the present time than has been evident since the ice storm."[36]

Giants Felled—The Chestnut Tree Blight

The ice storm followed close on the heels of another, more insidious natural disaster that also had taxed the city's forestry budget. American chestnuts, the ubiquitous giants that so impressed Daniel Gookin when he first viewed Worcester centuries earlier, were dying. Once a dominant species from Maine to Georgia, comprising about a fourth of native eastern hardwood forests, chestnuts were succumbing to a rapidly spreading fungus that had entered the country around the turn of the century, probably with a shipment of Asian chestnut species. First observed in 1904, when American chestnuts at New York's Bronx Zoo developed telltale cankers, *cryphonectria parasitica* ravaged forests and cities, claiming three to four billion mature chestnuts throughout the species' natural range within a few decades, and remaining virulent in chestnut roots and stumps through the present day.

Entering bark through wounds or holes, the fungus attacks each tree by infecting the cambium (the growing part of the trunk that makes annual rings), creating sunken cankers. As the infection spreads, the cankers encircle the trunk, essentially strangling the tree by cutting off its supply of water and nutrients. The roots often survive, but the deadly fungus remains to choke off any sprouts that reach about 20 feet—condemning once 100-foot giants to linger only as shrubs for at least the rest of the century.[37]

In Worcester, the chestnut blight was already pronounced by 1912. Writing of the "chestnut bark disease which is gaining such a stronghold in this state," city forester Harold J. Neale advised that Worcester should "destroy all but perfect trees, which afford the greatest immunity from inoculation." Any hopes of saving the chestnuts would soon prove futile, however. Two years later, Neale gloomily described the plight of the chestnuts that filled Lake Park: "They are doomed in this section and in a few years the chestnut bark disease will have fulfilled its mission and the noble chestnut will be a thing of history."[38]

Salvaging infected trees for their valuable timber and tannin, the city made the best of its disaster. Chestnut wood was marketable within a year after a tree was killed by the fungus, though more valuable if the sickly tree was felled while still alive. Since it took about three years for the fungus to choke a mature chestnut, foresters could plan their harvest accordingly. For more than a decade, city workers continued to fell the dying giants; the year of the ice storm, chief forester Herman Adams reported the removal of 604 chestnuts, most from Lake Park. Finally, in 1923, Adams glibly recorded what was by then a foregone conclusion: "Blight has taken the last of our chestnut trees. Over four hundred were removed during the year. These trees were cut into lumber and cordwood, both are very useful in our various parks. It will require two more years to removed the remaining dead chestnuts. This work is done during the winter months."[39]

Insects, too, plagued city trees. Brown-tail and gypsy moths infested limbs and stripped foliage bare, prompting massive spraying with lead arsenate. Elm leaf beetles and leopard moths wreaked havoc on the graceful elms that shaded the Common. And the maturing urban forest simply needed attention. "The trees on our parks must soon receive consideration," warned chief forester Neale in 1914. "The trees on the Common—beautiful, stately elms—are gradually dying. Although not discernible to the average eye, a few years hence will find them beyond recall."[40]

Indeed, as the insect infestations, chestnut blight and ice storm drained resources, the challenge of simply maintaining the city's 50,000 public trees became more difficult. Basic tree trimming suffered, as did new plantings. In 1914, after surveying all the public trees in Worcester, city forester Neale concluded that only half had received appropriate care, due to inadequate resources. New plantings to replace dead and diseased trees reached a low of 33 in 1920, a stark contrast with previous years when 500 to 1,000 new trees were planted annually. With appropriations strained by damage control, planting levels did not pick up again until the mid-1920s, after the removal of thousands of chestnuts and ice-ravaged trees left gaping holes in the city's landscape. But even under the O'Hara administration, forestry appropriations never reached more than 50 cents a tree, not enough to combat the stresses of an urban environment. "A large number of our older trees are dying off very rapidly due, no doubt, to the present day methods of street development," wrote forestry superintendent Herman Adams in 1925, a year in which 493 trees were planted and 287 removed, for a net gain of barely 200 trees. Lacking a vocal advocate like an Edward Winslow Lincoln, municipal trees took second place to a more popular cause—developing the city's recreation facilities.[41]

Building Strong Minds and Sound Bodies—The Rise of Recreation

The shift in priorities mirrored a national shift in attitudes toward the ideal purpose of parks. Where 19th-century reformers had viewed urban parks as a means to uplift the masses by imbuing them with aesthetic sensibilities, early-20th-century advocates argued that parks were valuable as a space to build strong minds and bodies through healthy athletic competition—in the process, increasing civic pride and reducing crime among idle youths.[42]

The transition was formalized in Worcester in 1917, when the city merged supervision of its parks and playgrounds to create the Commission on Parks and Recreation. Articulating the change in public priorities, superintendent G. A. Parker described parks as a tool of social reform: "[I]t is certain that whenever a city provides, through its park department, efficient equipment to combat the evils of its city, as it does through its Fire Department to combat fires, then it will lessen the evils and prevent their spread, just as surely as the Fire Department puts out fires and prevents conflagration, for the Park Department is the only function of a city that can cope with these evils."[43]

Parker's successor, Thomas Holland, defined that mission as nothing short of patriotic duty in his first report for the newly formed Parks and Recreation Commission: "Every man, woman and child of this city ought to be healthy. It should be considered a paramount duty for one and all. The great things in a nation's advancement are those which the whole people accomplish and the establishment by the city of recreational grounds which will be accessible to the multitude will not only promote wholesome enjoyment but aid materially in promoting the health and happiness of mankind."[44]

To carry out that mission, Worcester had 1,166 acres of parks, playgrounds and bathing beaches, with nearly half the land located in Green Hill Park. A popular spot for picnics and play, Green Hill's 520 acres of rolling lawns, woods and spectacular panoramic views made it a natural focal point for many of the city's recreation programs. Tennis, basketball and swimming in the summer, skating and tobogganing in the winter, Sunday afternoon band concerts in the gazebo and holiday parties in the mansion were just a few of the park's popular offerings. In 1928, Green Hill Park became home to a new municipal golf course; the following year, the city added a public bowling green.[45]

Green Hill was also home to a nursery of over 6,000 saplings that were used for all new municipal plantings, as well as the site of a seven-acre Memorial Grove of 281 sugar maples, planted to honor Worcester soldiers who died in World War I. But, like most of the city's parks, its primary use was now recreational.[46]

Much of the credit for new priorities went to Parks and Recreation chairman George F. Booth. Publisher of the *Worcester Evening Gazette,* Booth was also the prime mover behind the city's recreation renaissance. Keenly interested in the needs of city youth, Booth had formed and headed a voluntary group called the Playgrounds Association early in the century, which raised funds for new play spaces and sports equipment. The group's success led to the creation of the city Playground Commission in 1911, which Booth chaired for five years. He then persuaded the Holmes administration to consolidate the Playground and Parks Commissions into one body and was immediately appointed as head of the new board, a position he held until he resigned in 1925.[47]

A prominent member of many other community boards, including first president of the local Boy Scouts chapter, president of the Chamber of Commerce, president of the YMCA and a trustee of Worcester Polytechnic Institute, Booth was a Republican who was active in party politics but shunned public office as a conflict of interest with his journalism. His influential connections and editorial page more than compensated for that choice, however, in his ability to champion pet causes. Much as Edward Winslow Lincoln had effectively argued the case for creating municipal parks, Booth pushed recreation: "We are becoming a more and more out-of-doors people," he wrote in 1922, "appreciating the benefit to health and to happiness that getting out in the open and away gives, even if only for an hour or two, from the hurly-burly of every day life."[48]

That assessment was no exaggeration. In 1917, when Booth first took over the consolidated commission, nearly 7,000 children had enrolled in beach and playground programs. Fifteen years later, in the depths of the Depression, annual attendance levels at city recreation facilities had skyrocketed to just over 1.2 million people.[49]

Though the city was able to meet the growing demand for play spaces during the 1920s, with appropriations for parks, playgrounds and the golf course topping $200,000 by decade's end, expansion ceased with the Depression. The year after the stock market crash, 1930, recreation

Green Hill Park today
©*Robert Nash*

funding dropped by nearly a fourth and continued its downward slide for another three years. Focusing on basic upkeep, superintendent Holland wrote his terse assessment in the commission's 1932 report—no longer printed on glossy stock, but on thin, pale white paper—"Considerable reductions in all city appropriations did not allow for extensive improvements."[50]

No longer blessed with wealthy benefactors as in previous centuries, Worcester's municipal parks languished for four years, even as the public thronged to the free beaches and playgrounds that had become their only affordable form of recreation. Without adequate resources to match demand, Holland and his staff struggled to maintain parks plagued by "malicious vandalism." Finally, in 1934, federal relief became available, first through the Federal Emergency Relief Administration, and the following year through the newly organized Works Progress Administration (WPA). Holland immediately used the money and federally funded employees to build major improvements, such as community houses and other permanent structures.[51]

Still, ongoing maintenance remained a problem. With a budget of just over $70,000 in 1937—barely a third of what had been allocated a decade earlier—commission chairman George Richardson lamented: "With hardly enough money for proper maintenance to run the Department, there was little for the members of the Commission to do when attending meetings. Permanent improvements that were completed were due entirely to the WPA Projects."[52]

Then the hurricane hit. For city parks and trees, alone, the September 1938 disaster caused over $1 million in damages—smashing buildings, downing more than 15,000 public trees and ripping limbs off thousands more. So many trees were lost that commission chairman Paul Kneeland, himself in the lumber business, set up a sawmill for the Parks and Recreation Department to salvage the timber. "When the work is completed," wrote Holland in the 1938 commission report, "we will have cut between seven and eight hundred thousand feet, board measure."[53]

Among the downed trees were several giants that had earned a place in local history and lore, including the huge yellow locust that had grown in front of the old Green family mansion in Green Hill Park since the days of the Revolution. All that remained after the storm was part of its lower trunk, measuring 13 feet in circumference. Another tree from the same era, the Revolutionary Oak in Grafton—the site where townspeople had gathered to pledge allegiance to the new nation 163 years earlier—also fell victim to the powerful winds. In neighboring Sutton, on the grounds of Reverend Dr. and Mrs. John Ellery Tuttle, the so-called Beecher Elm was decimated; the landmark tree had been named for Henry Ward Beecher, whose wife was the daughter of the original owners of the estate, and who had preached many sermons beneath the elm's graceful boughs. And in the Worcester Arboretum so carefully tended by Obadiah Hadwen, between 150 and 200 trees were felled, including a towering tulip tree, one of the largest in Massachusetts, which crashed onto Hadwen's former home, knocking off the conservatories and front and side porches.[54]

With manpower and a $50,000 loan from the WPA, plus $40,000 in hurricane disaster relief, Worcester began to replant. In 1939, the Parks and Recreation Department planted 3,574 trees; the next year, the department set out over 1,525 street trees, and another 1,977 the year after that—making up about half the number downed by the storm. "There is nothing which adds more to the attractiveness of a city than continuous lines of well developed trees," wrote department head Herman Adams, the former chief forester who had succeeded his longtime boss, Thomas Holland, in 1940. "With this in mind, it is quite evident that a systematic planting of trees must continue to be an important part of our program."[55]

But even as public trees gained an important advocate in the new department head, at a time when residents were acutely aware of how much they had lost in the storm, plans to continue redeveloping the city's urban forest were once again blocked. As the war effort gained momentum and the WPA went out of business, Worcester was left with neither the funding nor manpower to undertake any more significant improvements regarding trees or parks. Another severe ice storm in late December of 1942 again damaged thousands of trees, but due to the war, no men were available to repair the damage. Even routine trims and maintenance went untended; new plantings of 4,000 pines and spruces from the state Department of Conservation in 1944 were due solely to the efforts of local Boy and Girl Scouts. "The Forestry Division is somewhat handicapped," wrote Adams, "and will continue to be until the war is over, because it is impossible to obtain young men as tree climbers."[56]

The Urban Forest Decimated—Dutch Elm Disease

Compounding Adams's worries was a new scourge—Dutch Elm disease. Like the chestnut blight, the fungus was imported to the United States in a contaminated shipment of wood. Within a decade of its arrival around 1930, *Ceratocystis ulmi* was rampant throughout the eastern states, reaching as far north as Quebec. A deadly disease with no known cure, carried by the tiny elm bark beetle, the fungus claimed 100 million American Elms by midcentury.

First identified in France in 1918, the fungus had quickly spread to trees in Holland, Belgium and Germany, reaching England by 1927. Initially thought to be the result of gunpowder fumes from World War I, the blight was ultimately identified by Dutch botanists as a pathogenic fungus. Transmitted when the beetles bore holes into an elm's trunk to lay their eggs, the fungus spreads rapidly via the tree's sap, which carries nutrients along transport vessels throughout the trunk and branches. To protect itself, the tree seals off the infected vessels; but by thus stopping the spread of the fungus, the elm also seals off its flow of nutrition and starves to death.[57]

Worcester started tracking the fungus soon after its arrival in the United States. In 1934, Holland noted that although the disease had spread to Ohio, New Jersey, New York, Connecticut and Maryland, it had not yet attacked any trees locally. The next year, Adams wrote in his forestry report that one or two cases had been identified in eastern Connecticut, but that Worcester's elms were still healthy. "There is nothing we can do but keep a lookout and seek expert advice to check the disease if necessary," he added.[58]

And so the deathwatch continued. By 1941, the relentless enemy had invaded Massachusetts, claiming at least 200 elms in 37 cities and towns, mostly in the western part of the state, over the next five years. It reached Quincy, near Boston, by 1946—"altogether too close for comfort," Adams wrote in his annual report, adding he "would not be surprised if it were found in Worcester at any time." The inevitable happened in 1951, when the city's first infected elm was discovered. Two years later, as Worcester watched, helpless, while its graceful elms died, Adams recorded the grim statistics: 37 elms lost so far in Worcester, 23,396 elms lost in 306 communities statewide.[59]

It was a crushing blow after a half-century of struggle to keep the city green. There would be no WPA to help with this emergency, no army of war heroes who could vanquish the enemy. There was only the hope that new trees would grow where old trees had fallen, and that the inevitable loss of thousands of elms would teach a lesson known by those who first planted them—of the inestimable value of urban trees.

[1] *Worcester Evening Gazette,* Sept. 21, 22, 1938.
[2] *Worcester Telegram,* Sept. 23, 24, 1938.
[3] *Evening Gazette,* Sept. 22, 1938.
[4] *Annual Report of the Board of Parks Commissioners of the City of Worcester, MA,* 1921, 1938. Note: The 50,000 tree census figure is from 1921.
[5] *Parks Reports,* 1911–12, 1921, 1923, 1924, 1934.
[6] *Parks Report,* 1920.
[7] Charles Nutt, *History of Worcester and Its People,* Vol. 3, p. 81.
[8] Rudy J. Favretti, *A History of Elm Park, Worcester, Mass.,* Olmsted Historic Preservation Project, Commonwealth of Massachusetts, Department of Environmental Management, 1985, p. 26.
[9] Charles W. Estus, Sr., and John F. McClymer, *gå till Amerika: The Swedish Creation of an Ethnic Identity for Worcester, Massachusetts* (Worcester, Mass.: Worcester Historical Museum, 1994), pp. 91–92; Norman T. Newton, *Design on the Land: The Development of Landscape Architecture* (Cambridge, Mass.: Harvard University Press, 1971), p. 475.
[10] *Parks Reports,* 1929–40.
[11] *Worcester Telegram,* Sept. 21, 24, 1938.
[12] *A City Plan for Worcester, Massachusetts,* 1924; Edwin Theodore Weiss, Jr., *Patterns and Processes of High Value Residential Districts: The Case of Worcester, 1713–1970,* PhD dissertation, Clark University, 1973, p. 193.
[13] *City Plan,* p. 19.
[14] Ibid., pp. 20–22.
[15] Martin R. Healy and Robert W. Mack, *Massachusetts Zoning Manual,* Vol. I (Boston: Massachusetts Continuing Legal Education, Inc., 1995), pp. 1–2.
[16] *Zoning Manual,* pp. 1.2–1.3; Peter Wolf, *Land in America: Its Value, Use and Control* (New York: Pantheon Books, 1981), pp. 86–87.
[17] *City Plan,* p. 10; "Manual for the City Council of the City of Worcester, Massachusetts, 1996–1997." Despite the optimistic projections of the early 1920s, Worcester's population in 1975 was actually about 7,000 less than in 1924—172,342 versus 179,754 in the year the plan was published.
[18] Newton, pp. 447–49.
[19] David Schuyler, *The New Urban Landscape: The Redefinition of City Form in Nineteenth-Century America* (Baltimore: The Johns Hopkins University Press, 1986), p. 150.
[20] Schuyler, pp. 150–52.
[21] Schuyler, pp. 154–56.
[22] Schuyler, pp. 157–59.
[23] Schuyler, pp. 162–65.
[24] Schuyler, p. 165; Philip Langdon, *A Better Place to Live: Reshaping the American Suburb* (Amherst: University of Massachusetts Press, 1994), p. 39.

[25] Newton, pp. 474–78.

[26] Newton, p. 479; *Worcester Magazine*, Vol. 17, Apr. 1914, pp. 92–96.

[27] The discussion of Norton Co. and Indian Hill draws from Estus and McClymer, pp. 66–96.

[28] Estus and McClymer, pp. 92–93.

[29] Weiss, p. 193.

[30] Ibid.

[31] *Polk's Worcester House Directory* (R. L. Polk & Co.), 1935, 1936, 1940, 1942. Although the vast majority of names listed for Westwood Drive during the mid-1930s and early 1940s are of Yankee origin, two Irish names appear: Joseph W. O'Connor at 3 Westwood in 1935, and Edward F. O'Brien at 20 Westwood in 1940.

[32] The discussion of the fall and rise of Worcester's Yankee-Irish coalition follows Estus and McClymer, pp. 104–119.

[33] Estus and McClymer, pp. 122–141.

[34] *Parks Reports*, 1917–29. Though appropriations remained in the $50,000 range for the first two years of the Holmes administration, in 1919, funding increased 125%, from $55,000 to $123,827. The next year, Sullivan's first term, funding dropped to $96,500 and then climbed by roughly $20,000 for each of the next two years. Part of the increase can be attributed to cleanup funding for the 1921 ice storm. Major increases did not take hold until O'Hara's fourth term, in 1927, when appropriations jumped from $152,000 the prior year to $201,000. For the next three years, parks appropriations topped the $200,000 mark, until the Depression took hold in the early 1930s.

[35] *Parks Report*, 1921.

[36] *Parks Reports*, 1922–25, 1928.

[37] Sandra L. Anagnostakis, "Chestnuts and the Blight," *Massachusetts Wildlife,* Fall 1989, pp. 30–35; Charles R. Burnham, "The Restoration of the American Chestnut," *American Scientist,* Sept./Oct. 1988, Vol. 76, pp. 478–87; Joseph R. Newhouse, "Chestnut Blight," *Scientific American,* July 1990, pp. 106–111; Rebecca Rupp, *Red Oaks & Black Birches: The Science and Lore of Trees* (Pownal, Vt.: Garden Way Publishing, 1990); Walter Sullivan, "New Techniques Revive Hopes for Blighted American Chestnut," *New York Times,* Nov. 15, 1988.

[38] *Parks Reports*, 1912–14.

[39] *Parks Reports*, 1913–14, 1921, 1923.

[40] *Parks Report*, 1914.

[41] *Parks Reports*, 1911–12, 1914, 1920, 1925.

[42] Roy Rosenzweig, *Eight Hours for What We Will: Workers and Leisure in an Industrial City 1870–1920,* (Cambridge [Cambridgeshire]; New York: Cambridge University Press, 1983), pp. 142–43.

[43] *Parks Report*, 1917.

[44] *Parks & Recreation Commission Report,* 1917. (Parks Commission changed to Parks & Recreation in 1917.)

[45] Ibid.; *Parks Report*, 1928.

[46] *Parks Reports*, 1926–27.

[47] Nutt, Vol. 3, pp. 80–81; *Worcester Evening Gazette,* June 14, 1940.

[48] Ibid.; *Parks Report*, 1922.

[49] *Parks Reports*, 1917, 1932.

[50] *Parks Reports*, 1929–32.

[51] *Parks Reports*, 1933–37.

[52] *Parks Report*, 1937.

[53] *Parks Report*, 1938.

[54] Margaret Parsons, "The Fate or Fortune of Some Famous Trees That Grew Up with Our History," *Sunday Telegram*, Oct. 23, 1938, (Collection of Worcester Historical Museum).

[55] *Parks Reports*, 1939–40.

[56] *Parks Reports*, 1940–44.

[57] Rupp, pp. 153–56; Hugh Johnson, *The International Book of Trees* (New York: Simon & Schuster, 1977), pp. 136–39; Elbert L. Little, *The Audubon Society Field Guide to North American Trees, Eastern Region* (New York: Alfred A. Knopf, 1980), p. 419.

[58] *Parks Report*, 1934.

[59] *Parks Reports*, 1941, 1946, 1951, 1953.

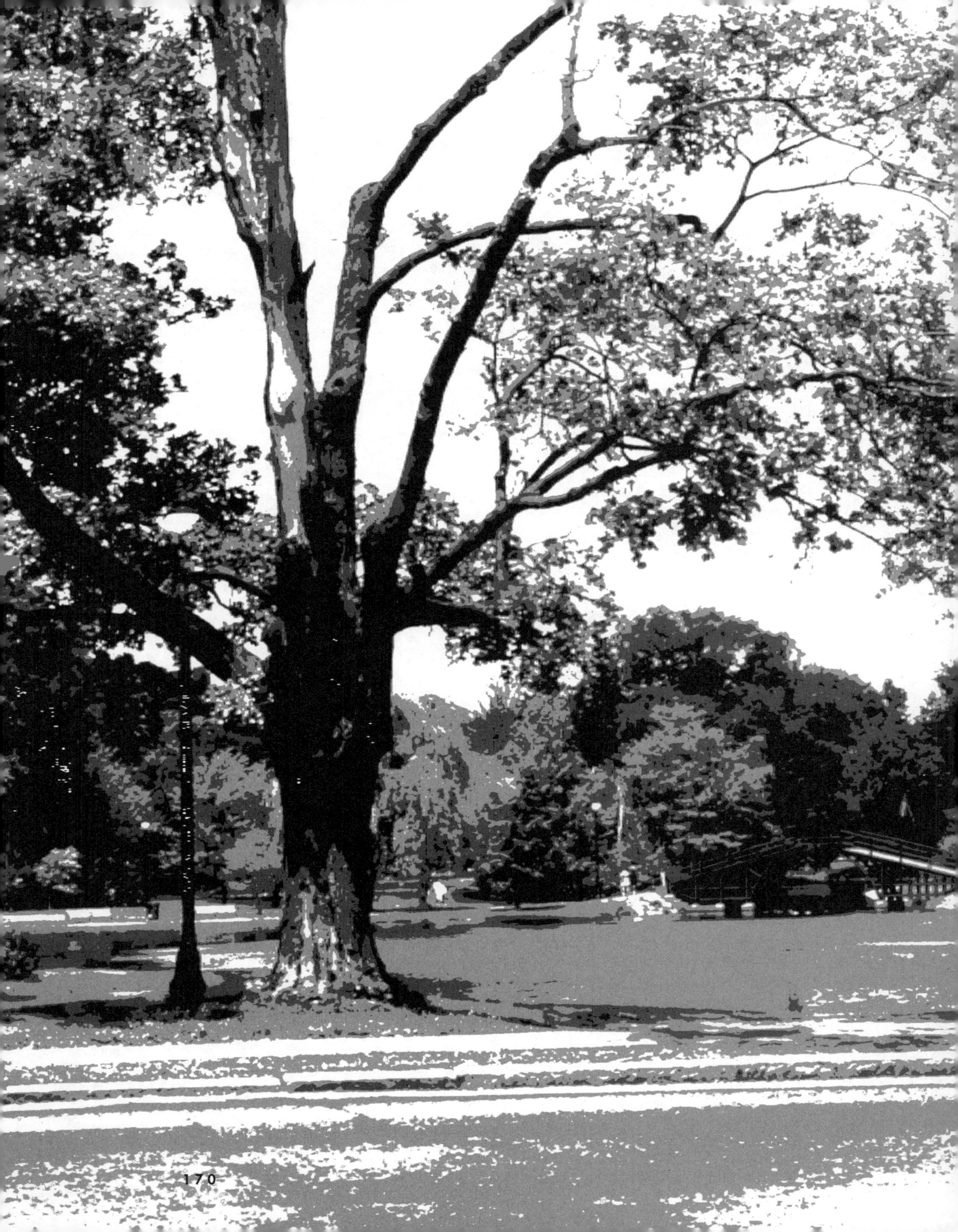

A LEGACY SQUANDERED
Chapter Seven

After a hard winter, spring can never come too soon to Worcester. All too often, it arrives late. It is the second week of May 1997, and the maples are just beginning to unfurl their tender leaves. Pale green foliage stipples brown hillsides, and along city streets, the Schwedler Norway maples and copper beeches add splashes of maroon and amber to the chartreuse of new growth. Following weeks of chill winds and gray skies, the mercury has finally hit 70 and the dogwoods are opening their cream and rose bracts to the sun's rays. Crabapples swell with magenta blossoms, and forsythias wave golden arms in the breeze, beckoning the office-bound to escape, if only for an hour.

In Green Hill Park this blissful day, a jogger trots down pock-marked Skyline Drive, and a young couple lolls in the grass with their puppy. Nearby, two women slap a racquetball against the back wall of an aging cinderblock court. Painted in mismatched layers of green, evidence of attempts to cover last year's graffiti, the court stands at the foot of a small bluff overlooking a lake—the former site of the Green family estate. The old, rambling mansion has long since been replaced by a drab green-and-brick municipal building, headquarters for the Department of Parks, Recreation and Cemeteries. The estate's magnificent, banana-shaped flower beds are long gone, as well; in their stead are a few stingy rows of daffodils and red tulips.

A few yards up the bumpy, winding drive, several adults stretch out on the grass near the lake, while farther up the hill, children shout and laugh as they slip down curly slides on a huge steel jungle gym. On the lake's far side, golfers steer white carts across the front nine of the municipal course—a rolling expanse of emerald grass and manicured trees, with one of the city's best views. The shoreline is litter-free today, thanks to a citywide Earth Day cleanup just two weeks before. But it won't be long before the park returns to its familiar state of disregard. Already scattered on the grass are a crushed pack of Marlboros and an empty box of Wolf-Pack caps, a plastic juice bottle and, near the edge of the jungle gym, several ashtrays worth of cigarette butts, left, no doubt, by parents and baby-sitters supervising their children's play.

Detritus of spring's promise, the litter hints of more insidious problems in the park. A short walk up the road, across from the barnyard petting zoo, orange-and-white metal signs on a chain-link fence warn of stiff fines for those who would toss their garbage here. This is the city's mulching operation, a place where residents can bring yard wastes to create mounds of rich compost for municipal plantings and home gardens. But the warnings do little to scare away would-be offenders from the remote wooded site. Around the perimeter of long rows of black-brown humus is fresh evidence of illegal dumping. Down one embankment, someone has tossed a closetful of old clothes. Nearby are the rusted frame of a broken kitchen chair, a mangled ironing board, and behind a rock, the crushed remains of a vacuum cleaner. Just past a fragrant mound of rotting Christmas trees, a red plastic toy gun perches on a sapling's branch.

And there is more garbage in Green Hill. Beyond the mulching site, around the hairpin turn, just past the Air National Guard headquarters, two soccer fields with rusting goalposts stand on a short, uneven plateau overlooking Worcester's surrounding hills and Mt. Wachusett. The plateau is not a natural landform, but the top of an old municipal landfill that fills a rock quarry. After years of controversy, the landfill was capped. But the cap was not done properly, and now glass is working its way to the surface of the fill—a phenomenon that reportedly necessitates glass patrols to remove shards that could injure young soccer players.

It has been a long time since Worcester's children flocked to Green Hill. But three years later, on a brisk Sunday afternoon in February 2000, families are here, sliding down the snowy hill near the Memorial Grove on everything from plastic sleds to inflatable mattresses, catching just one more ride before the rose and lavender sunset fades to dusk. The roads are neatly plowed, smooth and comfortable to drive, thanks to a new asphalt surface. The mulching site is gone, replaced by a primary-colored playscape—empty on this chilly afternoon but surrounded by the imprints of hundreds of small boots. The old steel jungle gym, with its long winding slides, is gone; in its place are dozens of young trees, anchored against the wind with tension wires and stakes. Farther down the hill, the newly renovated perfectory, an open fieldstone shelter, sports a red-tiled, pagoda-like roof. Another, smaller shelter is located closer to the pond, and along the shoreline are several wooden railed decks—overlooks for feeding the ducks or just contemplating the water. On lightpoles, dark green banners celebrate the changes: "Green Hill Park Renaissance, 1905–1999."

The $2 million transformation of Green Hill Park, whose natural beauty and spectacular vistas inspired Andrew Haswell Green to invest so much energy in New York's Central Park, represents an important shift in public priorities—both by city officials and citizens' groups—to begin to address the problems created by decades of benign neglect of Worcester's urban forest and public parks. Until the debate over appropriate land use in Green Hill gained media attention in the mid-1990s, the now 500-acre park had become Worcester's backyard—a place to build a compost heap and toss junk where the neighbors couldn't see. Budget cuts worked against the park; its vastness and remote location made it expensive to maintain and easy to ignore. In truth, until the recent improvements, the only part of Green Hill that didn't look worn out was the golf course, which is supported by greens fees and other revenue not tied to property taxes. The course commands nearly a third of the park, but until 1996 it was enjoyed by relatively few city residents. Leagues and restricted tee times had effectively limited play to a select group of golfers who viewed the municipal course as their private club.

Problems with golf course access, the improperly capped landfill and the mulching operation

CANADIAN HEMLOCK
Tsuga canadensis

A shade-loving evergreen with lacy, drooping branches, the Canada or Eastern hemlock is a popular ornamental that may soon go the way of the American elm. Under attack by the hemlock woolly adelgid, *Adelges tsugae,* thousands of acres of hemlocks throughout the Northeast are now coated with cottony white tufts, the woolly coats of the tiny migrating insects that feast on their sap and eventually suck the trees dry.

First reported in British Columbia in the 1920s, the parasites spread across North America during the first half of the 20th century, arriving on the East Coast in Virginia by the mid 1950s. Aided by Hurricane Gloria in 1985, the adelgid infestation swept north to Connecticut and has since reached Rhode Island and Massachusetts. Originating in Japan, the insect has no natural predators on this continent, and thus proliferates unchecked.

Damage is done by nymphs that produce the waxy white tufts, and brownish-red, oval adults, about 0.8 millimeters long. Adults lay eggs in late winter; about half the eggs develop into winged insects that migrate to the next hemlock, while the others, wingless, remain behind on the host tree. Uncontrolled by insecticides, the nymphs and adults can kill a hemlock in one year.

Applying horticultural oils to an entire hemlock smothers the adelgids and can save the tree; fertilizing, on the other hand, will only exacerbate the infestation, providing an even greater feast for the woolly parasites. In blighted hemlock groves, the only solution may be cutting down and removing infested trees. Such was the case in April 2000, when 50 acres of blighted, 60-year-old hemlocks were felled in Clinton, Massachusetts, around the Wachusett Reservoir, near the Clinton Dam. The infestation was more severe than in a natural forest, where hemlocks are only one component of the ecosystem; around the reservoir, however, the large grove had been planted in the 1940s to landscape the dam's banks—providing an ideal setting for the adelgids to spread from hemlock to hemlock.

When healthy, Canada hemlocks are tall, conical trees that grow to 70 feet, with trunks up to three feet in diameter. Two rows of short, flat needles grow on either side of flexible leaf-stalks. Dark green above, the needles are distinguished by two narrow white stripes on their undersides; small, brown, rounded cones with soft wings droop from branch tips. The bark of the Canada hemlock is a cinnamon brown, with deep, thick furrows and scales—once an important source of tannin for the commercial production of leather. For pioneers, the leafy twigs, boiled in water, made a fine tea. Along with its cousin, the Carolina hemlock *(Tsuga caroliniana)*, the Canada hemlock makes a beautiful ornamental shade tree as well as an effective hedge.

prompted the Massachusetts Department of Environmental Management in 1996 to withhold a $500,000 grant to the city for park improvements until those issues were appropriately addressed. The state's action, tipped off by a group of concerned park neighbors, resulted in months of debate over a park master plan, the first for Green Hill since 1979. Among the more controversial recommendations was a proposal to remove eight acres of trees and create a driving range for the golf course—a proposal that was endorsed by the city's Parks and Recreation Commission over the objections of a multi-interest, 34-member citizen's advisory committee.

Persistent pressure by the Green Hill Park Coalition—a citizens' advocacy group that formed in response to the controversy—succeeded in swaying the Worcester City Council to overturn plans for the driving range as well as another proposal to use the former landfill-cum-soccer fields as a disposal site for street sweepings over a period of 16 years, ultimately to be capped by state-of-the-art athletic fields. That vote reopened the planning process, resulting in a master plan that, among other things, called for the removal of the mulching operation, rerouting park traffic and returning Green Hill to recreational use. To fund the proposal, a $1 million state grant for park improvements was matched by a $1 million bond issue that the city is repaying from golf course revenues over the next decade.

But other land-use controversies persist: in particular, the Green Hill Park Coalition and the city have locked horns over a proposal to construct a new home for the Worcester Vocational High School behind the former Belmont Home on 19 acres of park woodland. The legal debate centers on potential destruction of wetlands, but the underlying conflict involves appropriate use of city parkland. As has been the city's history since the colonial Common was gradually diminished to meet other civic and commercial priorities, so the fight over the school's location is just the latest chapter in a clash of values regarding the importance of maintaining urban green space.

Budget Cuts and Benign Neglect—The Decline of Worcester's Urban Forest
The fight that erupted in 1996 over the future of Green Hill Park and continues today goes to the heart of Worcester's struggle to define the value of its sylvan legacy: nearly a century after the philanthropic champions of city trees and parks passed from the political arena, concerned citizens must organize to ensure that Worcester preserves its urban greenery. Without focused public pressure to redefine civic priorities, Worcester's once magnificent trees and municipal park system will continue to languish from budget cuts, benign neglect and abuse. In this era of civic retrenchment, when any use of tax dollars is suspect, maintaining municipal trees and parks takes last place on a priority list of urgent needs, topped by police and fire protection.

In fact, since Massachusetts passed Proposition 2 1/2 in 1980, a property tax cap referendum fueled by a nationwide tax revolt that began in California in the late 1970s, Worcester has had no local revenues to plant new trees. Garnering state grants and private donations, the city managed to plant 1,200 trees between 1981 and 1997; during the same 16 years, however, the city had to

©Robert Nash

remove some 5,000 dead and dying trees, for a net loss of 3,800. In other words, for almost a generation, Worcester has been able to plant only one tree for every four removed.[1]

Those losses follow three decades of fighting a losing battle against Dutch Elm disease, which claimed thousands of Worcester's elms, beginning in the early 1950s. When added to the cumulative cost of the century's earlier natural and economic disasters, the price of that epidemic and subsequent revenue-driven decisions to cut plantings has been to shrink the city's street tree population by at least half. As recently as 1987, boilerplate language in annual Parks and Recreation Department reports claimed a street tree census of 36,000; but a citywide inventory published the following year revealed that the census had actually dropped to just over 20,000. A decade later, a state-funded pilot program to update that survey has uncovered more significant losses in one inner-city neighborhood, with many trees in poor health and two streets, formerly lined by nearly a dozen trees each, today nearly barren. Although the update is limited in scope, based on those findings and dismal planting ratios—one tree planted for every ten removed in 1994, one for every five in 1995—probably about 17,000 street trees are left in Worcester. Of those, the city's chief forester estimates that nearly a third are dead, damaged or diseased.[2]

The figures are sobering. And for anyone who looks up while walking or driving along city streets, the evidence is blatant. Lopsided crowns, barren branches, gashed trunks—these are the hallmarks of Worcester's public trees. Crisis management is the norm for the overwhelmed forestry crew; only those trees that present the greatest danger to public safety are trimmed or removed. A few hundred trees are planted annually with grant funds, yet their maintenance is a matter of chance and their life span is short. Public parks are tended to the extent they are used, while more remote sites go to seed. Some of the smallest parks, like Dodge Park on the city's north side, have been so neglected, they have become barely recognizable. In the case of Dodge Park and a few others, such as Green Hill, Elm Park and Stephen Salisbury's Bancroft Tower, neighborhood groups have begun advocating for improvements and preservation. But these are the exceptions. Without a vociferous advocate like an Edward Winslow Lincoln, Worcester's public trees and parks remain the city's stepchildren.

Across the country, public trees in many communities fare no better. A 1991 survey of urban tree care programs in 20 major American cities by the national conservation group American Forests revealed that nearly three-fourths of those communities had cut back funding for street trees, despite the fact that they had collectively planted only about one tree for every four needed just to maintain their current tree census. Eighty percent of the cities surveyed had a backlog of dead trees for removal, and all were facing damage claims due to fallen trees or branches. In addition, 75 percent of the cities reported they were unable to do routine surveys of their street trees to identify trouble spots and do preventive maintenance. Like Worcester, most of the cities were reduced to crisis management, responding only to emergencies and the most pressing problems.[3]

©*Robert Nash*

That trend in urban tree care was further documented in a 1994 survey of communities of all sizes throughout the United States, conducted by the Davey Resource Group of Kent, Ohio. According to the study, when dollars are adjusted for inflation, the average municipal tree management budget dropped from $4.14 per capita in 1986 to $2.49 per capita in 1994—a 40 percent decline. Nonetheless, the study found that only a few communities have invested in public education programs or outreach to public or private groups in order to create the local support needed for better tree care. The authors also note, "though many municipalities are aware of the importance of a systematic maintenance program, the greatest percentage of tree management activities are performed on an as-needed basis"—this despite the documented fact that it costs more in the long run to care for trees on an emergency basis than it does to maintain a healthy forest that minimizes the number of ailing, hazardous trees.[4]

It costs even more to lose trees. In Worcester alone, the 1988 inventory priced the appraised value of the city's street trees at $42 million, with an average replacement value per tree of just over $2,000. In other words, the net loss of 3,800 street trees since Proposition 2 1/2 represents a sacrifice of $7.6 million in city property. For every 100 trees that the city removes each year—a figure that ranges from 150 to 300 trees—Worcester loses $200,000 of its sylvan inventory. Since the replacement trees are young, it will be several generations before their value equals that of the mature trees being removed, assuming they live as long. And given that most of the dying trees are centenarians, and that downtown street trees planted today live an average of only 13 years, this second-growth urban forest is unlikely to ever equal in value or stature that which has been lost.[5]

The loss of street trees represents the forfeiture of secondary financial benefits, as well, including energy savings to homeowners and businesses. According to American Forests, the urban tree cover nationwide saves about $4 billion in energy costs each year—a figure that could double with a careful planting strategy. Advocates also argue that city trees raise property values—and thus provide more tax revenue for the very services that take precedence in city budgets: police and fire protection. To bolster such arguments, there is now computer software to help communities price the costs and benefits of changing their sylvan landscape. Such are the modern weapons needed to protect public trees. Arguments for aesthetics and quality of life ring hollow in city halls; the fight to save urban forests is won or lost on the bottom line.[6]

A Call to Action—The Global Fight to Save Forests

Ironically, but perhaps not coincidentally, the decline in urban forestry programs has paralleled a growing awareness of the need to conserve trees in the wild. With ozone depletion and global warming now household phrases, children learn from the time they begin watching *Sesame Street* that saving trees is good and destroying forests is bad. By the time they get to high school, they learn the science behind those values: when trees are burned to clear land for agriculture or development, they release carbon into the atmosphere. The carbon is converted into carbon dioxide, the gas that traps solar radiation and warms the earth. A rapid increase in global deforestation in the past 50 years, combined with the exponential acceleration of fossil fuel consumption and methane gas production, have raised the amount of carbon dioxide in the earth's atmosphere by about 25 to 30 percent above levels that have prevailed for the past 160,000 years; if current consumption patterns persist, that percentage will probably double in the 21st century.[7]

Significantly increasing the volume of carbon dioxide in the atmosphere (as well as the amount of heat-trapping, ozone-depleting chlorofluorocarbons) means raising the globe's average temperature by several degrees, a phenomenon that would alter weather patterns, seacoasts and seasons. Predictions are dire: flooding along the coast, drought in continental interiors, infestations of migrating insects that spread disease. Extreme global weather patterns in the early 1980s provided a taste of the future, with severe drought, crop losses and spontaneous brush fires in Africa and Oceania. Though some of the extreme weather was attributable to El Niño—a cyclical phenomenon that disrupts global climate—recent computer models of global temperatures indicate that there has been a definable upward trend in the globe's average temperature over the past century. Responding to such findings, the 2,000 scientists and policy makers who comprise the United Nation's Intergovernmental Panel on Climate Change have sounded a clear warning that people are responsible for heating up the planet.[8]

Despite mounting evidence that something is fundamentally wrong, however, governments have been slow to respond. Nine years after the hopeful proclamations of the 1992 UN Earth Summit in Rio de Janeiro, the World Watch Institute reports that "global environmental trends have reached a dangerous crossroads as the new century begins."[9] At a time when global climate talks have come to an impasse, there is evidence that the Artic ice cap has thinned by 42 percent and 27 percent of the world's coral reefs have disappeared—danger signs that key ecological systems are severely compromised.

The globe's forests are at greater risk than at any previous time in history. Victims of rapacious consumption and waste, tropical rainforests in Africa, Asia and Latin America are destroyed at a rate of 100 acres a minute. Economic demand for development, crop land, timber and cattle pasture have reduced these valuable ecosystems from 14 percent to less than 7 percent of the earth's cover—experts predict that if current trends continue, rainforests could all but disappear in the next 25 to 50 years. Acid rain, too, is ravaging the world's forests. From the red spruce of Vermont to the forests of industrialized Central Europe, damage linked to chemical fallout from fossil fuel plants has been widely observed and reported. In the former West Germany, one of the hardest hit nations, over half the forests in 1988 were ailing from what scientists believed was a combination of air pollution and acid rain, a more than fivefold increase in just five years.[10]

Describing the exponential rate of global deforestation, the World Watch Institute's Alan Thein Durning envisions a time-lapse film of the earth viewed from outer space. The film opens

Dinosaur National Monument in Utah and Colorado, focus of a political controversy that led to passage of the federal Wilderness Act in 1964
Courtesy, www.americansouthwest.net

with a blue-green ball suspended in darkness, a third of its surface covered by forests. For the next nine minutes, the equivalent of 9,000 years, that image barely changes. During the last minute, the recent millennium, scattered patches of green are thinned and erased around the globe, but the ball is still green. Then, Durning writes, in the final three seconds of the metaphorical film, since 1950, "the change accelerates explosively. Vast tracts of forest vanish from Japan, the Philippines, and the mainland of Southeast Asia, from most of Central America and the horn of Africa, from western North America and eastern South America, from the Indian subcontinent and sub-Saharan Africa. Fires rage in the Amazon Basin where they never did before. Central Europe's forests die, poisoned by the air and the rain. Southeast Asia looks like a dog with the mange. Malaysian Borneo is scalped. In the final fractions of a second, the clearing spreads to Siberia and the Canadian north. Forests disappear so suddenly from so many places that it looks like a plague of locusts has descended on the planet."[11]

Rainforests and Old Growth Stands—Wilderness Preservation in the United States

Alarmed by the rate of global deforestation, conservation groups that first mobilized more than a century ago in response to deforestation here in the United States are now focused on saving wilderness, especially endangered forests. Highly publicized efforts to preserve old growth stands in Washington's Olympic Peninsula have pitted environmentalists against loggers, timber companies

A LEGACY SQUANDERED

and the U.S. Forest Service in a bitter fight to protect rare ecosystems and endangered species like the spotted owl. Success has been mixed; though swaths of ancient forest, with their mossy, giant spruce and cedars, have been spared, other areas have been stripped to stumps.[12]

The battle for the Olympic Peninsula is but one of the latest in a series of charged struggles to protect American wilderness during this century. Wilderness was first designated a national treasure in 1924, with the creation of New Mexico's Gila Wilderness Area in 1924, under the auspices of the U.S. Forest Service. But the momentum to preserve wild places faded after World War II, when the rich mineral deposits and natural resources contained in wilderness areas were deemed essential to postwar development. As pressure mounted to declassify wilderness, a major political fight ensued in 1950 over the fate of Dinosaur National Monument, located in Utah and Colorado. The six-year struggle to spare the monument by blocking plans to dam Colorado's Green River united all of the nation's major conservation groups for the first time, and ultimately resulted in the drafting and passage of the Wilderness Act of 1964. Other legislation followed, but for all their successes, conservation groups remained frustrated that they were unable to create a single government body that would oversee all national wilderness preserves—more than 90 million acres.[13]

Instead, government agencies that have managed national lands for over a century retain oversight, including the U.S. Forest Service and Bureau of Land Management. Both have come under fire in recent decades for kowtowing to commercial interests that would exploit timber and other natural resources located within or under public lands. In particular, critics claim that the Forest Service has bowed to pressure from private timber companies, permitting too much logging in national forests and selling the timber at a loss, well below market value. Underpricing the timber has created a false economy that fuels consumption. As a result, each week the nation loses about one square mile of ancient forest, mostly from the West Coast and Alaska.[14]

Fortunately, the news is not all grim. In September 1996, President Bill Clinton set aside 1.7 million acres of wilderness in Utah to create the Grand Staircase-Escalante National Monument—the largest area of protected public land in the lower 48 states. A rough-hewn labyrinth of canyons and cliffs that links the Grand Canyon to Bryce National Park, the monument includes some of the nation's most remote and pristine landscape. During the remainder of his second term, Clinton added 328,000 acres to federal forests in order to protect 34 groves of California sequoias. In a flurry of executive orders at the end of his presidency, Clinton created an additional 13 national monuments to protect environmentally sensitive land from gas and oil drilling. Whether those designations will be upheld by the new Bush administration is unclear. But Clinton left office with a conservation legacy that would have earned praise from Theodore Roosevelt.[15]

There is good news, too, in the East, where the nation's great Northeast Forest has made a comeback. What was mostly open farmland 150 years ago is wooded again—a transformation due in part to the westward migration of loggers who had depleted the ancient forests and farmers who sought richer, rock-free soil, and also due to the foresight of citizens and lawmakers who set aside protected tracts of forest at the century's turn. Today, upstate New York's Adirondack Park is a dense, mountainous forest that encompasses more land than the entire state of Vermont. Contiguous parcels of second-growth forest constitute a 26-million-acre wilderness stretching from the Adirondacks to Vermont's Northeast Kingdom, from New Hampshire's White Mountains to Maine's North Woods.[16]

The catch is that most of the land is privately owned, leaving it vulnerable to clear-cutting, which has riddled the Maine Woods, and development. The latter risk was made painfully clear in the 1980s when Diamond International Company, which owned about a million acres throughout the Northeast Forests, was sold to an international financier who chose to recoup part of his investment by selling off large parcels of timberland to developers. A startling departure from the way business had always been done in the region, where timber companies often bought out other timber companies but left the landscape intact, the transaction spurred a flurry of activity by conservationists and government officials to purchase tracts for preservation, and creation of an interstate task force to reevaluate historic land-use patterns. No easy solution has emerged. Ultimately, those who appreciate the forest for its haunting beauty and those who depend on it for their livelihood must work together toward a common goal of stewardship.[17]

Beyond Earth Day—The Struggle to Save City Trees

With media attention focused on such charged conflicts, the plight of urban trees has gone largely ignored. Although Earth Day and Arbor Day inspire an annual crop of tree-planting ceremonies, once the photo opportunities fade from memory, the new trees rarely get the attention they need to thrive. Urban parks are ailing too, suffering from intensive use, compacted soil, vandalism and inadequate maintenance. Despite admirable tree-planting campaigns, such as American Forest's Global ReLeaf program that has planted upwards of 15 million trees since its inception, public dollars are simply not there for long-term tree maintenance. In fact, according to the Davey Resource Group's study, the average municipal tree management budget amounts to just 0.31 percent of the total average municipal budget—less than a third of one cent of every dollar spent on city services.[18]

There are some notable exceptions. Among them, Milwaukee, Wisconsin, stands out for its model urban forestry program. A city of lush boulevards, Milwaukee employs a staff of 200 full-time workers to care for its 200,000 street trees. About 3,000 street trees are planted annually—one for each removed—using stock from the 160-acre municipal nursery. All trees are pruned on a three- or six-year cycle, depending on their size, to ensure continued health and strength. A $10 million budget funded by property tax revenues pays for it all. According to chief forester Preston Cole, the community made public trees a priority after Dutch Elm disease devastated the city. "During the '50s, we were removing 18,000 trees a year," says Cole. "People remember what Milwaukee looked like during that turmoil. We will not allow that to occur again."[19]

Most communities, however, lack such long-range perspective. At worst, public trees are planted just for show, expendable objects to spruce up downtown for a special occasion. That happened in Atlanta, where just a month after the 1996 Summer Olympics concluded, up to a fourth of the 3,000 elms, crape myrtles and willow oaks planted for the event were already dying from neglect—trees that had been planted to replace hundreds of mature trees felled to accommodate Olympics construction.[20]

It is an ironic but predictable reversal of 18th- and 19th-century sensibilities about trees. Wilderness, reviled when abundant, is now prized when scarce. And lush urban forests, once planted to heal the industrial wasteland, are now denigrated as expendable window dressing. Barring a major shift in municipal priorities, public trees that cleanse the air, moderate climate, control soil erosion and flooding, shelter wildlife, enhance property values and provide an oasis for body and spirit, will continue to fail until city streets and parks look more gray than green. At that point, perhaps, the public will begin to reevaluate spending priorities—when the cost of restoring the forest will be significantly higher and length of recovery several generations long. Once again, something precious must be lost before its true value is discovered.

Worcester's Urban Forest in Decline—The Ravages of Dutch Elm Disease

Veiled in late spring's leaves, Worcester's trees adeptly hide their wounds. Gouged bark and dead branches are cloaked by surrounding green, softening the truth. In this annual ritual of rebirth, ailments go unnoticed: all that matters is the long winter's end.

But even leaves couldn't cloak the appearance of Dutch Elm disease in 1951. Browning foliage, well before fall, was the giveaway that the fungus had arrived. Parks superintendent Herman Adams had been tracking the blight's grim progress across Massachusetts since it crossed the state border a decade earlier; now, with the discovery of the first dying elm, he began to meticulously record the city's losses—one in 1951, 14 in 1952, 22 in 1953.[21]

At least 3,000 elms probably existed in Worcester when the blight first struck—majestic trees whose fountain-like branches brushed the sky. From statewide data, Adams knew Worcester's elms were doomed; after the first few years, annual losses would double and triple until only the hardiest, most isolated elms remained. Perhaps because the end was inevitable, or perhaps because of a change in forestry personnel, Adams stopped recording elm deaths after 1953 and simply summarized the facts. For his 1955 Parks and Recreation Department report, he wrote only that staff from the University of Massachusetts Shade Tree Laboratory discovered a large number of infected elms.[22]

To curb the spread of the highly contagious fungus, the state required all diseased elms to be removed immediately and burned. The city forestry department also sprayed public elms two or three times a year with a combination of lead arsenate and DDT. Despite that chemical warfare, the disease continued to spread, in part, no doubt, because privately owned elms were not part of the city insecticide program and thus had a higher rate of infection. In 1960, forestry superintendent John Nugent reported that 2,641 public elms had been treated with the poisonous spray; five years later, the number had dropped to 1,785. The elms continued to die well into the 1970s, until only a smattering remained.[23]

Just three years after the disease was first detected, another natural disaster, more destructive than the Hurricane of '38, hit Worcester. On the muggy afternoon of June 9, 1953, a ferocious tornado dropped out of a roiling black cloud near the Quabbin Reservoir and hurtled southeast toward the city on a 42-mile, 84-minute course of utter destruction. Packing winds of up to 338 miles per hour, the mushroom-cloud-shaped funnel exploded homes, pulverized stores, scattered cars like playing cards and sucked out trees by the roots. It ripped the roof off of Norton Company's brand new machine tool division, crushed half of Assumption College and leveled its convent. When the storm finally lost force, 94 people throughout Central Massachusetts were dead, hundreds were injured and thousands were homeless; in Worcester alone, the twister had caused more than $37 million in property damage, including more than $285,000 in damage to the city water system, streets and trees. To help rebuild, the Parks and Recreation Department replanted 1,000 street trees that had been tossed and shredded by this, one of the most powerful tornadoes ever recorded in the United States.[24]

Spurred by tree losses from the tornado and Dutch Elm epidemic, the city began an aggressive planting program. To build up the Green Hill Park nursery, the forestry department set in thousands of maple whips and young maple trees. By the late 1950s and early 1960s, street tree plantings ranged from 400 to 600 trees annually; as a result, in 1960, the Parks and Recreation Department claimed an inventory of 39,000 public trees. Planting levels remained high through the end of the decade, as the forestry department set in 600 to 1,000 maples a year.[25]

Aftermath of the 1953 tornado: Toppled three-decker on Fales Street, Worcester, Massachusetts.

Aftermath of the 1953 tornado: Fires on Francis Street destroyed four homes when fire engines were blocked by downed trees.

Shifting Priorities—Public Funds Diverted from Tree Plantings

By the early 1970s, priorities had shifted again. Even as the city continued to condemn elms, plantings dropped off to between 200 and 300 trees annually—and in some years, significantly fewer. In 1977, the same year the federal government and commonwealth passed new laws restricting chemical spraying, Worcester condemned 248 trees and planted only six. The following year, as the Parks and Recreation Department geared up for a planning study of Green Hill Park's future, forestry staff were busy removing "dead and decayed trees" from the Green Hill Nursery, which would eventually be closed. Proposition 2 1/2, passed by statewide referendum in 1980, was the final nail in the coffin for Worcester's public trees. For the rest of the 1980s, tree condemnations averaged about 250 annually—with the notable exception of 1986, when Hurricane Gloria downed 600 trees—while privately funded plantings hovered around 10 or 15 a year.[26]

City parks fared no better under the department's new austerity budget. In 1982, the year after Proposition 2 1/2 went into effect, Parks and Recreation Commissioner Frederick Gay, Jr., wrote that the department had "made the most of what it had to work with. A reduced budget, with increased costs, created an almost impossible task. Some programs had to be reduced and in some cases eliminated. Emphasis was placed on those programs that would reach the most people and do the most good." Responding to the cuts, department staff began aggressively seeking and securing private, state and federal grant funds for park improvements and tree planting, including a $1 million Olmsted historic landscape preservation grant for improvements to tattered Elm Park. But local tax dollars remained scarce. In 1990, following another wave of budget cutting, the department was combined with the city-run Hope Cemetery, spreading the work of forestry staff even thinner.[27]

Department efforts to maintain and plant trees, despite the austerity budget, earned Worcester its first of many subsequent Tree City USA awards from the National Arbor Day Foundation in 1986, praising the city for its sylviculture. The following year, in an effort to beef up its lagging forestry program, the Parks and Recreation Department hired a consulting firm to inventory all of Worcester's street trees. The results, published in 1988, presented the harsh reality of decades of neglect and poor planning: the city had 20,227 street trees left—44 percent less than what had been assumed for the previous two decades. Equally as significant, the survey found that 90 percent of the city's street trees were maples: 68 percent were Norway maples; 16 percent, sugar maples; 4 percent, red maples; and 2 percent, silver maples. Despite the drastic loss of elms over three decades, the city had repeated the same horticultural mistake: planting a monoculture at risk for species-specific diseases and pests. That risk to the city's street trees is no longer hypothetical; in September 1996, the Asian long-horn beetle was detected in Brooklyn, New York—an imported parasite that destroys maples and other hardwoods, with no known predators.[28]

Despite ambitious plans in 1990 for a comprehensive, five-year urban street tree management program—including a stated goal of planting 1,050 trees annually throughout the decade—resources have continued to go elsewhere. Even a creative program to use grant funds to plant trees near clusters of small businesses in target neighborhoods has faltered: lack of communication between and within city departments resulted in the trees being planted without the forestry division's involvement or commitment to tend them, and agreements between the city and neighborhood business associations to maintain the trees have been only sporadically fulfilled.

With no one taking responsibility for their care, many of the hundreds of new trees planted since the beginning of the decade are showing signs of stress and neglect. Along heavily traveled Shrewsbury Street, there are gaps in the median strip of columnar crabapples where trees have been downed by careless drivers and never replaced. Outside mom-and-pop stores in Rice Square, Webster Square, along Main South and Green Street, young trees compete with weeds in iron grates. Some slim branches have been snapped by vandals; a few trunks grow askew. On a windy day, a handful of the slender trees will inevitably snag plastic bags and other airborne trash that no one will bother to remove from their crowns; the fluttering garbage will hang there for days and even weeks, until it disintegrates in the rain or is yanked free by another strong gust.[29]

Redrawing the Landscape—Urban Renewal and the 1980s Real Estate Boom

And so Worcester's urban forest continues to decline. More pressing issues have predominated since World War II: the loss of industry to regions with cheaper labor, migration to the suburbs and resulting shrinkage of the city's tax base and, most recently, out-of-state and international takeovers of business and industry. Far from the rosy predictions of untrammeled growth in the 1924 master plan, Worcester's population peaked in 1950 at just over 200,000, then began a long slide, bottoming out around 162,000 in 1980 before rising gradually to its present census of nearly 170,000. A city that once thrived on a diverse mix of locally owned large and small manufacturing concerns, Worcester has struggled to redefine itself in the past 20 years as a center for commerce, finance, health care and biotechnology, whose economy is no longer homegrown.[30]

It has been a long and painful metamorphosis for a city that does not weather change easily. In 1960, the same year the U.S. Census revealed the sobering news that—despite the baby boom—lost manufacturing jobs and suburban growth had forced an 8 percent drop in Worcester's population over the previous decade, researchers from MIT and Harvard's Joint Center for Urban Studies characterized Worcester as a cautious, conservative city with dated government procedures, sluggish urban renewal and commercial development lagging behind cities of comparable size. The report attributed that pervasive resistance to change to a Yankee elite who had maintained tight control of the prevailing social order.[31]

That upper strata of Yankee Brahmins had succeeded in making one notable change over a decade earlier—leading a successful reform campaign to replace the 41-member, weak-mayor/bicameral council system that dated back to 1848 with a nine-member council-manager form of government. Responding to criticisms that the older, unwieldy arrangement fostered unholy alliances between ward politicians and racketeers, the reformers pushed through the so-called Plan E charter revision by a wide margin on the 1947 ballot. But that dramatic rearrangement of Worcester politics did not foster comparable upheavals in municipal development. Rather, the city continued to stagnate.[32]

In a report to the Worcester Redevelopment Authority in 1965, a Chicago consulting firm bluntly described a city in decline: "The extent of physical blight and deterioration in Worcester is of serious proportions. Twenty-three neighborhoods, consisting of 4,525 acres and representing 30 percent of the built-up city, were found to be in need of active renewal assistance. These areas are in addition to the 650 areas in the three presently-committed [urban renewal] projects. In all, some 103,000 people or 55 percent of the city's population live in neighborhoods that qualify for urban renewal programs. Almost 45,000 people live in the 17,000 substandard dwelling units that are concentrated in these 26 neighborhoods. This is probably the most serious problem that is facing the citizens of Worcester in the immediate years ahead."[33]

With the arrival of the federal bulldozer, nondescript brick apartment complexes replaced aging three deckers. Downtown changed, too, as groundwork began on a new, enclosed shopping center across from the Common. For the Worcester Planning Department, the mid-1960s was a perfect time for rethinking the Central Business District's (CBD) design; offering a variety of suggestions in a slim critique of the CBD published in 1966, the planners advocated for European-style public squares and green spaces, narrow streets and "intimate crossroads," gardens, fountains—and trees. "Worcester can have tree-shaded avenues if we will take but the least bit of trouble," the authors chided. They also cautioned the city not to continue sacrificing public open space for municipal and private development: "Land has been taken from Elm Park for school purposes; land will soon be taken from Chandler Hill Park for a new school; old school property is being sold to private concerns; land is being taken at Burncoat Park and Green Hill Park for new highways. No one is disputing the need for new schools or new and better highways, but thought should be given to the ever-increasing problem of diminishing open space in the city. And open space is needed most desperately in the most densely built-up area—downtown."[34]

Those prescient warnings went unheeded for 20 years, until the city woke up in the middle of a major building boom. Struggling for years in Boston's shadow, Worcester in the 1980s was suddenly a desirable place to buy and develop property. Compared to Boston land prices, Worcester's land was a bargain—and only an hour's commute to the west. In addition, a tax revaluation during the 1970s had adjusted past inequities that had penalized new development, making land sales even more attractive. The resultant crush of land speculation and development came as something of a shock to a municipal government more accustomed to acquiring tax title property than issuing new building permits. As one *Sunday Telegram* reporter observed, with a dash of mixed metaphor, "Worcester's government has been about as well-equipped to deal with the recent development boom and its attendant rush of fancy, well-dressed and ardent suitors as a plain lonely bachelor who just inherited $100 million might be, which is not very well at all."[35]

Pressures of Growth—The Push for Conservation Lands

As Boston developers snapped up vacant factories and Victorian office buildings for investments, the housing market soared. By the end of 1984, over 30 new housing developments, accounting for 1,500 units, were either under construction or in various stages of the planning or approval process. Following a long-outdated zoning ordinance, construction permits were issued for every available lot of buildable land; and, as developers rushed to cash in on the development boom and buildable land grew scarce, some marginal sites on steeper grades were approved as well, despite the risks of soil erosion. Heady with all the attention and eager to shed its dowdy image, the city welcomed the onslaught—until mid-decade, when some concerned citizens began broadcasting the fact that Worcester's open space had shrunk from 50 percent of the city in the mid-1960s to less than 10 percent. In a stinging critique of the city's failure to control development, Dennis Ducsik of the Central Massachusetts Regional Environmental Council described the dramatic change in Worcester's landscape: "At certain locations on the West Side . . . a glance upward at the surrounding hills will reveal that what had always been a skyline of continuous forest is no longer an unbroken visual contour: in at least one place, walls of particleboard now can be seen where trees alone once stood."[36]

Ducsik warned that if the current rate of development continued, no open space would remain. This time, local officials heard. Among them was John Anderson, a member of the city council from 1976 to 1997, who served as mayor in 1986, the year after Ducsik sounded his alarm. One of Anderson's first actions as mayor was to create a land-use committee to review development issues; in a highly controversial move, he also recommended a moratorium on all new development, to give city officials a chance to assess the situation and update the master plan.

Sharing Ducsik's concern that the city was at risk of losing its green spaces, Anderson worked with the Regional Environmental Council and Massachusetts Audubon Society's Worcester office to persuade his fellow counselors that a yearlong moratorium on new large-scale residential and commercial development was critical in four key areas of the city. Over strident opposition by the local builder's association and the pro-development *Worcester Telegram* and *Evening Gazette* (both owned by the same publisher), the moratorium passed in the summer of 1986. The following year, the Worcester Conservation Commission published an open space update that targeted 17 undeveloped parcels for protection. Among them was a 350-plus acre parcel of unspoiled forest, field and wetlands known as Broad Meadow Brook, owned in various contiguous segments by the city, Catholic Charities, New England Power and a private family. Following several years of negotiations with owners for conservation restrictions and land acquisition, Broad Meadow Brook opened in 1990 as a 272-acre nature sanctuary managed by Massachusetts Audubon, the largest urban wildlife sanctuary in New England.[37]

Other key parcels have gained conservation status, as well, including the Cascade Green Belt, over 300 acres of woods on the northwest side, now owned jointly by the Worcester Parks and Recreation Department and the Greater Worcester Land Trust. In addition, since the late 1980s, the city has adopted a series of progressive conservation ordinances to protect wetlands, aquifers, and floodplains, as well as updated local zoning ordinances to protect environmentally sensitive lands.[38]

Challenge of the New Millennium—Preserving Worcester's Green Legacy

For all that progress, however, the city still has a long way to go in preserving the public landscape it has owned for well over a century—its parks and public trees. Citizen groups, such

©*Robert Nash*

as the Green Hill Park Coalition, have successfully raised awareness of their concerns over key public spaces, but the public at large has yet to identify trees and parks citywide as a civic priority. To some extent, this reflects a change in social values due to improved living standards. As more individuals have the means to invest in private landscaping and play spaces in their own backyards, the shared public recreation space has simply lost significance.

Adding to this general shift in social priorities here and elsewhere is Worcester's transition away from locally owned businesses. Bowing late to the pressures of a global economy, firms like Norton Company have been acquired by international or out-of-state corporations that have replaced paternalistic civic investment with a less beneficent concern for the bottom line. Insurance companies, banks, hospitals, health care providers, the local newspaper—all have been bought out in the past 20 years—weakening community links.

The result is a subtle but insidious withering of the city's landscape. A few summers after the downtown Worcester Center Galleria was transformed into the upscale Worcester Common Outlets amid much fanfare, weeds encroached on browning turf lawns and at least a fourth of the dozens of saplings planted for the grand opening were ailing. In Webster Square, on the city's southwest side, 125 trees donated by BASF Corporation in 1991 to mark its 125th anniversary have grown so large that the neighborhood business association that originally accepted the gift turned back the responsibility of tending them to the city. Even as Worcester has recently completed several major downtown development projects, including a new convention center and a hospital–health care complex, plans for landscaping and planting new trees have been scaled back, due to funding constraints—and indifference.[39]

Without a communal consensus that trees matter in this city and need tending to thrive, the view here will continue to brown around the edges until it fades into a bleak monotony of brick and granite and steel. Time remains to rescue the forest. But absent another major catastrophe that decimates trees, one that mobilizes public sentiment for planting and maintenance, as the elm blight did for Milwaukee, any hope of saving Worcester's urban forest rests in the hands of concerned individuals who value shared greenery as much as their own backyards—and can motivate others to do the same.

One such individual is Sheila Reid. A concert violinist who teaches violin and viola at the Performing Arts School of Worcester, Reid is a petite, dark-haired woman with an infectious smile and a gracious but insistent way of getting things accomplished—especially when it comes to planting trees. Appalled by the decline of so many aging maples that had once made her West-Side neighborhood so attractive when she moved there more than 30 years ago, Reid decided to take action. Joining the board of the Greater Hammond Heights Neighborhood Association to create a constituency for her cause, in 1994 she began hounding the city to remove the 15-inch stumps and dead trees that dotted the streets, vestiges of giant shade trees. Once that work was complete, she drove around the neighborhood to identify potential planting sites, then worked with the Parks and Recreation Department to determine which sites were viable. After contacting over 40 homeowners to enlist their cooperation, Reid secured grant funds from the Nathaniel Wheeler Trust, a local trust established for city beautification, and garnered the support of the Hammond Heights board and neighbors to subsidize the cost of trees for each homeowner. After three years and hundreds of hours of persistent effort, she achieved her goal: 43 new street trees.

The first of those trees to be planted, a sturdy ginkgo, stands in a newly dug pit in front of a gray stucco house at 10 Beechmont Street, its two-inch trunk wrapped in burlap and neatly staked on either side, a pile of fresh cedar chips on the grass nearby. Despite overcast skies, a small crowd is gathering by the tree on this May 19, 1997—businessmen in suits and bow ties, women in dresses and chinos, a baby in a blue pram. John Anderson, who lives down the street, arrives with his dog, Shamrock, as do another city councilor, the parks commissioner, and a bank officer for the Wheeler Trust. In the center of the group is Reid, elegantly dressed in a flowing violet and turquoise print jumpsuit, braided white jacket and gray pumps—this tree-planting ceremony marks the realization of her dream, and she does it with style. After an officer of the Hammond Heights group reads Joyce Kilmer's "Trees," Reid briefly recounts the work that went into this tree's arrival. "I hope this will be a prototype for the rest of the city, and that other neighborhood groups will contact us," she says earnestly. "I'll be glad to meet with them." Then, picking up a shovel, she throws some mulch onto the tree's roots.

The moment is marred only by the frightful demise of an old maple next to the young ginkgo; just hours earlier, the city forestry division had confused a work order for a tree removal elsewhere in the neighborhood and started sawing off limbs of the healthy tree. By the time they realized their mistake, they had carved the maple down to one main leader and a few branches. Its lopsided skeleton overlooks the ceremony, a grotesque reminder of all that has prompted Reid and her neighbors to take matters into their own hands.

Six weeks later, in the midst of a blistering summer heat wave, the gingko lifts its jade, fan-shaped leaves to the sun. Up and down the street, 15 other young trees stand neatly staked, their roots buried in mounds of fresh mulch. The savaged maple has been removed; all that remains is a pile of sawdust and wood chips. A long green garden hose snakes from the side of the gray stucco house, across the lawn, to the foot of the gingko. There the water seeps, gently, to its roots.

[1] *Parks & Recreation Reports, Worcester City Documents* 1980–92.

[2] Ibid.; *Worcester, MA Street Tree Management Plan, Executive Summary,* ACRT, Inc., 1988; Evelyn Herwitz, "Our Trees Are Dying," *Worcester Magazine,* Apr. 24, 1996; I am indebted to Colin Novick, formerly of the Central Massachusetts Regional Environmental Council, and Phil Rodbell, formerly of the Massachusetts Department of Environmental Management's Urban Forestry division, for sharing their unpublished data on Worcester's trees. The REC survey update covered an area of Main South bounded by Piedmont, Murray, Jaques, Wellington and Irving Streets.

[3] "The Sad State of City Trees," *American Forests,* Mar./Apr. 1992, pp. 61–64.

[4] Barbara A. Tschantz and Paul L. Sacamano, *Municipal Tree Management in the United States: A 1994 Report,* Davey Resource Group, 1994, pp. 2, 10–11.

[5] *Worcester Street Tree Management Plan,* p. 61.

[6]"Citygreen: Measuring urban ecosystem values," *Urban Forests*, Oct./Nov. 1994, p. 27; Herwitz, *Worcester Magazine*.

[7] Bill McKibben, *The End of Nature* (New York: Random House, 1989), pp. 3–46; Chris Bright, "Tracking the Ecology of Climate Change," *State of the World 1997: A World Watch Institute Report on Progress Toward a Sustainable Society*, Lester R. Brown, ed. (W. W. Norton & Co.: New York, 1997), pp. 78–94.

[8]Ibid.

[9]Christopher Flavin, "The Legacy of Rio," *State of the World 1997*, pp. 3—22; *State of the World 2001: A World Watch Institute Report on Progress Toward a Sustainable Society*, Lester R. Brown, ed. (New York: W. W. Norton & Co., 2001).

[10]Richard Admur, *Wilderness Preservation*, Earth at Risk Series (New York: Chelsea House Publishers , 1993), pp. 85–93; McKibben, pp. 35–37.

[11]Alan Thein Durning, "Redesigning the Forest Economy," *State of the World 1994*, p. 22.

[12]William Detroit, *The Final Forest: The Battle for the Last Great Trees of the Pacific Northwest* (New York: Simon & Schuster, 1992).

[13]Admur, pp. 73–83.

[14]Admur, pp. 48–62.

[15]"Utah park a seldom-seen treasure," *Worcester Telegram & Gazette*, Sept. 20, 1996; "Clinton Extends Protection for California's Sequoias," *Worcester Telegram and Gazette*, Apr. 1998; "Big Fight Likely for Bush Cabinet," *Boston Sunday Globe,* Jan. 14, 2001.

[16] Norman Boucher, "Whose Woods These Are," *Wilderness 25,* The Wilderness Society, Fall 1989, pp. 18–40; Bill McKibben, *Hope, Human and Wild: True Stories of Living Lightly on the Earth* (Boston: Little, Brown & Co., 1995), pp. 5–56.

[17]Ibid.; *Report Summary Northern Forest Land Study,* US Forest Service, May 1990; "Northeast Forests, Too, Get Congress's Interest," *New York Times*, Oct. 29, 1989.

[18]Sacamano, p. 12; Joseph M. Keyser, "Crisis in Our Urban and Historic Parks," *American Forests,* Mar./Apr. 1988, pp. 61–64.

[19]Herwitz, *Worcester Magazine*, Apr. 24, 1996.

[20]"Olympic trees already dying," *Boston Globe*, week of Aug. 12, 1996.

[21]*Worcester City Documents*, 1953.

[22]*City Documents*, 1954–79.

[23]Ibid.

[24]John M. O'Toole, *Tornado! 84 Minutes, 94 Lives* (Worcester: Databooks, 1993); "Tornado: A Record in Pictures of the Catastrophe That Struck Worcester and Central Massachusetts, June 9, 1953," *Worcester Telegram & Evening Gazette*, June 18, 1953; *City Documents*, 1953.

[25]*City Documents*, 1950–69.

[26]*City Documents,* 1970–89.

[27]*City Documents,* 1982–90.

[28]*Worcester Street Tree Management Plan*, 1988; "A beetle bores in Brooklyn," *Boston Globe,* Sept. 21, 1996.

[29]*City Documents*, 1990; Herwitz, *Worcester Magazine*.

[30]Worcester Planning Board, *Comprehensive Plan for Worcester, MA*, Aug. 1964; *City of Worcester Open Space and Recreation Plan*, Sept. 1994.

[31]Robert H. Binstock, "A Report on Politics in Worcester, Massachusetts," Joint Center for Urban Studies of MIT & Harvard (Cambridge, Mass., 1960), p. I-17

[32]Binstock, p. II-1.

[33]Worcester Redevelopment Authority, "A Community Renewal Program, Worcester, MA," Barton-Aschman Associates (Chicago, Ill.: May 1965).

[34]Worcester Planning Department, "Transition: A View of the Worcester Central Business District 1966," Nov. 1966.

[35]"Development Boom: Worcester Is Planning Ahead; Public Input Starts Tomorrow," *Sunday Telegram*, Oct. 26, 1986.

[36]Dennis W. Ducsik, 'Open Space Preservation in Worcester: A Tale of Neglect," REC White Paper, Mar. 2, 1985.

[37]Worcester Conservation Commission, *What's Left: An Update on Worcester's Open Space*, Aug. 1987; *Open Space Plan* 1994; *Sunday Telegram* editorial, Oct. 26, 1986.

[38]*Open Space Plan*, 1994.

[39]Herwitz, *Worcester Magazine*; "Where did all the trees go?" *Worcester Magazine*, Oct. 25, 1997.

EPILOGUE

On a wintry weekday morning in Green Hill Park, yet another layer of softly falling snow frosts Sky Line Drive with just enough white to cover the sandy grit that has accumulated since the roads were last cleared, a few days earlier. There is not much traffic in the park today, due to the snow, and only a few cars are parked in the lot outside the Massachusetts National Guard Armory, just up the road. In front of the low brick structure, a freshly painted green sign announces the building's new tenant—the Worcester Department of Parks, Recreation and Cemeteries.

The move from the Department's old offices in the dilapidated buildings on the former site of the Green family homestead was completed just a few weeks ago, with the official beginning of the new millennium in January 2001. Inside the Armory, recently renovated offices are clean and well-lit, a cheerful departure from the older, worn space, now scheduled for demolition. Staff members are still learning the ins and outs of their new home; as Parks Director Michael O'Brien leads a guest to a large meeting room, he takes a few minutes to locate the light switch.

Dressed in a plaid flannel shirt and brown corduroys, O'Brien is all business when it comes to discussing the status of Worcester's publicly owned trees. "My goal is to put Worcester on the map as a community that has turned itself around and reversed the pattern of neglect of city trees," he says earnestly. "I want us to become a leader in the Commonwealth, if not the nation, in caring for our urban forest."

No easy task, he admits. But he has taken some significant first steps in the right direction. With the support of environmental groups and private citizens, and the prompting of the four-year-old Urban Tree Task Force, a coalition of environmentalists spearheaded by the Worcester County Horticultural Society, O'Brien last year gained approval from the City Manager and Worcester City Council for increased funding for the Forestry Division. Modest staff increases and a reorganized line of command within the division have improved teamwork among tree climbers; in addition, the department added a fulltime urban forester to the Forestry Division in 1999. Now O'Brien's staff is preparing to purchase street tree management software that is compatible with the city's Geographic Information System, to enable mapping of all city-owned trees. The Department also has received approval for a nursery of 1,000 tree whips to be ready for planting on city streets in 2004. Another updated tree survey is in the works for Fall 2001, the first comprehensive inventory to be undertaken since 1988.

O'Brien suspects the findings will be grim—perhaps only 17,000 street trees left, many in fair to poor condition, the inevitable outcome of decades of underfunded tree planting and maintenance. This year alone, the Department has removed approximately 400 condemned trees. Working with community groups that commit to maintaining saplings, the Department intends to plant 120 new trees by the end of the fiscal year on June 30, 2001. It's a continuing pattern of net loss for the city's green canopy.

But O'Brien is determine to do better by partnering with as many community groups as are willing to take on the responsibility of tree stewardship. Striving to keep the issue before the public, he has engineered a series of public relations events over the past year, including the naming of a massive, century-old red oak in Elm Park as a Heritage Tree, earning a State special maintenance grant. The Department also teamed with Elm Park neighbors to plant 30 young trees last May and is working with at least two other neighborhood groups on similar projects for this spring. In addition, a team of students from Worcester Polytechnic Institute is helping the Department develop a comprehensive manual for neighborhood groups interested in tree stewardship projects, due out Arbor Day 2001.

To encourage more community partnerships, O'Brien has identified funds within the Department's budget to cover the cost of up to 300 new trees—a departure from past years when the only way to get money for tree planting was through grants. He senses a shift in public priorities; not only are more community groups expressing an interest in tree planting but attitudes are changing within the city government, as well. The next step, says O'Brien, is to get the public schools involved.

But no significant shift in public priorities will take place without strong grassroots support and help from the business community and developers. And that takes vision. "We need to understand what this means to the next generation," says O'Brien. "Worcester was so progressive. Imagine where we'd be if that momentum had continued. If I'm lucky, I may see the fruits of my labors when I retire."

◆ ◆ ◆

Four years have passed since I completed the original manuscript for *Trees at Risk*. In that interim, there have been encouraging signs of shifting public priorities. The formation of the Urban Tree Task Force, the hiring of the city's first urban forester, neighborhood groups' growing interest in street trees, and the Parks Department's renewed efforts to address the needs of city trees—all give reason to hope that Worcester may well rescue its declining urban forest. But the specter of treeless streets and dilapidated parks by midcentury still hovers.

Without heightened public awareness and significant support, our green canopy will continue to disappear. It is my sincere hope that the publication of this book and the funds it raises for tree planting will be the catalyst for a new era of public tree stewardship—an era distinguished not only by the restoration of Worcester's once magnificent urban forest but also by a civic commitment to invest in enhancing that sylvan legacy for generations to come.

Evelyn Herwitz,

Worcester, Massachusetts,

February 6, 2001

BIBLIOGRAPHY

Books

Admur, Richard. *Wilderness Preservation*. Earth at Risk Series, New York: Chelsea House Publishers, 1993.

Alexopoulos, John. *The Nineteenth-Century Parks of Hartford: A Legacy to the Nation*. Hartford: The Hartford Architecture Conservancy, 1983

.Binstock, Robert H. *A Report on Politics in Worcester, Massachusetts*. Cambridge, Mass.: Joint Center for Urban Studies of MIT & Harvard, 1960.

Brooke, John L. *The Heart of the Commonwealth: Society and Political Culture in Worcester County, Massachusetts, 1713–1861*. Amherst: The University of Massachusetts Press, 1989.

Brown, Lester R., ed. *State of the World 1994: A World Watch Institute Report on Progress Toward a Sustainable Society*. New York: W. W. Norton & Co., 1994.

———, ed. *State of the World 1997: A World Watch Institute Report on Progress Toward a Sustainable Society*. New York: W. W. Norton & Co., 1997

.———, ed. *State of the World 2001: A World Watch Institute Report on Progress Toward a Sustainable Society*. New York: W. W. Norton & Co, 2001.

Burke, Mrs. L. *The Language of Flowers*. Los Angeles: Price, Stern, Sloan, 1965.

Bushnell, Horace. *The Beginnings of Bushnell Park*. Hartford, Conn.: [s.n.], 1936.

Cooke, H. O. *The Forests of Worcester County: The Results of a Forest Survey of the Fifty-Nine Towns in the County and a Study of Their Lumber Industry*. Boston: Wright & Potter Printing Co., 1917.

Coombs, Zelotes W. *Worcester and Worcester Common*. Worcester: [s.n.], 1945.

Cronon, William. *Changes in the Land: Indians, Colonists, and the Ecology of New England*. New York: Hill & Wang, 1983.

———. *Nature's Metropolis: Chicago and the Great West*. New York: W. W. Norton & Co., 1991.

Dietrich, William. *The Final Forest: The Battle for the Last Great Trees of the Pacific Northwest*. New York: Simon and Schuster, 1992.

Emerson, George B. *A Report on the Trees and Shrubs Growing Naturally in the Forests of Massachusetts,* Vol. I, 2nd ed. Boston: Little, Brown and Co., 1875.

Epler, Percy H. *Master Minds at the Commonwealth's Heart*. Worcester: F. S. Blanchard & Co., 1909.

Estus, Charles W., Sr., and John F. McClymer. *gå till Amerika: The Swedish Creation of an Ethnic Identity for Worcester, Massachusetts*. Worcester: Worcester Historical Museum, 1994.

Foster, D.R. *Thoreau's Country: Journey Through a Transformed Landscape*. Cambridge, Mass.: Harvard University Press, 1999.

———. "Land-use History and Forest Transformation in Central New England," in McDonnell, Mark J. and Steward T. A. Pickett, eds, *Humans as Components of Ecosystems*. New York: Springer-Verlag, 1993.

———. "Land-use History and Four Hundred Years of Vegetation Change in New England," in B. L. Turner, A. G. Sal, F. G. Bernaldez & F. DiCastri, eds, *Global Land Use Change: A Perspective from the Columbian Encounter*. SCOPE Publications, Madrid: Consejo Superior de Investigaciones Cientificas, 1995.

Gould, Lewis L. *The Presidency of Theodore Roosevelt*. Lawrence, Kans.: University Press of Kansas, 1991.

Green Hill. Worcester: [privately published for the Green family], 1906.

Harris, Neil. *The Artist in American Society: The Formative Years 1790–1860*. New York: George Braziller, Inc., 1966.

Hedrick, U. P. *A History of Horticulture in America to 1860*. New York: Oxford University Press, 1950.

Johnson, Hugh. *The International Book of Trees*. New York: Simon & Schuster, 1977.

Kingsley, Elbridge and Frederick Knab. *Picturesque Worcester, Part I.* Springfield, Mass.: W. F. Adams Co., 1895.

Kolesar, Robert J. *Urban Politics and Social Conflict: Worcester, Massachusetts, in the Nineteenth Century*. PhD dissertation, Clark University, 1992.

Kowsky, Frank. Country, Park & City: *The Architecture and Life of Calvert Vaux*. New York: Oxford University Press, 1998.

Langdon, Philip. *A Better Place to Live: Reshaping the American Suburb*. Amherst: University of Massachusetts Press, 1994.

Lincoln, Waldo. *History of the Lincoln Family*. Worcester: Commonwealth Press, 1923. (AAS)

Lincoln, William. *History of Worcester, Massachusetts from Its Earliest Settlement to September, 1836: With Various Notices Relating to the History of Worcester County*. Worcester: Charles Hersey, 1862.

Little, Elbert L. *The Audubon Society Field Guide to North American Trees, Eastern Region*. New York: Alfred A. Knopf, 1980.

Marx, Leo. *The Machine in the Garden: Technology and the Pastoral Ideal in America*. New York: Oxford University Press, 1964.

McKibben, Bill. *The End of Nature*. New York: Random House, 1989.

———. *Hope, Human and Wild: True Stories of Living Lightly on the Earth*. Boston: Little, Brown & Co., 1995.

Morris, Edmund. *The Rise of Theodore Roosevelt*. New York: Coward, McCann & Geoghegan, Inc., 1979.

Moynihan, Kenneth. *Worcester: A New History*. Unpublished manuscript, 1993.

Muir, John. *Our National Parks*. New York: AMS Press, 1970.

Newton, Norman T. *Design on the Land: The Development of Landscape Architecture*. Cambridge, Mass.: Harvard University Press, 1971.

Nutt, Charles A. B. *History of Worcester and Its People*. Vols. I–III. New York: Lewis Historical Publishing Co., 1919.

Nye, Russel Blaine. *The Cultural Life of the New Nation 1776–1830*. New York: Harper & Row, 1960.

O'Toole, John M. *Tornado! 84 Minutes, 94 Lives*. Worcester: Databooks, 1993.

Peattie, Donald Culross. *A Natural History of Trees of Eastern and Central North America*. Boston: Houghton Mifflin Co., 1950.

Perry, Joseph H. *The Physical Geography of Worcester, Massachusetts*. Worcester: Worcester Natural History Society, 1898.

Porte, Joel, ed. *Ralph Waldo Emerson: Essays & Lectures*. New York: Library of the Classics of the U.S., Inc, 1983.

Porteous, Alexander. *Forest Folklore, Mythology, and Romance*. London: Unwin Brothers, Ltd., 1928.

Pruit, Bettye Hobbs, ed. *The Massachusetts Tax Valuation List of 1771*. Boston: G. K. Hall & Co., 1978. (AAS)

Ranney, Victoria Post, ed. *The Papers of Frederick Law Olmsted: Volume V, The California Frontier 1863–1865*. Baltimore: The Johns Hopkins University Press, 1990.

Rice, Franklin P., ed. *Worcester Town Records from 1753–1783*. Worcester: The Worcester Society of Antiquity, 1882.

———, ed. *Records of the Proprietors of Worcester, Massachusetts*. Worcester: The Worcester Society of Antiquity, 1881.

———, ed. *Worcester Town Records 1801–1816*. Worcester: The Worcester Society of Antiquity, 1895.

———, ed. *Eighteen Hundred and Ninety-Eight: Fifty Years a City, A Graphic Presentation of Its Institutions, Industries and Leaders*. Worcester: F. S. Blanchard & Co, 1899.

Rosenzweig, Roy. *Eight Hours For What We Will: Workers and Leisure in an Industrial City, 1870–1920*. Cambridge [Cambridgeshire]; New York: Cambridge University Press, 1983.

——— and Elizabeth Blackmar. *The Park and the People: A History of Central Park*. Ithaca, N.Y.: Cornell University Press, 1992.

Rupp, Rebecca. *Red Oaks and Black Birches: The Science and Lore of Trees*. Pownal, Vt.: Garden Way Publishing, 1990.

Sandrof, Ivan. *Your Worcester Street*. Worcester: Franklin Publishing Co., 1948.

Schuyler, David. *Apostle of Taste: Andrew Jackson Downing 1815–1852*. Baltimore: The Johns Hopkins University Press, 1996.

———. *The New Urban Landscape: The Redefinition of City Form in Nineteenth-Century America*. Baltimore: The Johns Hopkins University Press, 1986.

——— and J. T. Censer, eds. *The Papers of Frederick Law Olmsted, Vol. VI, The Years of Olmsted, Vaux & Co., 1865–1874*. Baltimore: The Johns Hopkins University Press, 1992.

Southwick, Albert B. *More Once-Told Tales of Worcester County*. Worcester: Databooks, 1994.

Spears, John Pearl. *Old Landmarks and Historic Spots of Worcester, Massachusetts*. Worcester: Commonwealth Press, 1931.

Stilgoe, John R. *Common Landscape of America, 1580 to 1845*. New Haven: Yale University Press, 1982.

Summerfield, Geoffrey, ed. *John Clare, Selected Poetry.* New York: Penguin Poetry Library, 1990.

Thornton, Tamara Plakins. *Cultivating Gentlemen: The Meaning of Country Life among the Boston Elite 1785–1860.* New Haven: Yale University Press, 1989.

Tucker, Arabella H. *Trees of Worcester: A list of trees both native and introduced.* Worcester: Putnam, Davis & Co., 1894.

Tymeson, Mildred McClary. *Rural Retrospect: A Parallel History of Worcester and Its Rural Cemetery.* Worcester: Albert W. Rice, 1956.

———. *The Norton Story.* Worcester: Norton Co., 1953.

———. *Two Towers: The Story of Worcester Tech, 1865–1965.* Worcester: Worcester Polytechnic Institute, 1965.

Washburn, Emory. *Memoir of Hon. Levi Lincoln, Prepared Aggreably to a Resolution of the Massachusetts Historical Society.* Cambridge, Mass.: John Wilson & Son, 1869.

Weiss, Edwin Theodore, Jr. *Patterns and Processes of High Value Residential Districts: The Case of Worcester, 1713–1970.* PhD dissertation, Clark University, 1973.

Whitney, Peter. *Worcester County: America's First Frontier. Worcester, 1793*—reprinted edition. Worcester: Isaiah Thomas Books & Prints, 1983.

Willey, Basil. *The Eighteenth-Century Background: Studies on the Idea of Nature in the Thought of the Period.* London: Chatto, 1949.

Wolf, Peter. *Land in America: Its Value, Use and Control.* New York: Pantheon Books, 1981.

Worcester Bank and Trust Co. *Some Historic Houses of Worcester.* Boston: Walton Advertising and Printing Co., 1919.

———. *Forty Immortals of Worcester and Its County.* Boston: Walton Adverstising and Printing Co., 1920.

———. *Historic Events of Worcester.* Boston: Walton Advertising and Printing Co., 1922.

Zaslowsky, Dyan, and the Wilderness Society. *These American Lands: Parks, Wilderness and the Public Lands.* New York: Henry Holt & Co., 1986.

Journal Articles

Beales, Ross W., Jr. "The Reverend Ebenezer Parkman's Farm Workers, Westborough, Mass., 1726–82." *Proceedings of the American Antiquarian Society* Vol. 99, Part I (1989): 121–149. (AAS)

Bender, Thomas. "The 'Rural' Cemetery Movement: Urban Travail and the Appeal of Nature." *New England Quarterly* 47 (June 1974): 196–211.

Brown, Richard D. Introduction to "Farm Labor in Southern New England during the Agricultural-Industrial Transition." *Proceedings of the American Antiquarian Society* Vol. 99, Part I (1989): 113–119. (AAS)

Burnham, Charles R. "The Restoration of the American Chestnut." *American Scientist* Vol. 76, (Sept./Oct. 1988): pp. 478–87.

Cronon, William. "A Place for Stories: Nature, History, and Narrative." *The Journal of American History* (Mar. 1992): 1347–1376.

French, Stanley. "The Cemetery as Cultural Institution: The Establishment of Mount Auburn and the 'Rural Cemetery' Movement." *American Quarterly* 26 (Mar. 1974): 37–59.

Foster, David R. "Land-use history (1730–1990) and vegetation dynamics in central New England, USA." *Journal of Ecology* 80 (1992): 753–772.

———, et al., "Post-settlement history of human land-use and vegetation dynamics of a *Tsuga canadensis* (hemlock) woodlot in central New England." *Journal of Ecology* 80 (1992): 773–786.

——— and Emery R. Boose. "Patterns of forest damage resulting from catastrophic wind in central New England, USA." *Journal of Ecology* 80 (1992): 79–98.

——— and T. M. Zebryk. "Long-term Vegetation Dynamics and Disturbance History of a *Tsuga*-dominated Forest in New England." *Ecology* 74-4 (1993): 982–998.

Goodman, Paul. "Ethics and Enterprise: The Values of a Boston Elite, 1800–1860." *American Quarterly* 18 (Fall 1966): 437–451.

Larkin, Jack. "'Labor is the Great Thing in Farming': The Farm Laborers of the Ward Family of Shrewsbury, Massachusetts, 1787–1870." *Proceedings of the American Antiquarian Society* Vol. 99, Part I (1989):

Lincoln, Waldo. "Mrs. Penelope S. Canfield's Recollections of Worcester One Hundred Years Ago." *The Worcester Historical Society Publication* Vol. I, No. 4 (Apr. 1931).

Lyman, Richard B., Jr. "'What is Done in My Absence?' Levi Lincoln's Oakham, Massachusetts Farm Workers, 1807–20." *Proceedings of the American Antiquarian Society* Vol. 99, Part I (1989). (AAS)

Meyer, William B. and Michael Brown. "Locational conflict in a nineteenth-century city." *Political Geography Quarterly* Vol. 8, No. 2 (Apr. 1989): 107–122.

Newhouse, Joseph R. "Chestnut Blight." *Scientific American* (July 1990): 106–111.

O'Keefe, J. and D. R. Foster. "An ecological history of Massachusetts forests." *Arnoldia* 58 (1998): 2–31.

"The Diary of Christopher Columbus Baldwin, Librarian of the AAS 1829–1835." *The Transactions and Collections of the American Antiquarian Society* Vol. VIII (1901). London: Johnson Reprint Corp. (1971) (AAS).

Newspaper and Magazine Articles

Anagnostakis, Sandra L. "Chestnuts and the Blight," *Massachusetts Wildlife,* Fall 1989.

Allen, Scott. "N.E. seeing the forest through the trees," *Boston Globe,* 13 Nov. 1995.

Allis, Sam. "Re-rooting Boston," *Boston Globe,* 2 Apr. 2000.

Boucher, Norman. "Whose Woods These Are," *Wilderness 25,* Fall 1989.

Astell, Emilie. "Open space pursued in city," *Worcester Telegram & Gazette,* 18 Jan. 2000.

Bumiller, Elisabeth. "'Go Out, Go Forth and Count' Volunteer Corps Will Give Street Trees a Checkup," *New York Times,* 29 July 1995.

Burnham, Charles R. "The Restoration of the American Chestnut," *American Scientist,* Vol. 76, Sept./Oct. 1988.

Erskine, Margaret A. "Returning to Green Hill: A city treasure lies in tatters," *Worcester Magazine,* 1 Jan. 1997.

Faber, Harold. "Insect Threatening Survival of Hemlocks in the Hudson Valley," *New York Times,* 11 Nov. 1991.

Hall, Jon. "A final wish helps tree city to branch out," *Boston Globe,* 10 Nov. 1997.

Herwitz, Evelyn. "Park Avenue: Some Call It 'The New Main Street'; Others Describe It As Example of Unplanned Growth," *Business Digest/Central Massachusetts,* Nov. 1985.

———. "For Trees' Sake," *Inside Worcester,* Apr. 1991.

———. "Our Trees Are Dying," *Worcester Magazine,* 24 Apr. 1996.

Higgins, Richard. "Of Leaves and Loss," *Boston Globe Magazine,* 8 June 1997.

Hopps, Michael W. "How Science Changes the Urban Forest," *Urban Forests,* Aug./Sept. 1994.

Howe, Peter J. "A beetle bores in Brooklyn," *Boston Globe,* 21 Sept. 1996.

Kaplan, Fred. "Looks count: When it comes to fighting crime, cleaning up the urban landscape may be the most effective strategy," *Boston Globe,* 19 Jan. 1997.

Kentworthy, Tom and Gary Younge. "Squeezed budget taxes nation's park system," *Boston Globe,* 25 Aug. 1996.

Keyser, Joseph M. "Crisis in Our Urban and Historic Parks," *American Forests,* Mar./Apr. 1988.

Kranish, Michael. "Big fight likely for Bush cabinet," *Boston Globe,* 14 Jan. 2001.

Kotsopoulos, Nick. "Land use plan a prelude to zoning study," *Worcester Telegram & Gazette,* 14 Mar. 2000.

———. "Parks dept. move set," *Worcester Telegram & Gazette,* 21 Nov. 2000.

Kuntsler, James Howard. "Home from Nowhere," *Atlantic Monthly,* Vol. 278, No.3, Sept. 1996.

Kush, Bronislaus B. "Elms make a comeback," *Worcester Telegram & Gazette,* 27 Oct. 1995.

———. "City tree program digs in: Effort re-leaves Elm Park," *Worcester Telegram & Gazette,* 13 May 2000.

Lueck, Thomas J. "City Asks Tree Lovers to Fill Their Buckets," *New York Times,* 8 June 1996.

Martin, Douglas. "Mother Nature Never Intended This," *New York Times,* 30 May 1994.

McDonald, Carol. "Elm Park trees honor fallen heroes," *Sunday Telegram,* 30 Apr. 2000.

Melady, Mark. "Renovation of park set to begin," *Worcester Telegram & Gazette,* 5 July 2000.

Montgomery, M. R. "The Emerald Necklace at 100," *Boston Globe,* 21 Sept. 1996.

O'Connor, Ellen. "Fighting for Green Hill Park," *Worcester Magazine,* 10 July 1996.

———. "Teed off over Green Hill Park," Parts I–II, *Worcester Magazine,* 28 May 1997, 4 June 1997.

Parsons, Eugene O. "Obadiah Hadwen, We Salute You!" *Evening Gazette,* 31 Jan. 1963.

———. "Worcester Horticultural Society to Observe 100th Anniversary in April," *Worcester Sunday Telegram,* 29 Mar. 1942.

Parsons, Eugene and Margaret. "One Hundred Years of Worcester Horticulture," *Sunday Telegram,* 15 Sept. 1940.

Parsons, Margaret. "The Fate or Fortune of Some Famous Trees That Grew Up with Our History," *Sunday Telegram,* 23 Oct. 1938. (WHM)

Semrau, Anne. "Digging Deeper into the Urban Forest," *Urban Forests,* June/July 1993.
Shaw, Kathleen A. "Venerable oak in Elm Park designated 'Heritage Tree,'" *Worcester Telegram & Gazette,* 27 Jan. 2000.
Skiera, Bob. "Building the Ideal Urban Forest," *Urban Forests,* Oct./Nov. 1991.
――――― and Gary Moll. "The Sad State of City Trees," *American Forests,* Mar./Apr. 1992.
Stevens, William K. "Amid Insult and Injury, Urban Forests Hang On," *New York Times,* 12 Nov. 1991.
Sullivan, Erin. "Trees for Tatnuck Square," *Worcester Magazine,* 9 July 1997.
―――――. "Money Growing on Trees? No, but Study Finds Next Best Thing," *New York Times,* 12 Apr. 1994.
―――――. "Want a Room with a View? Idea May Be in the Genes," *New York Times,* 30 Nov. 1993.
Sullivan, Walter. "New Techniques Revive Hopes for Blighted American Chestnut," *New York Times,* 15 Nov. 1988.
―――――. "American Trees Besieged by Alien Blights," *New York Times,* 28 Sept. 1993.
Taylor, Tricia. "The Greening of North Philadelphia," *American Forests,* Jan./Feb. 1993.
Watson, Tom. "Atlanta tries to preserve a shady side," *Boston Globe,* 7 Apr. 1999.
Woolhouse, Megan. "Hope for a park in Piedmont," *Worcester Magazine,* 3 Apr. 1996.
"A Home for Every Citizen," *Worcester Magazine,* Vol. 17, Apr. 1914.
"A menace to maple trees," *Boston Globe,* 30 Sept. 1996.
"Citygreen: measuring the urban ecosystem values," *Urban Forests,* Oct./Nov. 1994.
"Clinton extends protection for California's sequoias," *Worcester Telegram & Gazette,* Apr. 1998.
"Cutting Down the Great Elm in Front of the Lincoln House," *Worcester Evening Gazette,* 31 May 1870; *Worcester Daily Spy,* 3 June 1870. (WHM)
"Development Boom: Worcester Is Planning Ahead; Public Input Starts Tomorrow," *Worcester Sunday Telegram,* 26 Oct. 1986.
"Greening Our Cities," *Co-op America Quarterly,* Spring 1991.
"Hadwen Arboretum Renewal." *Clark Now,* Apr. 1968.
"Infested With Tramps, Lakeview in the clutches of an Organized gang of Hoboes," *Worcester Telegram,* 13 Sept. 1894
"Local Matters: The Makeshifts of Poverty—How the Poor Obtain Fuel," *Worcester Evening Gazette,* 15 Mar. 1876.
"Mr. Obadiah Brown Hadwen," *Worcester Magazine,* Vol. 10, No. 11, Nov. 1907.
"Northern Forests, Too, Get Congress's Interest," *New York Times,* 29 Oct. 1989.
"Old Trees Near Worcester," *Sunday Spy,* 2 Aug. 1891. (WHM)
"Olympic Trees Already Dying," *Boston Globe,* 12 Aug. 1996.
"Roosevelt Visits Indian Hill," *Norton Spirit,* Vol. 3, No. 2, Sept. 1916. (WHM)
"Shade Trees—A Plea for More Greenery," *Worcester Evening Gazette,* 15 July 1879.
"Shade Trees—A Practical Suggestion," *Worcester Evening Gazette,* 16 July 1879.
"Sold Beer in the Woods," *Worcester Telegram,* 24 July 1895.
"Teddy Tree Found," *Worcester Evening Gazette,* 4 June 1964.
"The Art of Arboriculture—A Gentleman Farmer's Legacy," *Clark Now,* Spring 1981.
"The Lumber Supply: The Canadian Pineries Less Extensive than has been Supposed," *Worcester Evening Gazette,* 17 Nov. 1883.
"The Tree That Grew in Brooklyn Is Dying All Over New York," *New York Times,* 8 June 1996.
"Tornado: A Record in Pictures of the Catastrophe That Struck Worcester and Central Massachusetts, June 9, 1953," *Worcester Telegram & Evening Gazette,* 18 June 1953.
"Trees of Many Climes on Farm," circa 1902. (WCHS)
"Trial of Henry J. Chamberlin for Larceny of Trees and Plants," *Worcester Evening Gazette,* 23 May 1876.
"Utah park a seldom-seen treasure," *Worcester Telegram & Gazette,* 20 Sept. 1996.
"Wachusett Dam hemlocks cleared out to stop insects," *Worcester Telegram & Gazette,* 14 Apr. 2000.
"What the Citizen Has Done for Our Public Parks," *Worcester Magazine,* Vol. 7, No. 2, Feb. 1904.
"What the Citizen Has Done for Our Public Parks, Part II," *Worcester Magazine,* Vol. 7, No. 3, Mar. 1904.
"Where Did All the Trees Go?" *Worcester Magazine,* 25 Oct. 1996.
"Worcester Horticultural Society to Observe 100th Anniversary In April," *Worcester Sunday Telegram,* 29 Mar. 1942.
"Worcester Was One of Thoreau's Favorite Visiting Places," *Worcester Sunday Telegram,* 1 June 1941.
1938 Hurricane coverage, *Worcester Evening Gazette,* 21–22 September 1938; *Worcester Telegram,* 21, 23–24 Sept. 1938.
Abbot Street trees dispute, *Worcester Telegram & Gazette,* 13, 15, 21 May 1996.

City Council proceedings, *Worcester Evening Gazette*, 11 Sept. 1883.
Death of Stephen Salisbury III, *Worcester Telegram*, 17 Nov. 1905.
Deforestation in Canada, *Worcester Evening Gazette*, 17 Nov. 1883, 25 Oct. 1895, 23 Oct. 1896.
Editorial on Forestry Congress in St. Louis, *Worcester Evening Gazette*, 16 Aug. 1883.
First Agricultural Society Fair, *Massachusetts Spy*, 13 Oct. 1819.
First Arbor Day celebration in Worcester, *Worcester Daily Spy*, 29 Apr. 1885, 1 May 1885.
Green Hill Park controversy, *Worcester Telegram & Gazette*, 7 Apr. 1996, 17 July 1996, 11 Nov. 1996, 2 May 1997, 13 May 1997, 15 May 1997.
Letter to Editor regarding removal of telephone poles on old Common, *Worcester Evening Gazette*, 18 Dec. 1883.
Theodore Roosevelt Visit, *Worcester Evening Gazette*, 21 June 1905; *Worcester Telegram*, 22 June 1905.

Maps

Blakes, Francis E. *Plan of the Town of Worcester 1795, copied from the original in the State Archives*, Jan. 1883.
Bowring, Larry. A. *Map of the Town of Worcester, Mass. circa 1771*. 1975.
Trescott, S. *Map of Worcester, Mass., Showing Oldest Roads and Location of Earliest Settlers, Prepared expressly for C. A. Wall's "Reminiscences of Worcester,"* 1877.
Atlas of the City of Worcester, F.W. Beers, 1870; Charles E. Tuttle, 1971.
Map of Worcester by William Young, 1784. (AAS)
Map of Worcester Parks and Recreation System, 1942.
The Town of Worcester, Massachusetts circa 1776. (AAS)

Other

"Application for Initial Certification of a Workable Program for Urban Renewal for Worcester, Mass." Oct. 1958.
A City Plan for Worcester, Massachusetts, 1924. Technical Advisory Corp.—Worcester Planning Board, Nov. 1924.
Beveridge, Charles E. and Carolyn F. Hoffman, et al. "The Master List of Design Projects of the Olmsted Firm 1857–1950." National Association for Olmsted Parks.
Brigham, Joan-Carol and Daniel Prince. "An Evaluation of the Clark-Hadwen Arboretum concerning the rare and valuable trees." 1978. (WCHS)
Calloway, Brad, et al. "Preliminary Report on the Status of the Hadwen Arboretum." Clark University, Dec. 1971. (WCHS)
Celebration of the Two Hundredth Anniversary of the Naming of Worcester, October 14 and 15, 1884. Worcester: Charles Hamilton Press, 1885.
City of Worcester Open Space and Recreation Plan. Sept. 1994.
College of the Holy Cross Campus Arboretum. 2nd Edition, 1993.
Comprehensive Plan for Worcester, Massachusetts. Worcester Planning Board, Aug. 1964.
Curtis, Edwin P. et al. "A Few Facts About the Public Parks of Worcester Massachusetts." Board of Park Commissioners, 1 Sept. 1914.
Duscik, Dennis W. "Open Space Preservation in Worcester: A Tale of Neglect." Regional Environmental Council White Paper, 2 Mar. 1985.
Favretti, Rudy J., *Early New England Gardens: 1620–1840* Sturbridge, Mass., 1996. (AAS)
———. *A History of Elm Park, Worcester, Massachusetts*. Olmsted Historic Landscape Preservation Program. Commonwealth of Massachusetts, Department of Environmental Management, 1985. (AAS)
Grimm, John and Paul Halloran. "A Picturesque Analysis of WPI and Institute Park." American Studies Seminar, 1986. (AAS)
Healy, Martin R. and Robert W. Mack. *Massachusetts Zoning Manual*, Vol. I. Massachusetts Continuing Legal Education, Inc., 1995.
Herron, Frances. "The Worcester County Horticultural Society—A Look at the Early Years," *The Worcester County Horticultural Society: Celebrating 150 Years*. Worcester County Horticultural Society, 1992. (WCHS)
Hope Cemetery at Worcester, Massachusetts. Board of Commissioners of Hope Cemetery, May 1952.
Hudson, Charles. "Character of the late Hon. Levi Lincoln of Worcester, Mass." 1870: (AAS)
Lincoln, Jr., Levi. *Address, Delivered Before the Worcester Agricultural Society, October 7, 1819, Being Their First Anniversary Cattle Show and Exhibition of Manufacture*. Worcester: Manniner & Trumbell, 1819.
———. *An Address Delivered on the Consecration of the Worcester Rural Cemetery*. Boston: Dutton and Wentworth, 1838.

Maine Historical and Geneological Recorder. Vol. VI, No. 4 (Oct. 1889): 449–453. (AAS)

Manual for the City Council of the City of Worcester, Massachusetts, 1996–97.

Memorial of Stephen Salisbury, LLD. 1885. (AAS)

O'Brien, Michael V. Memorandum to Thomas R. Hoover, "The Current State of the Urban Forest and Recommendations for the Maintenance and Management of this Natural Resource for the New Millennium," Worcester Parks, Recreation and Cemetery Department, 8 Oct. 1999.

Obituaries of Edward Winslow Lincoln. 15 Dec. 1896. (WHM)

Polk's Worcester House Directory. R. L. Polk & Co. 1935, 1936, 1940, 1942.

Reminiscences of the Original Associates and Past Members of the Worcester Fire Society, begun in an Address by Hon. Levi Lincoln, at the Quarterly Meeting, April, 1862, and continued in An Address by Hon. Isaac Davis, at the annual meeting, January, 1870. Worcester: Charles Hamilton, 1870. (AAS)

Report Summary Northern Forest Land Study. U.S. Forest Service, May 1990.

Roche, John. *Historical Sketch of the Parks and Playgrounds of Worcester,* Master's Thesis, Clark University, 1910.

Salisbury Family Papers. (AAS)

Will of Stephen Salisbury III. (AAS)

Shaarai Torah Synagogue cornerstone, Unpublished manuscript. (WHM)

Thirteenth Annual Report of the Trustees of the Rural Cemetery in Worcester. Worcester: C. Buckingham Webb, 1851.

Tschantz, Barbara A. and Paul L. Sacamano. *Municipal Tree Management in the United States: A 1994 Report.* Kent, Ohio: Davey Resource Group, 1994.

Worcester City Documents, 1849–1990.

Worcester County Horticultural Society Transactions. Worcester: Commonwealth Press, 1882, 1910, 1917.

Worcester Conservation Commission. *What's Left: An Update on Worcester's Open Space.* August 1987.

Worcester Fire Society. *Reminiscences and Biographical Notes of Past Members.* 7th series. Worcester: Commonwealth Press, 1916.

Worcester, Massachusetts Street Tree Management Plan, Executive Summary. ACRT, Inc., 1988.

Worcester Master Plan: Parks and Recreation Five Year Action Plan. On-site Insight, 1987.

Worcester Planning Department. "Transition: A View of the Worcester Central Business District 1966." Nov. 1966.

———. "Vacant Land Study in RG-5 and RL-7 Zones." Sept. 1969.

Worcester Redevelopment Authority. "A Community Renewal Program, Worcester, MA." Barton-Aschman Associates, May 1965.

Web Sites

Alliance for Community Trees: actrees.org
American Chestnut Foundation: chestnut.acf.org
American Forests: americanforests.org
City of Worcester: ci.worcester.ma.us
Elmcare.com
Massachusetts Department of Environmental Management: state.ma.us/dem/
Pennsylvania Horticultural Society: www.libertynet.org/phs/
The National Arbor Day Foundation: arborday.org
Trees New York: treesny.com
Urban Open Space, Manchester, NH: www.mv.com/ipusers/env/cultivars.html
Utah Guide: http://www.americansouthwest.net/utah/dinosaur/green_l.html
Virginia Cooperative Extension: ext.vt.edu

Key to Library Collections

AAS   American Antiquarian Society
WCHS   Worcester County Horticultural Society
WHM   Worcester Historical Museum